THE
MODERN
GARDENER

Thunder Bay Press
An imprint of Printers Row Publishing Group
9717 Pacific Heights Blvd, San Diego, CA 92121
www.thunderbaybooks.com • mail@thunderbaybooks.com

Thunder Bay Press
Publisher: Peter Norton • Associate Publisher: Ana Parker
Editor: Dan Mansfield
Acquisitions Editor: Kathryn Chipinka Dalby

Produced by HarperCollins*Publishers*
Editor: Sarah Vaughan • Designer: Gareth Butterworth
Author: Sonya Patel Ellis

Library of Congress Control Number: 2021949364

ISBN: 978-1-64517-945-0

Printed in Latvia

26 25 24 23 22   1 2 3 4 5

THE
MODERN
GARDENER

SONYA PATEL ELLIS

THUNDER BAY
P·R·E·S·S
San Diego, California

CONTENTS

INTRODUCTION

Personalize and inspire your own plant choices by connecting with your lifestyle, focus, and space, as well as more deeply and vitally with how nature works.

The main premise of this book is the idea of choosing plants based on the parameters of your own life. It's about thoughtful, personalized planting that requires you to look more closely at factors such as time available for gardening, people or animals you share your space with, nature-inspired passions or pastimes, and the light and humidity within a particular room.

The focus is also on container plants—or species that can be planted in pots as well as in the ground—as this provides scope for indoor and outdoor gardens, plus those increasingly inspiring areas in between such as conservatories, courtyards, and garden rooms. Being able to move your plants also allows for a seasonal reshuffle, or the creation of new vistas or productive yields.

Embrace the edit

Although it might seem as though you're limiting things at first, what you're actually doing is creating space for an ideal edit of plants—a selection that will provide you with exactly what you want or need: an ornamental garden that will grow with you, a houseplant family that will really thrive, or an edible garden that will reward in terms of a bountiful harvest.

Once you've established a workable vision—you want a low-maintenance, mainly ornamental garden for a semi-shady balcony, for example—you can start to layer up inspirations. This is the really fun part, taking cues from plant stores, a planting program, podcast or feed, or indeed the Planting Inspirations section (page 40) in this book. Take your time and enjoy the process, creating a "mood board," list of ideas, planting plan, or a simple hand-drawn design.

Be inspired by nature

The main inspiration, of course, is nature itself. Choosing to connect with nature bridges the gap between prescriptive and intuitive gardening. Neither one is possible without a degree of understanding about how plants grow or what they are capable of, whether that's through the applied learning of planting principles, or a lifetime experiencing the sensory qualities or growth habits of plants. This could be through gardening or growing your own food, or activities such as walking in the park or countryside, cooking, art, or even the simple act of preparing and drinking herbal tea. Every interaction we have with a plant, from observing a rose to tasting a tomato or inhaling the aroma of rosemary or thyme, leaves us with a nature-inspired memory. This is how we connect with plants every day.

Get personal

Modern gardening is simply about building on these connections with nature. We now know so much about plants—through thousands of years of recorded and shared botanical and horticultural knowledge and decades of modern science—that it makes sense to use these resources to help our gardens grow.

This doesn't mean using a plant's care label in a "one size fits all" approach. Rather, we should learn to read between the lines of such guides before or as we take their advice. Why does a plant prefer sun or partial shade? What benefits come from misting once a week? Or how does a particular cultivar work as a container plant whereas another might be too big?

Go deeper

The Personal Plant Selector (page 108) is designed to furnish the reader with a comprehensive list of container plants for indoors and out. But it also invites the reader to go deeper into a plant's backstory or narrative: Where does it come from? What is its natural habitat? How does it grow in the wild? How did it get here? How did it get its name?

Many houseplants hail from tropical rainforests, for example, where the natural climate is hot and wet, with little or no dry season. Some plants, such as *Syngoniums*, *Calatheas*, and *Sansevierias*, live in the partial shade of the forest floor. Others, such as philodendrons and devil's ivy (*Epipremnum aureum*), climb around tree trunks and in canopies, where they may receive brighter, filtered light. Epiphytic plants, including orchids and bromeliads, attach themselves to rocks and trees, absorbing nutrients from organic debris that collects around roots, from the air or other water supplies.

All this information provides the basis for an optimum care routine. And while some plants, such as the cast-iron plant (*Aspidistra elatior*), are helpfully versatile or hard to kill, most require at least a semblance of the light, water, food, and space that they need to grow well.

Be mindful

The Personal Plant Selector is also a guide to observing plants, in the wild and at home. It's arranged by plant type (see contents, page 111) so you can further personalize your garden or plant collection by using it interactively with the Planting Inspirations (page 40) and Your Personal Planting Guide (page 14).

The herb garden of your dreams, for instance, could be a south-facing terrace of sun-loving, drought-tolerant specimens such as lavender, rosemary, oregano, and thyme. Or it could be an indoor windowsill of cut-and-come-again basil and cilantro. Such plants could sit alongside potted-up edibles such as microgreens or lettuce.

Listening to your plants is key. You may have positioned, watered, and fed a plant correctly but it still doesn't seem to be flourishing as it should. Perhaps it has brown leaves, wilting stems, is outgrowing its pot, not blooming, or bolting instead of producing healthy foliage. What other factors could be involved? Use the section on Happy, Healthy Plants (page 76) to learn more about the ins and outs of plant care, from selecting and settling a plant into your home to the

reasons for choosing types of soils, containers, or fertilizers. Your otherwise well-tended plant may need better drainage or a pot made in a more breathable material such as terra-cotta. Or it may have picked up a pest or disease in the store or from another plant.

All the advice given in this section is nature-led, including the use of peat-free soil, organic fertilizer, and natural insecticides and fungicides. Learning how to propagate plants or grow your own can also save money and waste. It's all part of being a mindful gardener.

Explore and enjoy

Gardening mindfully means making smart, sustainable plant choices that ensure endangered species are conserved in the wild or that encourage suppliers to step up their ethical practices. Don't be afraid to ask about the provenance of a plant, and shop local where you can.

The plant kingdom includes nearly 400,000 known species, and while not all of them are suitable for your garden or your home, thousands of other species plus thousands more cultivars are. As new variants are discovered or cultivated every year, there really is an infinite world of plants to explore and enjoy.

HOW TO USE THIS BOOK

Create and nurture the perfect indoor or outdoor container garden, using **The Modern Gardener** *as your guide.*

Whether you need a Personal Planting Guide (page 14) to help you select the ideal plants for your lifestyle, focus, and space; Planting Inspirations (page 40) to help broaden your choices and edit things down; nature-led notes on nurturing Happy, Healthy Plants (page 76); or a Personal Plant Selector (page 108) filled with hundreds of beautiful species and cultivars ideal for indoor or outdoor container planting, let *The Modern Gardener* be your guide.

Personal Planting Guide
Need a little help designing an indoor or outdoor green space, or selecting container plants that have the best chance of surviving and thriving into the future? Use the Personal Planting Guide to make personalized choices based on how you live (Lifestyle Matters, page 18), how you enjoy or connect with nature (Find Your Focus, page 24), and the potential or limitations of your environment (Appraise Your Space, page 30).

Planting Inspirations
Now that you have some clarity about which plants might work best for you, find inspiration within Planting for Well-being (page 44), Planting for Style (page 52), Planting for Produce (page 60), and Planting for Seasonality (page 68). Ideas include The Mindful Garden (page 46), The Edible Garden (page 64), and The Holiday Garden (page 74), or you might be inspired to come up with your own theme. You will also find mini guides to enjoying plants through creative containers, crafting, and potting up, including how to make a terrarium (page 71) or force bulbs (page 73). Most of all, enjoy connecting with yourself and nature.

Happy, Healthy Plants

Choosing inspiring plants that suit your lifestyle, focus, and space is one of the best foundations for happy, healthy plants. A nature-led approach to their care and maintenance is another. Guides on Selection (page 80) and Pots and Potting (page 84), to Nurturing and Nourishment (page 90), Pruning and Propagation (page 98), and Listening (page 104) will help tackle common issues.

Personal Plant Selector

Time to get personal with plants. This section includes in-depth guides to over 200 ornamental and edible species suitable for container planting indoors, outdoors, or in between—including Ferns (page 114), Succulents (page 144), Other Flowers (page 168), and Herbs and Spices (page 194). In this section, the below symbols will help you to navigate each plant's safety and care ratings.

This symbol lets you know the plant is nontoxic to children and pets.

This symbol lets you know the plant may be toxic or harmful to children and pets.

"Easy," "medium," and "hard" care ratings let you know how challenging the plant is to nurture and grow.

GLOSSARY

A few words and contextual explanations to help you navigate your way through **The Modern Gardener.**

Aerial root
Roots that appear above the ground providing support for vining plants; also used to absorb water and nutrients from the air in the case of epiphytes, e.g., orchids.

Bonsai
An ornamental tree or shrub grown using the Japanese art of bonsai in order to keep it small enough to grow in a container.

Bract
A modified or specialized leaf that is found above the leaf but below the flower; most are inconspicuous, some are showy and petal-like as found in Arums.

Bulb
An underground storage organ, which lies dormant in winter, comprising a short stem base enclosed in overlapping membrane or fleshy tissue.

Container
A vessel in which plants can be grown when not planted directly into the ground, including pots and window boxes. Ensure containers have adequate drainage.

Crown
The area of a plant above the roots, potentially including stem, leaves, flowers, fruits, and seeds. In large shrubs or trees this usually means the area where the branches grow from the trunk.

Deciduous
Referring to a tree or shrub that sheds its leaves seasonally at a certain stage in its life cycle. Literally, the dropping of a part that is no longer needed.

Drainage
A method by which draining can occur in order to prevent waterlogging. Achieved through drainage holes in a pot or aided by materials such as sand and grit.

Edible
A plant, or plant part, that can be safely eaten by humans; potentially includes leaves, stems, flowers, fruits, seeds, and roots, and most pertinent to herbs, spices, fruits, and vegetables.

Epiphyte
A plant that grows non-parasitically on another plant or object such as a tree or rock, including species of orchids, bromeliads, air plants, and ferns.

Evergreen
A plant that retains green leaves throughout the year. May also include semi-evergreens when grown in consistently warm conditions, often as houseplants indoors.

Fertilizer
A substance added to soil or potting compost to deliver additional nutrients and thereby improve its fertility. Choose natural or organic alternatives where possible.

Foliage
The collective leaves of a plant. Commonly used to describe the leafier parts of a plant or specimens that are valued for their leaves rather than, or as well as, flowers.

Frond
A long leaf that usually has many divisions, as in the case of ferns, palms, and cycads. Can also refer to leaves that have a similar appearance to fronds.

Genus
A classification term that denotes plants categorized by one or more characteristics. More closely related than a plant family, less close than a species, e.g., *Rosa* (rose).

Herb
A plant with medicinal, aromatic. or savory properties that is used for preparing

therapeutic remedies or for flavoring or garnishing food, e.g. mint.

Houseplant
A plant grown primarily for ornamentation, in a container, within the home; or one grown in another indoor space such as an office. Needs to adapt well to indoor cultivation.

Humidity
Referring to atmospheric moisture or the concentration of water vapor present in the air. Required by many rainforest plants in order to thrive.

Nature
The phenomena of the collective physical world, including plants, animals, the landscape, and weather; fundamentally includes humans but not man-made creations.

Node
The part of a plant's stem from which one or more leaves emerge, often forming a slight swelling. Used most commonly when referring to propagation.

Nutrients
The chemical elements and compounds that are essential to a plant's health, including the big three: nitrogen (N), phosphorus (P), and potassium (K).

Offset
A lateral shoot that develops at the base of a mother plant via asexual reproduction, taking root to become a daughter plant; used in propagation.

Ornamental
Plants grown primarily for display or decoration rather than purpose. Usually have at least one beautiful feature, including flowers, leaves, fruits, and seeds.

Overwintering
The act of protecting plants from the cold or frost by moving them inside during winter; some plants also need overwintering to help them bloom.

Perennial
A plant that lives more than two years of its life cycle, typically cold-hardy plants that die down in winter and return again in spring.

Plant family
A grouping of plants with shared characteristics ranked between order and genus. Includes the palm family (Arecaceae) and the mint family (Lamiaceae).

Plantlet
Another word for offsets, although most commonly used to describe baby plants that grow at the end of a runner, as in the case of spider plants. Used in propagation.

Potting compost
Specially prepared soil designed to help plants grow, especially in containers; also known as potting soil. Choose coir-based rather than peat-based.

Propagation
The process by which plants grow or can be grown sexually or asexually via a variety of sources, including seeds, bulbs, cuttings, and other plant parts.

Rhizome
A modified, subterranean, starch- and protein-storing plant stem that sends out roots and shoots from its nodes. Edible rhizomes include ginger.

Rooting hormone
A combination of plant growth hormones that help stimulate a plant to switch from producing green cells for leaf and stem materials, to root cells. Used in propagation.

Rosette
Leaves that radiate from a center stalk at or close to ground level. Includes many rosette-forming succulents, including Echeveria and Sempervivum.

Runner
A horizontal branch extending from the base of a plant that produces new plants from buds at its tips or nodes, e.g., strawberries. Also known as a stolon.

Species
The basic unit of classification and a taxonomic rank of organisms, including plants that have the same main characteristics and are able to breed with each other.

Toxic
In this context, plants that include chemicals or compounds within one or various parts that have the potential to harm people or pets.

Variegated
Referring to leaves or foliage that are edged or patterned in a second or various other colors, including white, yellow, pink, red, and purple as well as shades of green.

YOUR
PERSONAL
PLANTING
GUIDE

YOUR PERSONAL PLANTING GUIDE

Want to create a garden or green space that really stands the test of time? Choose plants that match your lifestyle, interests, and space.

Whether you're creating a green space from scratch or adding to an established plant collection, choosing plants or flowers that really work for you is becoming an increasingly popular way to garden. This doesn't mean sidestepping all the plants you are intuitively drawn to—creating a visual "mood board" or list of the types of plants you instinctively like can be incredibly useful—it just means being more aware of which plants really suit your lifestyle, interests, and your space so that they can thrive.

Lifestyle matters
What's your lifestyle? Do you have the time to give plants lots of tender loving care or are you always on the go and would prefer a low-maintenance option? Factors such as family, pets, gardening expertise, and budget can all make a difference to the success of your planting. See page 18 to see how you fare.

Find your focus
How do you relate to plants? It could be that you enjoy the therapeutic act of gardening, relate to plants as part of a stylistic design vision, want to grow herbs for well-being, or have a steady supply of cut flowers. Or perhaps you'd like to grow your own fruits, vegetables, and flowers for cooking. See page 24 to help clarify further.

Appraise your space
Where you place your plants is hugely important to their survival, from the soil that supports their roots and growth to their immediate environment. Appraising the size and conditions of your space—including factors such as light, humidity, temperature, and room for growth—will help you edit your plant choices. See page 30 to explore further.

FIND YOUR PERFECT PLANT MATCH

A few key questions can help you find your perfect plant match and create a happy, healthy, long-term garden.

1

Where will my plant live?
Are you planning outdoor containers for a balcony or terrace, trying to find the perfect plant for a bathroom, bedroom, or hallway, or looking for an indoor-outdoor solution? Either way, environment really matters. Use the advice in Appraise Your Space (page 30) to help refine your choices.

2

Are there further space constraints?
There's no point buying a huge tropical plant if it doesn't have room to grow or can't be restrained. Plus there are lots of lovely smaller plants that work alone or in groups, in pots, on pedestals, or in hanging baskets. Visit the Personal Plant Selector on page 108 to help choose.

3

What are the key environmental factors?
Plants, like humans, are sensitive to their environment, preferring conditions that are similar to their native habitat in terms of light, moisture, ventilation, and nutrients. See Happy, Healthy Plants on page 76 to reap the benefits of going with the flow of nature.

4

How plant-friendly are you?
Having green fingers comes from experience and intuition but also relates to lifestyle and listening to nature. See Lifestyle Matters (page 18) to help choose the right plants for you, plus look for handy ease-of-care and pet/family-friendly keys in the Personal Plant Selector (page 108).

5

What kind of plants do you like?
Creating a garden or green space is a wonderful way to express your tastes and preferences, whether that's through choosing plants that suit your pastimes or the culmination of a particular style or vision. See Find Your Focus (page 24), then head to Planting Inspirations on page 40 for topical plant edits.

LIFESTYLE MATTERS

Listen to the limitations of your lifestyle and the innate possibilities of plants to create gardens and green spaces that really thrive.

What makes a plant survive? In nature, plants have adapted over millions of years to thrive in a range of conditions, and left to their own devices, in their natural habitat, should flourish into the future. When we bring them into our homes or gardens, we are assuming a certain responsibility for their ongoing survival. How and where we plant them, watering and feeding routines, and pest or disease control is all within our hands.

What makes modern gardening so exciting is that we now have so much access to key care knowledge about the plants that we want to grow: where they come from, how big they grow, what soil they prefer, how much water or extra nutrients they need. By listening to the limitations of our lifestyles—regarding time, space, expertise, budget, and dependents such as pets and children—and the innate possibilities of plants, we have the opportunity to create and maintain green spaces that truly thrive.

FREEDOM TO ROAM

Angel's trumpet

If you're lucky enough to have the freedom to roam around a large indoor or outdoor space, or even both, then your choices are similarly expansive in terms of relative plant size, from big tropical houseplants to trees or shrubs. Where you may need to be careful is in cramming too much in without leaving enough room for height and spread. Cherish the opportunity to take your time populating a space with plants that will grow with you.

Three to try:
Fiddle-leaf fig (*Ficus lyrata*)—page 122
Bird of paradise (*Strelitzia reginae*)—page 171
Angel's trumpet (*Brugmansia* spp.)—page 178

LIMITED SPACE

A lack of space may rule out some of the bigger specimens but it certainly doesn't restrict creativity. Limitations can, in fact, often inspire innovative ideas, from the clever use of trailers and climbers to making the best of containers or windowsills. Restricting plant choice to smaller or more compact specimens is also a first step toward a strong final edit. Focus on finding plants that really suit your lifestyle, environment, and interests.

Three to try:
String of pearls (*Senecio rowleyanus*)—page 163
Air plants (*Tillandsia* spp.)—page 142
Basil (*Ocimum basilicum*)—page 194

Air plant

FIRST-TIME GARDENER

Hyacinth

Creating a garden or a green space for the first time is an exciting proposition. Don't be put off by a lack of knowledge, as gardening is very much about learning on the job. It's a process involving a certain amount of trial and error. Do start with easy-care plants that suit your environment, as this will help build confidence—there's lots of choice. Also choose plant types that naturally inspire you, as this will sustain interest and dedication.

Three to try:
Hyacinth (*Hyacinthus orientalis*)—page 185
Jade plant (*Crassula ovata*)—page 149
Calendula (*Calendula officinalis*)—page 202

EXPERT HANDS

Gardenia

If you've been gardening or looking after houseplants for a while, there's lots of scope to take things to the next level. This could include attempting to grow plants that require more maintenance, creating a large and diverse collection of houseplants, mastering perennial or successive planting, or planning a themed garden. There may be some restricting factors involved, however, such as time or family, so remember to listen to your lifestyle.

Three to try:
Gardenia (*Gardenia jasminoides*)—page 176
Fishtail palm (*Caryota mitis*)—page 120
Meyer lemon (*Citrus* × *limon* 'Meyer')—page 208

SHORT ON TIME

Houseleek

How much time you have to devote to the care of your plants is probably one of the most important factors when it comes to choosing plants. Selecting low-maintenance specimens is the best foundation advice, followed by grouping together plants of similar likes and dislikes—plants that love humidity, for example—so they can be watered, misted, or fed at the same time. If you want to branch out, try adding new items in one by one.

Three to try:
Houseleek (*Sempervivum* spp.)—page 144
Cast iron plant (*Aspidistra elatior*)—page 135
Rosemary (*Salvia rosmarinus*)—page 196

HOURS TO SPARE

Auricula

If you've got the luxury of hours to spare, if looking after plants is part of your job, or if you're willing to go the extra mile caring for them, then there's lots of scope in terms of choice. It can be helpful to impose some limitations, however, as there are only so many hours in the day. Rather than dedicating all your time to a diverse array of plants, it could be the moment to develop a themed garden or collect a particular group of plants.

Three to try:
Pine bonsai (*Pinus* spp.)
Zebra plant (*Aphelandra squarrosa*)—page 129
Auricula (*Primula auricula*)—page 173

ON A BUDGET

Lettuce

A green space doesn't have to cost a lot of money. In fact, it's possible to create a garden or plant collection on little or no budget at all, by propagating from seed, cuttings, or offsets, or using donations of seedlings from fellow plant-lovers. A tight budget can also prompt the creative use of containers or pots made from upcycled materials, or force you to focus on just a few select plant specimens to which you can devote all your loving care.

Three to try:
Snake plant (*Sansevieria trifasciata*)—page 147
Missionary plant (*Pilea peperomioides*)—page 136
Lettuce (*Lactuca sativa*)—page 212

MONEY TO INVEST

Fiddle-leaf fig

If you do have money to invest in your garden, yard, or interior green space, then it's worth making a master plan so you make every penny count. Do invest in good-quality plants from a sustainably minded grower, but also take advantage of plants for free (see above). You could then free up some money for structural or decorative components such as pots, a trellis, or a pergola to create a strong, stylish foundation for all that lovely greenery.

Three to try:
Fiddle-leaf fig (*Ficus lyrata*)—page 122
Gardenia (*Gardenia jasminoides*)–page 176
Dahlia (*Dahlia* spp.)—page 179

FAMILY-FRIENDLY

Spider plant

Making a family-friendly garden can be lots of fun, especially if you can get the children to help. Children grow and change from one year to the next, so be prepared to adapt your space accordingly and make it easy on yourself by going low-maintenance. Create a sensory experience with plants to look at, listen to, smell, touch, and taste—just make sure plants are safe for little hands, mouths, and eyes (see the child-friendly key in the Personal Plant Selector).

Three to try:
Kentia palm (*Howea forsteriana*)—page 119
Spider plant (*Chlorophytum comosum*)—page 161
Viola (*Viola* spp.)—page 203

PET AWARE

Rattlesnake plant

As with children, it's important to keep your pets safe from harmful toxins or plant parts such as spikes, spines, or choking hazards. Some plants can be fatal if ingested by cats and dogs; others may cause a temporary stomach upset or dizziness. Either way, follow the pet-friendly key in the Personal Plant Selector for the ones to avoid. It's still possible to include some such plants in your garden—just make sure they are well out of reach.

Three to try:
Boston fern (*Nephrolepis exaltata*)—page 114
Rattlesnake plant (*Calathea lancifolia*)—page 130
Parsley (*Petroselinum crispum*)—page 198

FIND YOUR FOCUS

Edit your plant choices by finding an inspiring focus—from greening up your home or yard to growing your own food, herbs, or cut flowers.

If you're reading this book, it's already a given that you love plants and want to know more about how to incorporate them into your indoor or outdoor spaces. However, it's also likely that you relate to plants in a certain way or have certain plant preferences, whether that's ornamentals to enhance the beauty of a room or outdoor space, or useful herbs, edibles, or cut flowers with which to nourish, heal, or style.

Once you've found a focus, using the suggestions below as a guide, delve deeper into that area, using books or online reference sources to create a mood board of ideal plants and possible design or styling ideas. Think about inspiring arrangements, potential containers or structural components, and plants that will fit your lifestyle and your space. You're now well on the way to creating a perfect plant list for yourself.

ORNAMENTALS

Ornamental plants are primarily planted for decorative purposes and include tens of thousands of species, cultivars, hybrids, and varieties, including houseplants, outdoor trees, shrubs, foliage plants, and flowers, and those hardworking specimens that could feature inside or out. Let your intuition and your senses guide you in terms of color, scent, texture, and form, plus take inspiration from other gardens or green spaces that fit your bill.

Three to try:
Staghorn fern (*Platycerium bifurcatum*)—page 115
Tufted air plant (*Guzmania lingulate*)
Slipper orchid (*Paphiopedilum* spp.)—page 155

Staghorn fern

USEFUL PLANTS

Ginger

Useful plants include edibles such as fruits, vegetables, microgreens, and herbs, but also plants and flowers that can be used for floristry, crafting, artworks, and design. Such plants can be incorporated into your home or garden, either as a main focus, as part of a wider planting scheme, or grown in a dedicated area or in containers and pots. Many houseplants are useful in terms of purifying the air, too. See The Mindful Garden (page 46).

Three to try:
Peace lily (*Spathiphyllum wallisii*)—page 168
Lavender (*Lavandula* spp.)—page 207
Ginger (*Zingiber officinale*)—page 204

EVERGREENS

Peperomia

Evergreens are an invaluable lush, green part of any year-round planting scheme, and include a wide range of tropical houseplants, conifers, and some ferns, shrubs, climbers, vines, and grasses. It's entirely possible to create a whole garden or plant collection out of evergreens, or you can use them as anchors for reliable seasonal interest. See the Personal Plant Selector for ideas.

Three to try:
Peperomia (*Peperomia* spp.)
Philodendron (*Philodendron* spp.)—page 124
Hoya (*Hoya* spp.)—page 160

FLOWERING PLANTS

Kalanchoe

Flowering plants are by far the largest group in the plant kingdom, offering a diverse array of species, cultivars, hybrids, and varieties. This includes some evergreen plants plus many ornamental and edible trees, shrubs, perennials, annuals, and biennials suitable for borders or pots. For ideas on container planting for indoors or out, use the Personal Plant Selector.

Three to try:
Kalanchoe (*Kalanchoe* spp.)—page 175
Passionflower (*Passiflora* spp.)—page 166
Narcissus (*Narcissus* spp.)—page 184

ANNUALS

Tulip

Annuals include plants that complete their life cycle in a year, but many biennials (a life cycle of two years) and perennials are also grown as annuals, including various food crops, cut flowers, and seasonal bulbs. Such plants are often grown for a specific purpose and can be fun to grow from seed or plug plants over the years.

Three to try:
Tulip (*Tulipa* spp.)—page 187
Cornflower (*Centaurea cyanus*)—page 203
Tomato (*Solanum lycopersicum*)—page 213

PERENNIALS

Chili pepper

Perennial planting—using plants that often die down in winter but live for at least two years—has become increasingly popular. With a diverse range available for almost every situation in the garden, they are great for adding color and interest to tricky areas such as shade, used to fill pots and other containers, and can flourish year-round if brought indoors in winter. See the Planting Inspirations section for suggestions.

Three to try:
Painted leaf begonia (*Begonia* spp.)—page 174
False shamrock (*Oxalis triangularis*)—page 181
Chili pepper (*Capsicum annuum* spp.)—page 214

HERBS

Oregano

Herbs are a wonderful combination of both beautiful and useful, including a range of woody shrubs and herbaceous perennials, annuals, and biennials that can easily be grown in beds or containers. Many herbs have been grown for thousands of years, resulting in an in-depth knowledge of their optimum growing conditions and nutritional or medicinal benefits. Be inspired to grow herbs inside and out via the Personal Plant Selector.

Three to try:
Oregano (*Origanum vulgare*)—page 195
Thyme (*Thymus* spp.)—page 197
Chives (*Allium schoenoprasum*)—page 200

FRUITS AND VEGETABLES

Microgreen

Bring pot to plate by growing your own fruits, vegetables, salad crops, and even edible flowers. This is especially rewarding if you love cooking but can also be fun if growing with children or if you want to save money and wasteful packaging. It's also possible to produce crops indoors, from microgreens and cut-and-come-again lettuce, to tomatoes and strawberries.

Three to try:
Arugula microgreens (*Eruca vesicaria*)—page 212
Grapevine (*Vitis vinifera*)—page 210
Scallions (*Allium* spp.)—page 215

CUT FLOWERS

Dahlia

Growing your own cut flowers is a lovely way to connect with nature while filling your home with gorgeous color, scent, and texture at the same time. It also helps avoid buying non-sustainable flowers that have been imported from abroad. Many cut flowers, fillers, and foliage plants can also be grown in pots for those who don't have access to garden borders or raised beds. See Planting for Produce (page 60).

Three to try:
Mophead hydrangea (*Hydrangea macrophylla*)—page 179
Dahlia (*Dahlia* spp.)—page 179
Coleus (*Plectranthus scutellarioides*)—page 134

CREATIVE PURSUITS

Sweet plum

Lots of plants can also be grown for various creative pursuits, including natural dyeing, botanical drawing, and pressed flower crafting. Working with or observing plants in this way can be hugely therapeutic, promoting a sense of well-being from looking closer at nature. It's also a good way to get children interested in the science, art, and seasonality of plants. See Planting for Seasonality on page 68 for more ideas.

Three to try:
Staghorn fern (*Platycerium bifurcatum*)—page 115
Sweet plum (*Sageretia theezans*)—page 189
Dill (*Anethum graveolens*)—page 201

APPRAISE YOUR SPACE

Consider the size, light, humidity, and temperature of a room or outdoor container space to help select plants that will really flourish and thrive.

It's tempting to choose plants based on their visual appeal or use, but this doesn't mean that they will automatically thrive. All plants have inherent sensitivities and survival skills based on where they naturally grow in the wild, and these factors continue to come into play in your home or garden. So for the best chance of healthy, happy plants, try to echo nature as closely as you can by appraising or adapting your space before you buy.

Many lush, green houseplants, for example, are native to tropical rainforests where they have evolved to flourish in warm temperatures, dappled light that filters through jungle canopies, and increased humidity. If you can easily mimic, re-create, or control any of these conditions in your home—such as high humidity in a bathroom plus bright, indirect filtered light from an east-facing window—then your plant will be off to a good start. Use the following room and outdoor space guides to point you in the right direction.

INDOORS

A wide range of houseplants, bonsai, flowers, herbs, and edibles can be grown indoors. Some need constant warm temperatures or several hours of bright sunlight, while others prefer high humidity, cool shade, or room to spread out. Find the right plant match by observing the general light, warmth, ventilation, and humidity of each room but also specific zones such as windowsills, corners, tables, and shelves over the course of a day.

Three to try:
Swiss cheese plant (*Monstera deliciosa*)—page 158
Forest cactus (*Rhipsalis boliviana*)—page 153
Natal lily (*Clivia miniata*)—page 183

Swiss cheese plant

OUTDOORS

Outdoor plants in gardens or on balconies or terraces will be subject to climatic factors such as temperature, rainfall, and wind, but you can still control elements such as position and soil. This is especially true of container plants, which can be grouped together for optimum light or shelter, are easily moved (including overwintering indoors), benefit from a controlled balance of nutrients, and are great for greening up smaller or awkward spaces.

Three to try:
Boston fern (*Nephrolepis exaltata*)—page 114
False castor oil plant (*Fatsia japonica*)—page 137
Narcissus (*Narcissus* spp.)—page 184

Boston fern

KITCHEN

Aloe vera

This is often the heart of the home, where plants can be used ornamentally but also to purify the air or produce edible crops. Environmental factors to consider when choosing suitable plants include increased heat and humidity from cooking, use by family members or guests, and general indoor elements such as light and ventilation. Use the Personal Plant Selector to help pinpoint plants or crops that work best on a sunny windowsill, for example.

Three to try:
Devil's ivy (*Epipremnum aureum*)—page 160
Aloe vera (*Aloe vera*)—page 146
Cilantro (*Coriandrum sativum*)—page 198

DINING AREA

Moth orchid

Whether you have an open-plan kitchen or a seperate dining room, plants can be used for greening up the room, tablescaping, and to provide easily accessible edibles for garnishes. This is also a good space in which to mix and match plants of different sizes and shapes, including tropical trailers for shelves, herbs for windowsills, flowering plants or bulbs for tables or occasions, and floor plants for room corners.

Three to try:
Moth orchid (*Phalaenopsis* spp.)—page 154
Amaryllis (*Hippeastrum* spp.)—page 182
Bay (*Laurus nobilis*)—page 206

LIVING ROOM

Parlor palm

A living room is the place where you're most likely to relax, so it makes sense to include plants that enhance a feeling of well-being. This could be through favorite plant types or by including sensory plants or those that purify the air. It might also be the most obvious space for a collection of plants that includes trailers, climbers, and larger specimens. Be aware of drying heat sources in winter.

Three to try:
India rubber plant (*Ficus elastica*)—page 123
Parlor palm (*Chamaedorea elegans*)—page 118
Tail flower (*Anthurium andraeanum*)—page 169

HALLWAY

Peperomia

A hallway is the first and last port of call to your home, so it should be as welcoming and memorable as possible. Plants can add drama, sensory color or scent, or soften what can sometimes be a colder, less lived-in space. Choose plants that you intuitively love but also take light levels into account, as this is likely to be one of the darker areas in the house. Container plants or hanging baskets can be placed on steps or in porches for added green appeal.

Three to try:
Dragon plant (*Dracaena marginata*)—page 126
Kentia palm (*Howea forsteriana*)—page 119
Peperomia (*Peperomia* spp.)

BEDROOM

ZZ plant

Opt for plants that are restful and rejuvenating for both sleeping and waking moments, and that give out oxygen 24 hours a day as opposed to most plants that emit carbon dioxide at night (although it would take a lot of these plants to affect the air quality). Some herbs or flowering plants can also aid sleep. Choose nontoxic species for children's bedrooms and shade-loving plants for less sunny spots.

Three to try:
Devil's ivy (*Epipremnum aureum*)—page 160
ZZ plant (*Zamioculcas zamifolia*)—page 137
Vriesea (*Vriesea* spp.)—page 140

BATHROOM

Silver inch plant

The bathroom is the ultimate space for plants that love humidity, including many plants native to the rainforest, such as some ferns, palms, foliage plants, climbers, trailers, and orchids. Take advantage of moisture in the air from a bath or shower to help water such thirsty plants, but don't forget to check light levels. Although many jungle plants prefer bright, filtered light, direct sun can scorch the leaves. Hanging plants also work well.

Three to try:
Rattlesnake plant (*Calathea lancifolia*)—page 130
Silver inch plant (*Tradescantia zebrina*)—page 161
Bird's nest fern (*Asplenium nidus*)—page 115

CLOAKROOM

Lucky bamboo

If you have a separate space for your coats, shoes, and bags, a dedicated utility or boot room, or an extra bathroom, a plant can bring the space to life. These areas can often be dark and shady, so try and find plants that thrive in these conditions. Aromatic or air-purifying plants can also be helpful for naturally freshening and scenting a room. Also, small specimens, hanging plants, or trailers can be useful in small spaces.

Three to try:
Heart leaf (*Philodendron scandens*)—page 159
Prayer plant (*Maranta leuconeura*)—page 132
Lucky bamboo (*Dracaena sanderiana*)—page 126

OFFICE

Peace lily

If you work in an office at home or elsewhere, plants can make a real difference to your mood and job satisfaction. Greening up such spaces can help retain a connection to nature, especially if you're indoors all day, while some plants can improve humidity or actively purify the air. Plants can also enhance meeting rooms and communal areas. Just choose the ones that suit light levels and opt for easy care if you're not there every day.

Three to try:
Peace lily (*Spathiphyllum wallisii*)—page 168
Spineless yucca (*Yucca gigantea*)—page 125
African violet (*Streptocarpus* sect. *Saintpaulia* cultivars)—page 172

WINDOWSILL

Mint

Pretty much every house, apartment, or home has a windowsill where at least a few plants could thrive. Indoor windowsills allow you to more easily control conditions, but be sure to take increased ventilation into account if you frequently open the window. Study the daily light cycles to see which plants would work best where—see Nurturing and Nourishment on page 90. For outdoor sills, make up window boxes that can be watered easily.

Three to try:
Echeveria (*Echeveria* spp.)—page 145
Avocado (*Persea americana*)—page 213
Mint (*Mentha* spp.)—page 195

CONSERVATORY

Bird of paradise

If you're lucky enough to have a conservatory or garden room, you can potentially think big, from outsized tropical plants, flowering shrubs, small trees, and citrus fruits to wandering trailers and vines. Conservatories can be hot in summer and cold in winter and have through drafts, so assess your space over the year. Direct sun can also cause leaf scorch to plants that prefer bright, filtered light. This is an ideal space in which to overwinter tender plants.

Three to try:
Bird of paradise (*Strelitzia reginae*)—page 171
Calamondin (*Citrus* × *microcarpa*)—page 209
Bougainvillea (*Bouainvillea* spp.)—page 167

BALCONY

Passionflower

A balcony can be a very inspiring place for plants, utilizing floor space, table areas, shelves, railings, and walls to create a haven of houseplants, herbs, flowers, and edibles. The first thing to do is determine which way your balcony is facing, or do a light assessment through the day. Suitable plants—including pollinator-friendly species—can then be planted in containers to stay permanently outside or, if necessary, overwinter indoors.

Three to try:
Cacti (*Cactus* spp.)—page 150
Passionflower (*Passiflora* spp.)—page 166
Strawberry (*Fragaria* spp.)—page 211

TERRACE

Agave

A terrace is that wonderful area that joins the indoors and out, providing a lovely opportunity for merging the two zones. As well as considering the plants that suit the climate, level of shelter, and light, it's worth thinking about the kind of containers you want to use. Raised beds, large or small, are great for bedding flowers, herbs, or crops, containers can add sculptural interest or be moved indoors in winter, while a trellis or a pergola add height.

Three to try:
Chinese fan palm (*Livistona chinensis*)—page 121
American agave (*Agave americana*)—page 147
Snowdrop (*Galanthus* spp.)—page 184

COURTYARD

Jasmine

A courtyard may be located within the center of your home or be a covered area next to your house. Like balconies, these areas have lots of potential for the creative use of container plants, climbers, and hanging baskets, or for bringing the indoors out with a Japanese-inspired garden or cocktail garden. If it's a covered space, assess the light, temperature, and ease of care; for outdoor spaces, also take climatic conditions into account.

Three to try:
Jasmine (*Jasminum* spp.)—page 165
Japanese maple (*Acer palmatum*)—page 191
Lemon verbena (*Aloysia citrodora*)—page 202

PLANTING
INSPIRATIONS

PLANTING INSPIRATIONS

Design your dream garden, indoors or out, by homing in on elements of well-being, style, produce, and seasonality.

A garden is often defined as a piece of land, usually adjoining a house, where flowers and other plants are grown. But, increasingly, it is almost any place where plants are grown within or outside the home: the herb garden on your windowsill, containers of home-grown fruits and vegetables on a balcony, a tropical jungle in the conservatory, raised beds on a terrace, a huge plot in the backyard, or a single houseplant in the bathroom.

Planting for well-being
Plants can help promote mindfulness, stimulate the senses, boost your mood, and even purify the air—from oxygen-producing greenery or bright flowers to hardworking houseplants and herbs. See page 44 for design and planting ideas.

Planting for style
Using plants and flowers to ornament your home as well as your garden is a centuries-old way to bring a space to life and create ambience. Pick and choose a diverse array of plant types to suit a range of tastes and styles (page 52).

Planting for produce
Growing your own food, herbs, or cut flowers can be incredibly rewarding, whether it's a few choice species in pots or on a windowsill, or following an overall theme. Find inspiration for your space and preferences on page 60.

Planting for seasonality
Plants are intrinsically connected to the seasons, many with obvious periods of growth, bloom, or dormancy. Pay closer attention to these features for seasonal or successive interest or crop yields, plus "holiday plants" for special occasions (page 68).

DESIGN YOUR DREAM GARDEN

*You have a blank canvas and can have the garden of
your dreams. Which design or plants should you go for?*

1

What is the space like?
Appraise your space to find ideal plant matches for the size, position,
and environment. Think about how you could use the space in terms
of "hard landscaping," such as pots, containers, borders, and beds.
This also informs what you can potentially grow.

2

What's your budget?
Working within a budget can help you plan the foundations of your
space or plant purchases. What can you afford to spend on plants or
pots and how could you save money? Upcycling containers, making
plant hangers, and sowing from seed are all viable options.

3

What's your focus?
What kind of garden would bring you the most joy? Whether
ornamental, edible, indoors, outdoors, houseplants, flowers, or
herbs—or a mix of everything—the Personal Plant Selector (page
108) can help cultivate your ideas.

4

What's your lifestyle?
Lifestyle is a huge factor when
it comes to maintaining as well
as designing a garden. Make
sure that your creative vision
aligns with your commitments,
such as time, work, family, or
pets. Edit plant lists and planting
combinations so everything has
a chance to really thrive.

5

Any other preferences?
Are you a born minimalist or
do you prefer a bohemian vibe?
Are you turned on by bright
colors or feel happiest
surrounded by evergreens? Use
the Planting Inspirations to help
inspire a garden or planting
scheme that speaks volumes
about you.

PLANTING FOR WELL-BEING

Boost health and well-being by gardening or interiorscaping with plants such as aromatic herbs, mood-boosting flowers, and oxygenating houseplants.

Plants are proven to have positive effects on our health and well-being, from oxygenating the air that we breathe to the positive physical and mental effects recorded when we interact with nature. Different studies show that this is the case whether we are simply surrounded by plants or actually gardening, so combining the two is doubly beneficial.

Research shows that simply looking upon a view of nature—through a window, for example—can reduce stress or anxiety and boost mood and memory. Introducing plants into your immediate environment deepens this connection, while nurturing plants brings the added feel-good factor that comes from caring for something.

Houseplant heroes

Even one lush, green houseplant can lift the mood of a room, so try and incorporate that effect throughout your home. Humidity-loving houseplants can reduce dry air, while top-heavy specimens are said to promote feelings of security and calm. Some plants are also proven to remove harmful chemicals such as volatile organic compounds (VOCs) from the air (see opposite), although research into this is ongoing.

Healing herbs

Herbs are another group of plants that can naturally help promote health, well-being, or healing through aromatic or medicinal properties—lavender for sleep or rosemary to rejuvenate, for example—as well as providing beautiful foliage and flowers. Many herbs are quite compact, drought-tolerant, or thrive in full sun or shade, so are ideally suited to container gardening indoors or out.

Flower power

Flowering plants can stimulate the senses through appearance, scent, textures, or sound—the rustling of leaves, for example. In one study, patients with a daily view of flowers recovered significantly quicker than those without, while other research reveals that being around plants increases compassion, concentration, productivity, creativity, happiness, energy, and mindfulness—all good reasons to fill your home with them.

Ten to try: air-purifying plants

All plants help produce the oxygen that we breathe, with some having the potential to purify the air by removing harmful chemicals (based on a 1989 NASA clean air study).

1. Spider plant (*Chlorophytum comosum*)
2. Devil's ivy (*Epipremnum aureum*)
3. Peace lily (*Spathiphyllum wallisii*)
4. Bamboo palm (*Chamaedorea seifrizii*)
5. Snake plant (*Sansevieria trifasciata*)
6. Split leaf philodendron (*Thaumatophyllum bipinnatifidum*)
7. Boston fern (*Nephrolepis exaltata*)
8. Weeping fig (*Ficus benjamina*)
9. Aloe vera (*Aloe vera*)
10. Corn plant (*Dracaena fragrans*)

THE MINDFUL GARDEN

Aid mindfulness by combining the aromatic, purifying, and tactile elements of plants with the simple joy that stems from nurturing something.

The art of mindfulness is about learning to be fully present within your mind, body, and your feelings, which helps to promote peace, calm, awareness, and clarity. It's a state of mind that all humans can access given the right tools, including practices such as meditation and breathing exercises. Interacting with nature is also proven to aid mindfulness, from spending time in the garden and tending houseplants, to harnessing the proven benefits of calming herbs.

Lavender

Lavandula spp.
The relaxing benefits of lavender have been documented for thousands of years, with recent neurological studies showing that it can help combat anxiety and stress. The medicinal properties of this beautiful purple-blue flowered herb are incredibly easy to access, either through growing some of your own outdoors or in a pot, picking a few budded stems to breathe in while meditating, or using the essential oil. Try growing some in the bedroom, where it can also aid sleep.

Jasmine

Jasminum spp.
For much of the year jasmine appears as a pretty-leaved evergreen vine, but in spring, when the blooms begin to appear, it really comes into its own. Not only are the white, star-shaped flowers exquisite in their simple beauty, when evening comes they emit the sweetest scent. Used to fragrance teas and cosmetics since antiquity, this scent is also said to heal, ease stress, and promote sleep. Try keeping a sprig of flowers on hand to inhale while meditating or through the day.

Peace lily

Spathiphyllum wallisii
Transforming your home or even a small corner of it into a sanctuary
for practices such as mindfulness, meditation, or yoga will almost
certainly be enhanced by the addition of a few well-chosen plants.
The peace lily, by name and by nature, is a good place to start,
displaying energizing lush, green leaves and arching stems of pure
white spathes. They are also said to purify the air of harmful toxins
such as benzene, and will adjust to lower light levels or survive spells
of drought. If you see it wilting, give it some love.

Aloe vera

Aloe vera
Nature has all sorts of ways of promoting mindfulness, including
inviting us to look closer at a shape or provenance, take an active
role in helping plants grow, or asking us to explore our connection
to the plant kingdom. Aloe vera can help focus or anchor the mind
through its confident swordlike structure, heal the body through the
soothing gel within its succulent leaves, and requires a little mindful
commitment to keep it happy and healthy.

Missionary plant

Pilea peperomioides
Every home should have a missionary plant, which, thanks to its
giving nature—in the form of an abundance of plantlets—is entirely
feasible. The offshoots that sprout from the trunk of the parent
plant are traditionally given away as "friendship plants," which is a
lovely way to weave kindness into your mindfulness practice. These
compact plants are also perfect for smaller spaces or offices, helping
to maintain an everyday connection with nature at home or work.

**How to meditate
with plants**

1. Allocate some time out from the
hustle and bustle of everyday life—
even five minutes can be helpful.
Choose a plant to connect with in
your home, office, garden, or wider
environment. This may be an active
choice, or try letting your intuition
guide you to a particular plant.

2. Be open to the ways in which plants
communicate with other elements
of nature, including humans. Let
yourself be drawn to characteristics
such as color, scent, form, or even
the wind blowing through leaves. Sit
down or stand still, focus on the plant,
and breathe.

3. Observe how you feel. Does
connecting with nature make you
feel calm, relaxed, or reduce feelings
of stress? If so, stop, breathe, and give
thanks to the plant. If the opposite is
true, stop and use your breath to stay
focused and grounded.

THE SENSORY GARDEN

Engage the senses and reward body and mind with herbs and houseplants that stimulate via touch, sight, scent, taste, and sound.

Sensory gardens can be planted specifically with the five senses in mind—often with a therapeutic or rejuvenating focus—or contain elements that naturally make your garden a sensory experience, whether that's via a tactile houseplant or a window box of aromatic herbs. Stimulating the senses doesn't mean overloading them, as we all have varying sensitivities and preferences; rather, it's designing a thoughtful space that restores and revives you.

Rosemary

Salvia rosmarinus
Rosemary has been lauded for its stimulating properties since antiquity, with Roman soldiers said to have tucked sprigs of the aromatic leaves behind their ears to keep them alert. If you've got a sunny spot in your garden or on a terrace or windowsill, it should do well in a well-drained border, raised bed, or pot, rewarding with its camphorous scent, earthy flavor, soft, needlelike leaves, and beguiling purple flowers. Rub the leaves between your fingers and breathe in for the full rosemary effect.

Begonia

Begonia spp.
Some plants cry out to be touched, including soft or furry-leaved species such as lamb's ear (*Stachys byzantina*), Mexican bush sage (*Salvia leucantha*), African violet (*Saintpaulia ionantha*), and many begonias (*Begonia* spp.). Rex begonias (*Begonia rex*)—also known as painted leaf begonias—are particularly rewarding due to their showy red, pink, black, purple, silver, and green patterned leaves. They're a bit fussy but worth it for looks and touch.

Calendula

Calendula officinalis

Calendulas are particularly good for growing with children, as they are quick to mature—about six to eight weeks after sowing. They also produce uplifting orange, daisylike flower heads that open and close with the light like a clock. This colorful, sensory experience can also last for much of the year, with blooms appearing well into winter and the arrival of the first hard frosts. Known for their soothing and skin-softening properties, the petals can also be picked and dried, to be used in teas, salves, or soaps.

Ponytail palm

Beaucarnea recurvata

A breeze rustling the leaves of trees, or grasses that make a swishing noise as you brush past them, are both ways in which plants appeal to our sense of sound. It's harder to stimulate this sense in our environmentally controlled homes, which is where the power of suggestion comes in. Include plants with plumes of long leaves, such as the ponytail palm, and you can almost feel it swaying in the wind. It also doesn't mind being touched and is nontoxic, so don't be afraid to run your fingers through its foliage.

Gardenia

Gardenia jasminoides

Large, glossy evergreen leaves and almost obscenely beautiful and highly scented flowers make the gardenia a must for a conservatory—if you've got the time or location to give it the nurturing and environment it needs. Given constant warm temperatures, enough light, and high humidity, they should give back, producing the strongest, sweetest scent at dusk. For an easier option, try sherbet-perfumed roses, scented pelargoniums, or wisteria.

How to make a succulent garden

1. Make the most of wonderfully tactile and visually curious succulents such as *Sempervivum, Haworthia, Aeonium,* and *Sedum*. Start by sourcing species with the same needs—those that prefer full sun, are frost-hardy, or more drought-tolerant, for example.

2. Plant or pot in well-drained soil, adding sand or grit if necessary. Succulents have shallow root systems so can also be tucked into a little bit of soil in the crevice or depression of a large rock. Also think about planting smaller specimens around a large focal point.

3. Use rock mulch to retain heat around plants, and water and feed according to species. Be brave when it comes to maintenance, donating pruned offshoots to friends, plus make time every day to admire your sensory creation.

THE ZEN GARDEN

Let zen garden design philosophy help promote peace and purpose in your home or outdoor space by imitating the essence and pure beauty of nature.

Zen gardens were developed by Japanese Buddhist monks as miniature stylized dry landscapes designed to imitate the essence of nature and help aid meditation and contemplation, with key elements including carefully composed arrangements of rocks, water features, moss, pruned trees, and raked gravel or sand to represent ripples. Incorporating Zen-style purpose and meaning into your garden or home can promote a similar sense of peace, focus, and tranquility.

Bonsai

Various species
Gazing upon ancient-looking, carefully balanced bonsai or trees and shrubs such as cherry (*Prunus*), pine (*Pinus*), fig (*Ficus*), and ginkgo (*Ginkgo biloba*) can be a grounding activity in itself, while persevering in the process can require Zen-like patience and calm. Either way, a bonsai can be a wonderful addition to your home, courtyard, or an outside terrace if using hardy specimens such as conifers. See Bonsai (page 188) for suitable species.

Japanese painted fern

Athyrium niponium
Ferns of all types are ideal for a Zen or Japanese-inspired garden, with the Japanese painted fern—also known as the painted lady fern—one of the most beautiful. Ideal for brightening up borders or containers in shady spots, it has deep red stems and deeply fronded leaves that appear frosted with silver. Choose from varieties such as 'Pictum' or pink-toned 'Burgundy Lace', planting en masse to create a calming carpet of elegant feathery foliage. To grow indoors, provide bright filtered light and humidity.

Japanese rock hosta

Hosta kikutii
Hostas are naturalized throughout Japan, where native forms are known as *giboshi*. Forming large clumps of green or blue oval- or lance-shaped leaves, they are well suited to the Zen garden, pairing beautifully with other plants that thrive in partial shade and moist environments, such as ferns. The Japanese rock hosta is particularly apt, with narrow, deep-veined leaves and pretty white-blue tubular flowers in late summer to fall. Hostas are also suitable for container growing, with the Zen practice of watering regularly.

Japanese forest grass

Hakonechloa macra
A Zen garden must, this bright green, clump-forming grass brings verdancy to borders or pots, its arching leaves happily swaying in the breeze. Although it can tolerate full sun in cooler climates, it prefers shady spots, making it ideal for peaceful woodland areas or sheltered courtyards. Added interest comes in the form of delicate summer flowers and red-brown foliage in fall, and cultivars such as 'Nicolas', 'Aureola', and 'Samurai', which extend a base palette of calming green to cream and gold.

Japanese maple

Acer palmatum
Japanese maples are a mainstay of Japanese garden design, offering a small, elegant habit, finely divided or lacy leaves, and often-breathtaking color in fall. They also thrive in large containers, ideally of natural substances such as terra-cotta or stone, and are thus ideal for indoor-outdoor terraces. Marking the fleeting beauty or ephemerality of the seasons by incorporating changing leaf colors or emerging blossoms into a planting scheme is a good way to embrace Zen philosophy.

How to make a kokedama

1. *Kokedama* is the centuries-old art of displaying a plant in a ball of moss, stemming from the practice of showing containers of plants alongside bonsai. Ideal for indoor Zen gardens, the process of making the ball can also help deepen a connection with nature and promote peace.

2. Mix two-thirds peat moss with one-third *akadama* (granular clay) or bonsai soil and apply a 1-inch (2.5cm) ball-shaped layer of wet mud onto the exposed roots of your chosen plant—a Japanese bird's nest fern (*Asplenium osaka*) is ideal for a calm, green Zen garden vibe.

3. Squeeze the ball to release dripping moisture, then envelop with a soaked layer of sustainably sourced sphagnum moss. Secure in place by winding waxed polyester twine or cotton cord around the ball, leaving a looped section for hanging.

PLANTING FOR STYLE

Lush green foliage, architectural form, beautiful flowers, and evocative scent are just some of the ways in which plants can help style up your home.

Plants have been cultivated in gardens and containers for thousands of years, but the concept of the "houseplant" is a relatively new phenomenon, whereby plants were brought indoors to brighten up dark rooms and add interest, color, and texture to decor.

Several hundred years later, the use of indoor or container plants to ornament or style up our homes has never been more popular. How plants are positioned and potted up is more inventive, however, with classic rainforest evergreens sharing the space with flowers, cacti, succulents, herbs, and edible produce, and indoor and outdoor space often merging as one.

Aspect and arrangement

Assess your space in terms of size, aspect, and environmental conditions (page 92), but also decor and details such as paint color, period features, furniture, and textiles. Use cascading or frond-leaved plants to soften hard edges, architectural forms as focal points or to add depth, and group plants in odd numbers, experimenting with a range of textures, sizes, and shapes.

Pots and planters

Pots, planters, and containers (page 86) can be used to echo decor, hide less attractive but well-draining containers, and grouped together in different heights. Couple large floor pots with tall, big-leaf specimens, play with plain or patterned ceramic pots for tables and shelves, use plant stands or hangers to make the most of cascading plants, and remember: pots and containers are a movable feast.

Maintaining visual appeal

Plants need varying levels of ongoing care and maintenance, but if you're planting primarily for visual appeal, it's worth paying even closer attention to form and shape. Bushy, trailing, or vining specimens may need pruning or training, for example, while flowering plants may benefit from regular deadheading to fully bloom.

Ten to try: showstopping plants

Weave the wonders of the plant kingdom into your home via large architectural floor plants, variegated foliage, succulents, and blooms.

1. Staghorn fern (*Platycerium bifurcatum*)

2. Amazonian elephant's ear (*Alocasia × amazonica*)

3. Fiddle-leaf fig (*Ficus lyrata*)

4. Variegated Swiss cheese plant (*Monstera deliciosa* 'Variegata')

5. Fishbone cactus (*Epiphyllum anguliger*)

6. Agave 'Blue Glow' (*Agave* 'Blue Glow')

7. Venus slipper orchid 'Maudiae' (*Paphiopedilum* 'Maudiae')

8. Silver vase plant (*Aechmea fasciata*)

9. Air plant (*Tillandsia ionantha* 'Fuego')

10. Bird of paradise (*Strelitzia reginae*)

THE MINIMALIST GARDEN

Enhance the clean, simple, calming lines of a minimalist home or outdoor space with a similarly streamlined choice of plants, pots, and containers.

Whether you naturally embrace a minimalist lifestyle or are drawn to it as a way to declutter your home, garden, or even thoughts, plants can play a vital role. Where surfaces, furniture, or a color palette are pared back, a choice selection of plants can add pockets of color, texture, or contrasting form, or be used as focal points. Let pots speak the minimal language too, in sleek or natural materials, making space for the odd piece of standout ceramic art.

India rubber plant

Ficus elastica
The handsome, smooth-edged oval leaves of the rubber plant really stand out against a minimalist backdrop, especially when paired with a large concrete or cast-iron pot, or placed on a plant stand for smaller specimens. Free from surrounding clutter, it's also easier to observe its natural growth habit and other features, with both the shiny upper side and clearly veined lower side of the foliage catching the eye. Popular cultivars include the dark red-black 'Burgundy' and black-green 'Black Prince'.

Bird of paradise

Strelitzia spp.
A bird of paradise plant may seem at odds with the minimalist approach, but in this case it's the leaves rather than the flowers that are the main focal point. A large plant, ideal for the corner of a room or for softening edgy furniture, it displays huge paddle-shaped, banana-like leaves on long, upwardly arching dramatic stems. *Strelitzia reginae* has the well-known orange and blue flowers, while *Strelizia nicolai* has potentially more minimalist white ones. It can also be moved outdoors in warm summers.

Cactus euphorbia

Euphorbia ingens
Also known as a candelabra tree due to its multistemmed columnar growth habit, this is a perfect plant for making an architectural statement in an otherwise pared-back room. Although it looks like a cactus, bearing small stems along each of its leafless ridged stems, it is actually a succulent tree that can grow up to 26 feet (8m) tall in the wild. For minimal design schemes, pair with a plain pot and place on a table, sideboard, or plant stand where it should retain a compact size.

Snake plant

Sansevieria trifasciata
Snake plants have stiff, vertical, swordlike leaves that make them ideal for a minimal home. While the foliage is variegated in shades of green and yellow—like a snake, hence the name—it's a graphic design that goes well against a neutral palette or can echo geometric shapes or hard lines. Snake plants are also easy to care for, if a minimal lifestyle requires low-maintenance options as well, ideal for areas of low light or an office where an element of drought tolerance is required.

String of hearts

Ceropegia woodii
Just one plant can bring a room or corner of a room to life, from an eye-catching or unusual houseplant to a little pot of herbs. Limiting the number of plants can also help draw the eye to sometimes-overlooked features, such as leaf shape, stem color, or overall silhouette. The delicate string of hearts plant, for example, easily gets lost in a busy design scheme. While alone on a shelf or mantelpiece, its heart-shaped leaves, pretty patterning, and cascading nature can really come into their own.

How to make a himmeli air plant holder

1. To make this clean-lined, geometric air plant holder, source some 0.1-inch (2.5mm) brass tubes and cut into twelve 4-inch (10cm) pieces using wire cutters. Cut a 60-inch (150cm) piece of fine brass wire.

2. Take three pieces of brass tube and string them onto the wire. Connect the wire to make a triangle, leaving a 1-inch (2.5cm) tail end. Feed on two more pieces of tube, then connect the wire to make another triangle. Do this until you have five triangles in a row.

3. Feed on one more piece of tube and then connect your wire to the beginning piece using the tail end. Then feed the wire through the side of one of the loose triangles and use it to connect the tops of both triangle flaps. Place an air plant in the brass holder and hang.

THE BOHEMIAN GARDEN

Express yourself through a world of plants as well as colors, textures, patterns, and art to create an eclectic, individual, or retro boho style.

Bohemian style is all about weaving together an eclectic, often unconventional mix of colors, textures, patterns, art, and influences from around the world. Plants add an extra layer of wild, from dramatic floor plants and cascading hanging baskets, to walls of wandering vines or rooms full of tropical specimens. There are no rules—just remember to choose the right plants for your lifestyle, focus, and space in terms of maintenance and care, especially if it's a jungle out there.

Swiss cheese plant

Monstera deliciosa
This classic plant has been used in bohemian decor for decades, as illustrated by artists such as Henri Matisse, who had a giant specimen in his 1940s studio. Not only do the huge, holey leaves make for a dramatic focal point in a room, they're also an interesting conversation starter in terms of why this leaf fenestration is there. Is it to stop hurricanes, catch random rays of light, or tolerate heavy rains—the jury is still out. Either way, monsteras look fantastic in a large pot with a support or trained up a wall.

Devil's ivy

Epipremnum aureum
Also known as golden pothos, devil's ivy has a natural ability to live in relatively deep shade. This versatile, easy-care plant can be used in pots, cascading down from shelves, in a hanging basket, or trained up a wall. The latter option is an increasingly popular one, creating a green wall of vigorous green stems and lush, heart-shaped green-yellow leaves. If you're looking for an extra twist, there's also the white-green 'Marble Queen' and the zingy acid green 'Neon' golden pothos to choose from.

Prayer plant

Calathea, Maranta, and *Stromanthe*

Prayer plants, including species of *Calathea, Maranta,* and *Stromanthe,* all have exquisite variegated foliage, and leaves that close at night like hands in prayer, hence the name. The Personal Plant Selector (page 108) can help guide you through the various types, although don't be surprised if you end up with a collection, from the red-veined *Maranta leuconeura* or the dark purple undersided rattlesnake plant (*Calathea lancifolia*), to the pink, green, and creamy white stromanthe (*Stromanthe sanguinea* 'Triostar').

Bunny ear cactus

Opuntia microdasys

Weave a sense of escapism into your planting scheme with sun-loving desert plants such as succulents and cacti. Take inspiration from artists such as Frida Kahlo, Yves St. Laurent, and César Manrique, who wove such species into their respective homes and gardens in Mexico, Morocco, and Lanzarote in the Canary Islands. Furry-padded bunny ear cacti are great stand-alone specimens in colorful or patterned pots, or team with spiral aloe (*Aloe polyphylla*) or zebra haworthia (*Haworthia attentuata*).

Dahlia

Dahlia spp.

Flowering plants can also introduce aspects of color, pattern, and texture into your home, from small windowsill specimens such as bright purple African violets to large conservatory specimens such as camellias, bougainvillea, or angel's trumpets. Dahlias are particularly lovely vintage container plants, blooming through summer and fall if you have an outdoor balcony or terrace, with numerous cultivars to suit every taste.

How to make a macramé plant hanger

1. Cut four equal lengths of thick yarn or cord about 20 inches (50cm) long (size up for larger vessels). Fold the bundle of strands in half and loop the folded end through a small metal or wooden hanging ring. Feed the loose ends through the yarn loop and pull taut.

2. Separate the yarn into groups of two strands. Double knot each pair together about 2.5 inches (6cm) down. Then take the left strand of each pair and double knot it to the right strand of the pair next to it about 1.5 inches (4cm) down. Then knot the two outer strands to make a circular net.

3. Repeat the second part of the last step but knotting 1 inch (2.5cm) down. Then tie all the strands together in a large knot 1 inch (2.5cm) below that. Cut off the excess yarn to create a tassel. Then open out, place a potted-up plant inside, and find a suitable place to hang it.

THE COCKTAIL GARDEN

Embrace outdoor living and style up an al fresco area of your home in which to share botanically inspired drinks with family and friends.

Al fresco eating and drinking has become even more important in recent times, with an increasing trend for bringing the indoors out as well as the outdoors in. Creating a warm, comfortable outdoor space in which to host family or friends can be great fun, from dressing up the space with ambient lights, cushions, and throws, to creating a green oasis with plants and climbers, or growing your own herbs and flowers for botanically inspired drinks.

Mint

Mentha spp.
Grow mint in containers in full sun or partial shade in or near your drinks prep area so it's easy to pick fresh. This can then be used to make hot or cold drinks or herbal preparations, from fresh mint tea and mojitos to mint-infused syrup. There are lots of lovely mint types to try, including garden mint (*Mentha spicata*), peppermint (*Mentha × piperita*), chocolate mint (*Mentha × piperita f. citrata* 'Chocolate'), and apple mint (*Mentha suaveolens*). Grow them in separate pots to keep the flavors from merging.

Lemon verbena

Aloysia citrodora
There are several ways to get a lemon flavor into your drinks—from freshly squeezed lemon juice, slices, or wedges (try growing your own lemon tree, page 208) to lemon-scented and flavored herbs such as lemon balm, lemon thyme, and lemon verbena. The latter produces the most exquisite sherbet lemon aroma and taste from just one leaf and can easily be grown in pots and containers, then used to infuse hot and cold drinks.

Borage

Borago officinalis

Most classic summer drinks, alcoholic or mocktails, taste even better with the addition of home-grown fruit and flowers from your garden, terrace, or balcony, including fresh mint, cucumber, strawberries, and borage flowers. Borage's pretty blue star-shaped flowers can be added to a cocktail mix, used to garnish separate drinks, or frozen into ice cubes. Borage is also a great companion plant for growing next to outdoor vegetables such as tomatoes and squash, as it attracts beneficial pollinators.

Palms

Various species

Evergreen palms are great for creating a lush, green tropical landscape inside or out. For warmer indoor spaces, choose species such as the parlor palm (*Chamaedorea elegans*), kentia palm (*Howea forsteriana*), and the areca palm (*Dypsis lutescens*), coupled with verdant ferns such as the Boston fern (*Nephrolepis exaltata*). These can all be moved outside in summer. For colder or outdoor spaces, go for a hardy fern such as the umbrella-like dwarf fan palm (*Chamaerops humilis*).

Scented geranium

Pelargonium spp.

Use fragrant plants such as wisteria, jasmine, and roses to create an inviting ambience, placing in pots or around pergolas. A host of scented geraniums can also look fabulous on a terrace or balcony, with interesting foliage and flowers in a variety of shapes, shades, and colors. Crushing the leaves releases the scent, from apple-scented (*Pelargonium odoratissimum*) to chocolate peppermint (*P. tomentosum*) to rose (*P. graveolens*). The edible flowers can also be used as garnishes, and the leaves to scent sugars.

How to make a herbal syrup

1. Tie eight sprigs of a woody herb such as thyme, rosemary, or lavender into a bundle with kitchen twine. Combine 2 cups (475ml) water and ¾ cup (175ml) honey (preferably raw and organic) in a pan. Bring to a gentle boil, whisking until combined. Turn off the heat.

2. Add the herb bundle to the honey syrup. Cover and let steep for 30 minutes. Remove the herb bundle and discard in the green waste or composter. Strain the syrup through a fine mesh sieve into a sterilized 16-ounce (475ml) glass lidded jar. Seal and store in the fridge for up to six weeks.

3. Use the syrup in cocktail and mocktail recipes such as gin and tonics, garden gimlets, or mojitos. Thyme syrup, for example, is delicious mixed with smashed basil leaves, grapefruit juice, a squeeze of lime, tonic, and optional gin.

PLANTING FOR PRODUCE

Make indoor or container gardens really work for you by incorporating useful crops, including herbs, edible fruits, vegetables, and cut flowers

Whether you're bringing the outside in by greening up your home or bringing the inside out for that cozy al fresco experience, the lines between garden and home are increasingly blurred. This includes the types of plants that can be grown inside and out, from pots of herbs and edibles in the kitchen to tropical or tender specimens spending their summers on a patio or balcony.

If outdoor space is limited, it's especially useful to know that there is a wider range of crops that can be grown indoors or in containers than many people realize: a variety of nutritious microgreens on a windowsill, a whole herb garden positioned between the sunny and shadier spots of the kitchen, or tomatoes, cucumbers, and cut flowers on a terrace.

Herbs
There are so many positive reasons to grow herbs, from the sensory appeal of their beautiful and aromatic leaves and flowers to the ways in which they can be used to heal, nourish, and style. Herbs are also one of the most versatile plant groups, with specimens suitable for sun, shade, drought, and humidity. Their compact size makes them suitable for containers or raised beds.

Edibles
You don't need a backyard, large borders, or raised beds to grow fruit and vegetables. There are lots of viable crops that can be grown indoors or in small or large containers, from cut-and-come-again lettuce to strawberries and edible flowers such as violas or borage. For optimum, bountiful harvests, pay close attention to the care label.

Cut flowers

Cut flowers are a little harder to grow indoors, but many prefer to be started inside from seed. Plus lots of beautiful bloomers will thrive in containers for planting up indoor-outdoor spaces. Dahlias, roses, and hydrangeas provide blowsy blooms, while herbs and perennials are ideal for more delicate or aromatic posies or bouquets.

Ten to try: useful container plants

Plant containers up with plants that are beautiful and useful, including healing herbs, delicious fruits, salad crops and vegetables, and beautiful cut flowers.

1. English lavender (*Lavandula angustfolia*)
2. Rosemary (*Salvia rosmarinus*)
3. Common thyme (*Thymus vulgaris*)
4. Rose (*Rosa* spp.)
5. Fennel (*Foeniculum vulgare*)
6. Myrtle (*Myrtus communis*)
7. Lettuce (*Lactuca sativa*)
8. Tomato (*Solanum lycopersicum*)
9. Grapevine (*Vitis vinifera*)
10. Chili pepper (*Capsicum annuum* spp.)

THE HERB GARDEN

Grow herbs to nourish, heal, and style your body, mind, and home, from kitchen windowsill planters to a fully fledged apothecary garden.

Herbs are one of the most rewarding groups of plants to grow, with many species known for their culinary, medicinal, and beautifying properties. A wide variety of herbs are suitable for containers, from larger woody shrubs that can be trimmed into compact shapes to tender annuals or perennials that can be grown from seed. Just remember to read the care label so you get the very best from these wonderful plants.

Bay

Laurus nobilis
Add structure to a sunny or partially shaded terrace using larger but easy to prune evergreen herbs such as bay (*Laurus nobilis*) and myrtle (*Myrtus communis*). As well as providing handsome, glossy green foliage, the leaves of both these plants can be used in cooking. Harvest bay from trees over two years old, at any time of the year, laying them on parchment paper for two weeks in a warm, dry space to improve flavor and scent. Use in bouquet garnis or to make fragrant wreaths or garlands.

Thyme

Thymus spp.
Tiny-leaved, pink- or white-flowered thyme has been cultivated since ancient times for its warm, pungent flavor, decongesting scent, and naturally antibacterial and antiseptic properties. This small woody or creeping herb is also ideal for growing in pots using a gritty potting medium and placed in a warm, sunny spot. Harvest just before blooming for the most aromatic scent and flavor, then use fresh or dry in soups, roasts, and bakes or infused into syrup for drinks or to soothe coughs.

Oregano

Origanum vulgare

There are several herbs from the *Origanum* genus worth growing for their aromatic flavor and scent, including oregano (*Origanum vulgare*) and marjoram (*Oregano majorana*), the former being sweet, floral, and woody, the latter more pungent, citrusy, and camphorous. Oregano is particularly useful in cooking, adding a tangy note to pizza or pasta sauce or an earthy flavor to quick breads. Harvest in late summer before the flower buds open, or dry in loose bunches for a year-round supply.

Basil

Ocimum basilicum

Basil deserves a place on every kitchen windowsill, or can be grown outside in summer in terra-cotta pots. Given at least six hours of sunlight a day, adequate drainage, fertile soil, and a feed with a diluted organic fertilizer, such as liquid seaweed, a couple of times during the growing season, it should reward with a bounty of sweet, tender foliage. Plucking leaves also encourages new growth, so use in cooking as an ingredient or garnish, to make an aromatic oil, or as part of a decongestant steam.

Fennel

Foeniculum vulgare

If you have enough height in an outdoor space to grow fennel, the rewards are numerous. First come the anise-tasting feathery leaves, which can be used in sweet and savory dishes. Tall stems of yellow umbels then deliver a pungent pollen—ideal in cream, a roasting rub, or on fresh fruit—followed by the seeds that can be eaten to freshen the breath or used to make tea. This pollinator-friendly plant is also lovely as a lacy landscaping element, or press the flowers and foliage to make beautiful art.

How to harvest and store herbs

1. Pinch leafy annual herbs such as basil at the tip of the stems, gathering several leaves at a time. Cut longer-stemmed herbs such as cilantro, parsley, lavender, and rosemary near the base. And harvest sprigs of perennial herbs such as oregano, thyme, sage, and tarragon.

2. In general, don't remove more than one-third of a plant at a time. Many herbs are at their best just before flowering, others when they reach a certain height or maturity. Harvesting edible flowers, seeds, or roots depends on the season.

3. Pick herbs mid-morning, then wash and pat dry. Use fresh according to the recipe. Herbs with a low moisture content, such as marjoram, oregano, and thyme, can be air-dried. Herbs with more succulent leaves, such as basil, chives, mint, or tarragon, can be preserved in the freezer.

THE EDIBLE GARDEN

A surprisingly wide range of seasonal produce can be grown in containers inside or out, for accessible year-round crops.

You don't need a backyard or even raised beds or borders to grow your own fruits, salad, or vegetables. Many crops do just as well in containers and some can be grown indoors, potentially producing a harvest year-round. The key to successfully growing your own edibles in this way is to ensure that the plant is getting enough nutrients, light, and water to complete its necessary life cycle. Sourcing a cultivar or species that is ideal for indoor growing can also help.

Salad leaves and greens

Various species
Growing your own salad provides fresh, tasty leaves while crucially saving on plastic packaging and cost. There's a huge range of leafy vegetables that can be grown as cut-and-come-again crops, including loose-leaf lettuce, spinach, and arugula; the leaves of root crops such as beets, radish, and turnip; herbs such as basil and cilantro; and the flowering plant amaranth. Grow crops in a sunny spot that doesn't get too hot, harvesting tender leaves when at their freshest.

Tomato

Solanum lycopersicum
Tomatoes are ideal for containers, grown in well-draining pots or bags with suitable supports and given enough light, water, and organic feed. If you don't have a sunny south-facing window, supplement with grow lights. Small patio varieties or determinate tomato plants are best for indoors, although these fruit all at once, so plant a succession of varieties that ripen at different times, or sow new seeds every month or two. Tomatoes can also be grown outdoors in spring after the last frosts.

Bell or chili pepper

Origanum vulgare

The species *Capsicum annuum* includes various pepper varieties and cultivars, such as sweet and hot peppers, with the fiery sensation triggered by a compound known as capsaicin. All peppers can be grown in containers in a sunny greenhouse or conservatory, potentially moved outside during warm summer months. Choose your ideal specimen based on taste, heat, and color but also on space—bell peppers need more room to grow, whereas dwarf chili peppers are ideal for a sunny windowsill.

Ginger

Zingiber officinale

Ginger is easy to propagate from small pieces of leftover rhizome, by planting in a container of well-drained potting mix, with a visible eye or small yellow tip just level with the surface. Water in well, cover with a clear plastic bag, and place in a warm, sunny spot. Small green shoots eventually give way to a beautiful flowering houseplant with new rhizomes of ginger ready to harvest after six to eight months. Keep planting for a steady crop. You can also try cultivating the ginger family relative turmeric at home.

Strawberry

Fragaria × ananassa

You don't need to produce a huge harvest of strawberries to enjoy growing them. Even a handful of fruits can provide a delicious sweet treat or taste of summer. Strawberries are perfect for growing in a variety of containers, including space-saving hanging baskets, specially designed strawberry jars, or pots with pockets for inserting multiple plants. It's also worth exploring different cultivars, including summer-bearing, ever-bearing, and the more compact Alpine (*Fragaria vesca*).

How to grow microgreens

1. Microgreens are the first true leaves of leafy herbs, salad crops, or greens. Packed with health-giving vitamins, antioxidants, and minerals, they can be added to salads, sandwiches, and stir-fries and are easy to grow indoors in containers for a constant fresh supply.

2. Source a microgreen mix or ideal variety such as mustard, kale, endive, arugula, watercress, basil, lettuce, spinach, or radish greens. Fill a 2-inch (5cm) deep container with organic potting mix. Smooth the soil and scatter the seeds $^1/_8$ inch (3mm) apart. Cover with $^1/_8$ inch (3mm) of soil.

3. Water gently but thoroughly. Then place on a sunny windowsill or spot with at least 4 hours of direct sunshine. Keep soil moist and harvest when the first true leaves appear (after the seed leaves), generally around 10 days after sowing. Sow the next crop and repeat.

THE CUT FLOWER GARDEN

Experiment with a succession of container-grown flowers for cutting and drying as well as enjoying while in their pots.

Growing flowers for cutting and drying may require a little outdoor space and experimentation to see what works, but it's worth it even if you only manage to grow a few single stems. Remember to select plants that work for your lifestyle, focus, and space, as some flowers need specific environmental conditions or elements of care to make them really bloom. Plus, have fun collecting vases or pots in which to display your cut or dried arrangements.

Tulip

Tulipa spp.
Growing plants from bulb is a great way to produce a succession of beautiful flowers without the mad rush to sow seeds in spring. Many bulbs or corms such as snowdrops, crocuses, narcissi, hyacinths, muscari, alliums, and tulips are best planted in the fall and can be easily grown in containers, layering bulbs or corms to come up at different times. Tulips are one of spring's brightest and most rewarding bulbs, with a huge range of covetable cultivars, including parrot tulips and 'La Belle Epoque'.

Herbs

Various species
Herbs are another group of plants that can double up as cut or dried flowers, with many flourishing in containers or pots. Blooming species such as frilly blue cornflowers, orange daisylike calendulas, aromatic lavender, the purple-spired *Salvia*, and anise-scented *Agastache* are obvious for a herbal flower garden, bringing evocative fragrance as well as visual beauty. Herbs such as rosemary, lemon balm, bay, oregano, and marjoram are lovely used as filler foliage, less showy blooms, or in table displays.

Love-in-a-mist

Nigella damescena
Experiment with annual, biennial, and perennial flowers for cutting and drying. Growing in containers gives some control over soil type, drainage, and nutrition, but take factors such as light, shelter, and growth space into account. Love-in-a-mist is an easy-to-grow, medium-height self-seeder with beautiful lacy white or blue flowers and impressive seedpods that work fresh or dried. Or try cosmos, zinnia, scabious, astrantias, or strawflowers, choosing dwarf varieties for more compact growth.

Rose

Rosa spp.
Consider growing statement or focal point flowers such as roses, sunflowers, foxgloves, chrysanthemums, or dahlias. These larger-headed flowers can be grown in containers as well as beds, although you may need to feed, prune, or support certain specimens to get the most profuse blooms. Use roses to introduce exquisite scent and color, choosing from climbing, rambling, and bush forms as well as thousands of unique and romantic cultivars. To dry, hang rose stems upside down in a warm, dry place.

Hydrangea

Hydrangea spp.
Shrubby flowering plants such as hydrangeas or viburnums are ideal for larger containers on balconies, terraces, or patios, adding structure to a space. As plants mature, they will also provide prolific blooms with which to supplement cut or dried displays. There's also a wide range of hydrangeas in terms of color, shape, and foliage, from large puffball mopheads or flatter lace-caps, to pointed panicles and oak leaves. For pots, go for compact varieties such as *Hydrangea paniculata* 'Little Lime' or *Hydrangea quercifolia* 'Sike's Dwarf'.

How to condition flowers

1. Conditioning cut flowers is about bringing out their blooming best and prolonging vase life, starting with the best time to cut them: in the morning when the stems are still fully turgid (filled with water). Place stems straight into a bucket of water as soon as possible after cutting.

2. Most flowers are best picked when just starting to show color, but this can differ between species. Roses and dahlias, for example, may not open if picked in too tight a bud, while sweet peas will bloom over a longer period if picked regularly.

3. Strip all the leaves from the bottom half to two-thirds of each stem. Re-cut all stems to a clean, angled cut—woody or dropping stems may need a further cut or sealing. Place prepped stems in a bucket of clean water and in a cool place for 2–3 hours. Arrange in a clean vase.

PLANTING FOR SEASONALITY

Planting for year-round interest rewards with foliage, flowers, fruits, and seeds, including timely specimens for special occasions and holidays.

Planting the seasons is rewarding in terms of year-round ornamental interest and potential produce, but it's also one of the best ways to learn about plants in terms of growth patterns, life cycles, and basic needs. This follows through in terms of planning a garden around seasonal foliage, flowers, fruits, or seeds, but also inversely where plants can be forced to bloom early or act as evergreens.

Most gardens have elements of the seasons woven through them, from deciduous trees to perennial borders or cut flower patches. Container gardening can embrace many of these elements, but whether plants are grown indoors or outdoors does have a bearing. To fruit, flowering plants need to be pollinated for example, while winter-bare specimens are not generally ideal as houseplants.

Climate and environment

To plant seasonally, get in tune with your climate and environment. Temperate climates cycle through all four seasons: spring, summer, fall, and winter. These seasons happen at different times of the year around the world, with variations in temperature and precipitation. Tropical zones have either one hot season year-round or a dry and rainy season, the latter lasting one to three months.

Succession planting

Succession or successive planting, designed to stagger or extend a harvest or create a continuous flow of interest, is a great way to get the most out of containers or small spaces. There are several ways of doing this, including sowing crops to cut and come again, layering bulbs, ordering perennials to flower at different times in the same place, or deadheading to encourage more blooms.

Seasonal decor

Designing a seasonal garden also rewards in terms of foliage, flowers, fruits, or seed heads with which to decorate for special occasions or holidays. This could include spring blossom, fall fruits, flowers for birthdays, or traditional plants or forced bulbs for cultural, religious, or spiritual holidays.

Ten to try: plants to grow successively

Quick-maturing plants, those prone to bolting, plus bulbs and tubers that can be layered or forced are ideal for succession planting edibles and flowers.

1. Little gem lettuce (*Lactuca sativa* 'Little Gem')

2. Arugula (*Eruca vesicaria*)

3. Cilantro (*Coriandrum sativum*)

4. Basil (*Ocimum basilicum*)

5. Dill (*Anethum graveolens*)

6. Calendula (*Calendula officinalis*)

7. Cornflower (*Centaurea cyanus*)

8. Dahlia (*Dahlia* spp.)

9. Narcissi (*Narcissi* spp.)

10. Tulip (*Tulipa* spp.)

THE SPRING/SUMMER GARDEN

Celebrate the natural growth period of spring and summer with an array of lush, green foliage and seasonal blooms and fruits.

Warmer weather prompts the growth of new shoots and leaves, followed in some cases by flowers and fruits. This doesn't just apply to outdoor plants—many tropical houseplants have a warm weather or "dry season" growth period too, and appreciate a bit of fresh air if environmental factors allow. Team such tropical plants with containers full of brightly colored flowers, citrus fruits and berries, and tender herbs for the perfect spring or summer vibe.

False shamrock

Oxalis triangularis
This small, sensitive houseplant, a native of South America, with its distinctive purple-maroon, trifoliate leaves, is often bought or given in fully fledged leaf. In which case, many people don't realize that it actually grows from a bulb and thus has a dormant period when it can die right down. In spring and summer, however, it quite literally blooms with pretty pink-white flowers, its foliage opening and closing with the sun like a marker of the longer days.

Tropicals

Various species
Using plants to merge spaces between indoors and out is becoming increasingly popular, including moving suitable houseplants onto a terrace or balcony in summer for a bit of fresh air. The latter is a great way to create a lush, green, tropical vibe using plants such as palms, snake plants, figs, cacti, and succulents. Wait until the last frost has passed, then acclimatize plants for two weeks first by placing in a shady spot and bringing them in at night. Trailers can also be hung from trees or posts.

Passionflower

Passiflora spp.

Flowering plants are at their most bounteous during spring and summer, including climbers such as jasmine, wisteria, clematis, and passionflower, all of which can be grown vertically, bringing color, form, and scent to tighter spaces such as courtyards or balconies. The passionflower is particularly enticing due to its exotic-looking flowers, orange fruits, and self-clinging nature by way of springy tendrils. Choose from numerous cultivars, including frost-hardy *Passiflora caerulea* 'Grandiflora' or 'Amethyst'.

Cilantro

Coriandrum sativum

Many herbs are at their best during the spring and summer months, with aromatic oils being at their strongest on a warm morning, just before flowering (thyme or sage) or when in bud (lavender). Flowers such as calendula, camomile, and rose can also be harvested at this time. It's also the time to grow many tender herbs from seed or plug plants, such as cilantro, basil, and dill, placing in pots outside or on a sunny windowsill. Pick cilantro fresh to use in salads, sauces, and as a garnish.

Lemon tree

Citrus × limon

Citrus trees reward with handsome, shiny foliage, sweet-scented pretty blossoms, and the potential of zingy fruit to come—perfect for a warm conservatory or sunny spot in the house. They can also be brought outside in summer, creating a holiday atmosphere, although you'll need to allow plants time to adjust to light levels, giving them shelter and increasing watering during hot, dry spells. If you can get a lemon tree to fruit, including cultivars such as 'Meyer' and 'Variegata', you can also enjoy the tangy juice in cooking or cocktails.

How to make a terrarium

1. Terrariums are fully or partially closed glass structures that allow heat and light to enter while confining water, and are a lovely way to show off miniature plants or seasonal displays of foliage and flowers. Choosing a terrarium that is partially open will allow some airflow.

2. Line the base of a glass container or terrarium with sustainably sourced sheet moss or 2-inch (5cm) stones for drainage. Add a ½-inch (1cm) layer of activated charcoal to control odor. Add a second layer of moss, followed by at least 2 inches (5cm) of sterile, multipurpose potting mix.

3. The soil level should be low enough that plants will fit without touching the terrarium top. Take small potted versions of plants such as croton, pothos, ferns, or nerve plants. Cut off some of the roots to retard growth. Use a spoon and chopsticks to plant, and water gently so it is just moist.

THE FALL/WINTER GARDEN

Steer your indoor or container garden to reflect the changing, colder seasons, moving from colorful fall foliage to aromatic herbs to uplifting winter blooms.

Gardening for fall or winter is all about embracing the turn of the seasons, finding ways to brighten duller, darker days, and choosing plants that can survive elements such as outdoor frost or centrally heated rooms. Most tropical houseplants will appear lush and green year-round, but make sure you adjust watering and feeding regimes for the seasons. Supplement these with bright, variegated foliage, winter blooms, and aromatic herbs.

Flowering maple

Abutilon × hybridum
Fall is all about color, with true maple trees (*Acer* spp.) displaying some of the most arresting hues of red, amber, and gold. The flowering maple is not so hardy outdoors through the colder months and needs to be moved indoors before any risk of frost, but it does have similar-shaped leaves plus orange, yellow, salmon, or red mallowlike flowers depending on the cultivar. What you get instead is the essence of fall but within your home, ideal for a cool room with just a few hours of direct sunshine.

Flaming Katy

Kalanchoe blossfeldiana
Also known as Christmas kalanchoe, flaming Katy brings joy to the winter months through evergreen, shiny, scallop-edged succulent leaves, a pleasingly round habit, and late fall to early winter blooms ranging from dark red, pink, and orange to gold and white. Use to brighten a windowsill, sideboard, or table, providing bright filtered light to help it thrive. Removing dead flowers can encourage prolonged blooming, while pruning back can help promote plants to last from one year to the next.

Croton

Codiaeum variegatum
Create a fall-themed display using flame-hued foliage plants such as the vibrant, leather-leaved *Codiaeum variegatum*, available in a wide spectrum of varieties and cultivars, including different leaf shapes and colors ranging through yellow, orange, red, pink, green, cream, black, and purple. Just ensure that you follow the care label, as crotons can be slightly fussy specimens in terms of light, water, humidity, drafts, and being moved.

Hellebore

Helleborus spp.
Embrace the fall or winter months by designing outdoor container displays around seasonal foliage, flowers, fruits, and seedheads. Include jewel-colored cosmos, dahlias, *Verbena bonariensis*, and fennel as a final farewell to summer. Make the most of turning leaves and fading fall petals with containers full of hydrangeas, asters, and grasses. Also plan ahead for winter using early bloomers such as hellebores and snowdrops. A little bit of interest for the colder, darker months can go a long way.

Winter savory

Satureja montana
Pots full of aromatic herbs such as rosemary, thyme, sage, and winter savory deliver on woody structure and neat evergreen or semi-evergreen foliage, but also delicious flavor for soups, stews, roasts, and bakes. Winter savory is particularly good with beans or cabbage, aiding digestion while lending a spicy, earthy, warming taste. It can go dormant in winter in colder climes but will continue to flourish if brought inside, given well-drained soil and at least six hours of bright light.

How to force bulbs

1. Force spring bulbs such as paperwhites or hyacinths to bloom earlier than expected for winter color and scent. For best results, buy prepared bulbs in early fall that have been pre-chilled to trick them into thinking it's already winter.

2. For hyacinths, place bulbs close but not touching, tip side up, on a 2-inch (5cm) layer of potting compost. Fill with compost so the tips are visible. Water lightly, cover, and keep in a dark, cool place for around 10 weeks when shoots appear. Move to a light, airy spot to bring on flowers.

3. For paperwhites, allow 6 weeks from planting to bloom. Fill a shallow container with 2 inches (5cm) of gravel. Place bulbs on top, close together, filling in so the tips are visible. Water to the base of the bulbs. Keep somewhere cool. When roots develop, move to a cool, sunny spot to shoot and flower.

THE HOLIDAY GARDEN

Plant or style up your garden or home for festive occasions using visually on-theme houseplants and seasonal blooms, fruits, and vegetables.

Using nature to celebrate the seasons or festive occasions is a long-standing tradition that goes back thousands of years. Some plants, believed to hold certain properties or cultural, religious, or spiritual meaning, are used symbolically, often due to the timing of their foliage, flowers, or fruits. Others have elements that are simply used decoratively, from brightly colored flowers to evergreen foliage to dried seedheads. There is always a way to let nature be your guide.

Amaryllis

Abutilon × hybridum
Tall, stately, flamboyant-flowered amaryllis makes a wonderful gift for winter holidays such as Christmas. A tender bulb, it needs to be planted indoors, at some point between early fall and early winter, six to eight weeks before you want it to bloom. Which means you can also stagger blooms to appear until early spring or even Easter. Match colors to taste or follow a seasonal theme, from single-colored deep crimson 'Belinda', cerise pink 'Bestseller', or red-flowered 'Red Lion', to red and white 'Star of Holland'.

Christmas cactus

Schlumbergea × bridgesii
So named for its propensity to bloom from early to mid-winter—thus including the Christmas period for those in the Northern Hemisphere—this epiphytic rainforest-dwelling cactus has flat succulent segmented branches and red, white, yellow, pink, or purple blooms. Due to its naturally cascading habit, it works perfectly in hanging baskets, on high shelves, or on plant stands, and a preference for high humidity makes it ideal for a steamy bathroom. To force blooms, give plants twelve hours of darkness in the fall.

Myrtle

Myrtus communis

Using nature to create garlands, wreaths, or for tablescaping is another lovely way to mark the seasons, weaving in ancient symbolism and the language of plants and flowers. Myrtle, for example, was sacred to the Greek goddess Aphrodite, made into crowns by the Romans, is a sacred plant in Judaism, and has been historically used to celebrate the pagan festival of Beltane. Aromatic herbs or foliage such as thyme, rosemary, and eucalyptus are similarly mythical and great to craft with.

Tail flower

Anthurium andraeanum

Giving flowers as a token of love is nothing new. Using houseplants rather than cut flowers to convey your feelings—on a whim or for celebrations such as Valentine's Day—may offer a different route to explore. This could include plants with heart-shaped leaves, such as the sweetheart hoya (*Hoya kerrii*), the trailing string of hearts (*Ceropegia woodii*), or the cyclamen (*Cyclamen* spp.). Or opt for a brazen *Anthurium*, which has tall-stemmed, heart-shaped red or pink blooms as well.

Pumpkin

Cucurbita pepo

If you have a little outdoor space, fill containers with the pick of winter vegetables and fruits such as kale, ruby chard, squash, and pumpkins, to eat but also to use as seasonal decor. The latter may need a structure up which to climb, but twine, canes, or a small amount of trellis will do. Simply source a large container into which indoor plants can be potted in spring. Use fertile soil plus water, and feed well down to the roots. Pick fruits when ripe, eating fresh or storing over winter.

How to make a wreath

1. Hanging wreaths is a lovely way to be naturally festive and supplement other greenery in your home. Combining herbs such as rosemary, thyme, marjoram, and bay with eucalyptus, ivy, and dried flowers from your garden also adds a fragrant or personal touch.

2. Make a wreath base by weaving woody but pliable materials such as grapevine together, or source a rattan or metal hoop. Gather foliage, flowers, and other features such as berries, dried citrus, or cones. Cut stems into 4- to 8-inch (10–20cm) pieces, depending on wreath size.

3. Arrange stems in mixed bunches, tying with floristry wire. Layer bunches onto the wreath in a circular fashion, exploring full or half wreath designs. Secure with wire. Add focal and peripheral elements such as pine cones or feathery grasses. Hang with twine or nature-dyed silk.

HAPPY,
HEALTHY
PLANTS

HAPPY, HEALTHY PLANTS

Go deeper into the nature and nurture of your indoor or outdoor container plants to help them really flourish and thrive.

Getting the best from your plants is so much easier when you begin to understand their place in nature and what conditions they prefer or need to survive and thrive. Key factors include:

Selection

The selection of plants is key. Use the Personal Planting Guide (page 14) to help determine your final plant or plant family edit, then use the following section to hone the selection process, including shopping, settling in, and tools.

Potting

Choosing the right pot for your plant can be crucial to its ongoing health and happiness. Consider factors such as drainage, size, shape, and material in your final choice. See Pots and Potting (page 84) for notes on pots and containers, plus repotting and potting up.

Position

Position your plant for optimum light, humidity, shelter, warmth, and ventilation, using the Personal Plant Selector (page 108) as a guide to popular species and cultivars. Notes on Nurturing and Nourishing (page 90) also cover conditions and environment in more detail.

Nurturing

Nurturing plants can help boost your well-being as well as keep your plants happy and healthy. Ways to care include watering (page 94) and feeding (page 96); use the Personal Plant Selector to find out if your intuitive processes match the suggested regimes.

Pruning and propagation

Take notes on page 98 to help keep plants in shape, remove unsightly foliage, encourage growth, take cuttings for propagation, or explore ways to pass your plants on.

BE A BETTER PLANT PARENT

Asking a few simple questions before you buy can help develop or hone your green thumb.

1

What kind of plant is it?
Check the label or ask a supplier about the specifics of plants that interest you. Find out the species, cultivar, and maturity in order to supplement care advice or explore growth habits. This also comes in handy if you want to repeat buy.

2

What kind of pot does it need?
The container you buy a plant in might not be the right one for your plant, space, or style. Use the Personal Plant Selector (page 108) for necessary notes on size, drainage, or material. A well-drained pot, saucer of moist pebbles, or attractive outer pot (sleeve) can make all the difference.

3

What conditions does it prefer?
This is a question to ask before you get a plant home so you can fulfill any conditions it needs, such as adequate growth space, bright indirect light, or high humidity. See Appraise Your Space (page 30) and use the Personal Plant Selector (page 108) to make the best plan.

4

How often does it need watering?
Many people water or feed plants intuitively based on a plant's responses, although it can take a bit of trial and error to settle on the perfect regime. Supplement the process by reading up on nature-led watering and feeding needs.

5

Does it need pruning or other care?
Different plants require different levels of pruning or other care such as pest control, repotting, rotating, or training. Choose a care level that your lifestyle or space allows.

SELECTION

Spending time selecting plants is the best foundation for a healthy, happy plant family and can save you time and money in the long run.

Selecting plants from a garden center, store, or market can be a lovely process, so take your time and enjoy it. Approach plants that naturally attract you, but try to be selective about which ones will really work for you.

Enjoy the edit

Become inspired by an increasing ability to edit things down. This doesn't necessarily mean opting for a minimalist vibe—unless you want to, that is (see The Minimalist Garden, page 54). It's more about being aware of what plants need, which is especially important if you've got a whole eclectic family of them to take care of (see The Bohemian Garden, page 56), want plants that last well into the future, or are developing a cohesive indoor or outdoor garden design, including Planting for Well-being (page 44), Style (page 52), Produce (page 60), or Seasonality (page 68). Your plants will be healthier and happier for a little preparation and planning where you can.

Think sustainably

Plants reach our homes from all sorts of sources, including nurseries, shops, and donations from family or friends. But ultimately, they come from nature, which needs taking care of too. It's therefore

important to ask about the provenance of a plant. Is it native to this country or has it been imported from overseas? Has it been propagated by seed or harvested as a mature plant? Does buying a particular plant help preserve its heritage or contribute to rarity or extinction? Does your supplier use sustainable materials in terms of soil, pots, and packaging? It's not always possible to find answers to these questions, but it's important to try. If in doubt, find another supplier.

Ten to try: houseplant tools

It's worth acquiring a kit of key tools, equipment, and materials with which to grow and care for your selection of plants. This could include:

1. **Pots:** Use the Personal Plant Selector to help choose ideal pots, but also collect ones that attract you as you go.

2. **Drip trays:** Catch water dripping through pots with drainage holes by placing on a tray or saucer.

3. **Pebbles:** Increase humidity by placing plants on trays of pebbles, or use in terrariums or to plant bulbs.

4. **Small watering can:** Be motivated to water by investing in a good watering can with a removable sprinkling rose.

5. **Mister spray:** Source a dedicated plant mister or use a clean spray bottle with a fine-mist setting.

6. **Trowel:** Source general and narrower transplanting trowels with a sturdy steel blade and ergonomic handle.

7. **Secateurs:** Invest in a high-quality pair of carbon steel bypass secateurs and keep them clean and sharp.

8. **Pruning knife:** Explore the range of pruning and budding knives for clean cuts and ongoing healthy plants.

9. **Dibber:** Helpful for creating a hole for planting seeds, seedlings, or small bulbs.

10. **Soft cloth and brush:** For dusting plants or wiping or sweeping up spills. Source them in sustainable materials.

SHOPPING AND SETTLING IN

*Break down the list of things you need to do
when you're sourcing and settling in your plants.*

Take a shopping list

Taking a shopping list of edited-down species or cultivars, potential candidates, features you are looking for, or pitfalls you want to avoid can help you bring the perfect plant partners home. If you're a visual person, make mood boards of inspirational and then final ideas. For gardens or interiorscapes that require multiple plants, consider the time it may take to plant or pot them. It's better to slow down and do one section at a time rather than buying too much, potentially killing plants in the process.

Read the label

Always read the care label, and if there isn't one visible or information is limited, ask your supplier or source to fill you in on key details. This includes the species name and cultivar if relevant; ideal position in relation to light or shelter; potential sowing, planting, and blooming times; growth habit comprising height and spread; and watering and feeding requirements. Use the Personal Plant Selector (page 108) to compare notes and fill in any missing gaps. The index (page 216) may also help identify mislabeled plants.

Do a health check

Put potential plant purchases through a health check to ensure you're not bringing back unhealthy specimens or unwanted pests or diseases. First check for signs of wilting, which should be obvious at a glance. Look at leaves, stems, or foliage more closely for dark spots or streaks, which could indicate disease. Take time to turn over leaves and inspect soil to see if any pests are lurking there. Finally, ease the plant out of its pot to check if it is root-bound. Ideally look for a new specimen.

Transport with care

Whether you're traveling on foot, cycling, by public transportation, or in a car or van, make sure that you can carry the weight, support the structure, and protect any delicate features of the plant. If any elements get broken, use a clean pruning knife or secateurs to cut down to healthy growth to prevent diseases from entering through the wound. Tender plants may also need wrapping if transporting during cold weather, especially frost or below-freezing temperatures.

Be mindful

Your plant is a living organism with a potential range of nature-led needs and sensitivities, and may need a bit of help settling in or acclimatizing to your home. Carefully unwrap any packaging. Cut off any broken or damaged parts (see above). Repot if necessary (see Potting and Repotting, page 88)—this can be a vital step for plants that need more growing room or better drainage. Place on a drip tray or saucer or in a decorative outer plant pot (sleeve) and water well before positioning.

POTS AND POTTING

How you pot your plants can make a huge difference to their vitality, longevity, productivity, and style.

Planting in pots or containers is an incredibly versatile way to garden, whether you're after a space-saving solution, a movable feast, more control over your soil, or an eye-catching design. It's also perfect for indoors, outdoors, and those increasingly useful and beguiling spaces in between.

Potting for purpose

Plant pots are essential to the health and happiness of a plant, being a container that will hold the soil and the roots, a vessel into which water and food are added, and a base for supporting stems, leaves, flowers, and fruits. Pot sizes range from a seedling-suitable 3.5 inches (9cm) to a gigantic 25 gallons (95 liters) for small trees, with a wide range of choices in between suitable for potting or repotting herbs, houseplants, or shrubs. Good drainage is key, with a drip tray or sleeve to catch water from holes in the base, while porous materials help air circulate and cool. A well-potted plant also needs the right soil—use the Personal Plant Selector (page 108) for plant-by-plant advice. Also consider weight if moving pots around.

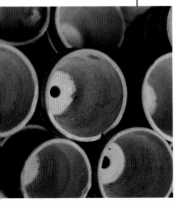

Potting for style

Pots also allow individual taste, style, creativity, or resourcefulness to shine through via proportions, shapes, materials, finishes, patterns, or homemade or upcycled designs. If you've got your heart set on a particular pot or planter, remember to factor in purpose first. Sacrificing drainage for decor will only result in an unhappy or unhealthy plant. What you can do is use that pot as a sleeve in which to place a potted-up plant. Measure up first so it's easy to slip the inner vessel in and out: increase the diameter 2 inches (5cm) for pots under 4 inches (10cm) in diameter, and 3 inches (7.5cm) for larger pots. If you only want to use one pot, follow the advice above, with more attractive choices often made of terra-cotta or ceramic (page 29).

Ten to try: reasons to pot up

Most plants need potting up from time to time, whether to allow more room to grow or more nutrients, or for pest or disease control.

1. **Plant size:** Some plants need potting up regularly when they get too big. Knowing your species can help.

2. **Root-bound:** Look for roots growing through drainage holes at the bottom of pots. Try to pry them out to check.

3. **Wilting foliage:** This can be a sign of congested roots, preventing water or nutrition from getting through.

4. **Leaf yellowing:** Another potential sign of congested roots. Carefully take the plant out of its pot to check.

5. **Nutrient boost:** Refreshing the soil in containers can be crucial, especially for hungry or edible plants.

6. **Disease prevention:** Help combat disease by using clean containers replenished with fresh soil.

7. **Plant divisions:** Transplant baby plants into new pots and fresh soil. Parent plants may need repotting, too.

8. **Promote growth:** Repot to promote new vigorous growth. A pot that's too big could slow things down, however.

9. **New purchase:** Repot new plants where possible for optimum drainage, nutrition, and overall health.

10. **Change of aesthetics:** Swap unattractive plastic pots for stylish well-draining alternatives, or cover in a sleeve.

POTS, PLANTERS, AND CONTAINERS

Transform potted plants into nature-led style statements using elements of design, vintage finds, and upcycled materials.

Size and shape

Have fun playing with the size and shape of pots and containers. This could include making a dramatic focal point out of one huge floor pot, grouping together pots of different heights, or matching containers of the same scale for a cohesive effect. Correspond size to space, usage, and growth—smaller pots for shelves or compact kitchen herbs, bigger vessels for larger shrubs or trees, and always use a container that accommodates growth below and above the soil.

Material and texture

For pots that will directly house a plant and its soil, it's often good to go for a well-drained pot of a natural, breathable material. Terra-cotta or ceramic pots are ideal, available in a range of shapes and sizes, from classic plant pots to strawberry planters to huge urns, often with accompanying drip trays. Ceramic pots also increase options in terms of color, pattern, and design. External sleeves come in numerous materials, including cast iron, concrete, zinc, wood, glass, and basket weave. Play around with textures to complement a plant's foliage.

Color and pattern

Choosing a pot according to its color or pattern is very much led by personal taste or style preferences. Certain colors or patterns can really enhance a plant's shading or markings—darker pots to display silver-gray succulents such as *Echeverias*, for example, or gray or silver containers to contrast with red-hued plants like false shamrock (*Oxalis triangularis*). Stripes or dots can also be used to mirror variegated foliage on a zebra or snake plant. Pots picked up on travels can help create an exotic or bohemian vibe.

Mounts, hangers, and stands

Make the best use of accessories that allow natural plant habits to really shine. This includes hanging baskets, plant hangers, and plant pedestals for trailing plants (see how to make a macramé plant hanger, page 57), wooden plant mounts for epiphytic ferns, geometric designs for air plants (see how to make a brass plant holder, page 55), and glass terrariums for succulents (see how to make a terrarium, page 71).

Repurposing

Last but not least, there are infinite ways to create plant pots and containers using vintage or upcycled finds. The best thing about this approach is that you will often end up with a container display that is truly unique to you. It can also save on cost and waste, repurposing items that may otherwise be thrown away. Plus tracking down or stumbling across such finds can be great fun, bringing an extra layer of creativity to a plant display or container garden. Look for ideas from books or online, from recycled zinc baths to tiny terrariums in mason jars.

POTTING AND REPOTTING

Transform potted plants into nature-led style statements using elements of design, vintage finds, and upcycled materials.

Choose a pot
Size matters, so choose the right pot width and depth to accommodate roots, although some plants—such as some orchids and bromeliads, snake plant, jade plant, peace lily, and agapanthus—like to be root-bound (check the Personal Plant Selector for specific plant details, page 108). For potting up, choose a pot that is one size larger than the container it is currently housed in, with adequate drainage holes. And remember, most plants need repotting every two to three years, so you have time to consider how to style up this new aspect of your plant's journey.

Select your soil
Fill your pot with suitable growing media. Soil or loam-based compost tends to be best for trees, shrubs, and perennial climbers. Multipurpose

compost suits most annual flowering plants, while houseplant compost caters for most houseplants except for those with special needs (see below). It's important to source peat-free options. Free-draining seed compost is best for growing seeds and taking cuttings. There are also special composts for cacti, succulents, and orchids. For edibles, use an organic potting compost that supports the health of home-grown food.

Additional materials

Soil or compost sometimes needs the addition of supplementary materials such as horticultural gravel, grit, sand, perlite, or moss. Gravel and grit can be added to the bottom of a pot or, if appropriate, smaller particles mixed with compost to improve drainage—ideal for drought-tolerant plants and succulents. Horticultural sand can also help create free-draining conditions. To retain moisture, try adding perlite or vermiculite, spongy minerals that hold water well. A top layer of sphagnum moss can benefit plants such as ferns.

Preparing your plant

Take the specimen you want to pot or repot and water well, letting the moisture sink in for around 30 minutes. It's now time to remove your plant from its pot, which can be a slightly tricky process if root-bound, often visible by the extension of roots through the drainage holes. Be patient, gently separating your plant until it is clear of the pot. Then tease apart any roots that are tightly packed, working from the bottom and the edges. Set the manipulated plant onto its new bed of compost so it is at least ½ inch (1cm) below the pot rim.

Layer up and firm down

The last step is to fill in around the roots with more compost, firming down with your hands to remove any air. Ensure that your plant is at the same depth as in its previous pot, leaving stems and any aerial roots visible above the soil. Then gently water, taking care to keep leaves dry. Larger plants and shrubs can also be repotted by trimming off roots around the sides, then returning to the same pot with fresh compost. Or simply remove the top 1 inch (2.5cm) of compost, apply a slow-release granular fertilizer, layer up, pat down, and water well.

NURTURING AND NOURISHING

Nurturing and nourishing your plants with mindful care routines can be just as rewarding as enjoying their visual beauty.

Encouraging plants to survive and thrive through mindful, everyday, or long-term care routines—from watering and feeding, to optimum positioning through the year—not only produces healthy, happy plants, it can also work wonders for your mental health and well-being.

Listen to nature

All plants need food, light, moisture, air, a suitable temperature, and space to grow. How much of these elements they need to really thrive, however, depends on their species or even cultivar. A plant's care label can give you a basic grounding in preferred position, growth habit, and watering/feeding regimes. But connecting with the bigger picture—the reason why a plant might prefer high humidity or gets by on minimal nutrients—is when you really start to understand how plants work. You can then apply this deep-seated knowledge to develop the most nurturing and nourishing routines for individual plants, and also to groups of plants that might have similar needs.

Feel your way

Start by carefully looking at your plant. Are the leaves smooth and shiny or thick and succulent, for example? Do stems grow tall and erect or arch and cascade? Does your plant have flowers, and when do they bloom? Get to know your plant in good health and it's easier to spot problems and potential causes further down the line. While the Personal Plant Selector (page 108) gives plant-by-plant advice about watering, feeding, and optimum position, such factors can be affected by season or weather. It's therefore important to also feel your way, from watering when the top layer of soil feels dry to replenishing soil or repotting if a plant appears to need more nutrients.

Ten to try: ways to care

There are lots of ways to care for your plants, from watering and feeding routines to giving them the perfect place in your home.

1. **Use the right size pot:** Help plants to flourish by giving the crown and roots room to spread out and aerate.

2. **Ensure adequate drainage:** Choose a pot with suitable drainage and growing medium for long-term health.

3. **Check the soil regularly:** Inspect soil routinely for moisture content and signs of pests or disease.

4. **Care according to plant profile:** Use the Personal Plant Selector (page 108) for the very best care.

5. **Use tepid distilled or rainwater:** Help remove any risk of shock or a buildup of harmful chemicals.

6. **Set up a watering system:** Set up a drip or soaking system or ask a friend to water while you're away.

7. **Clean leaves regularly:** Cleaning leaves helps remove dust and keeps them looking lush and healthy.

8. **Turn your plants:** Some plants need rotating toward the light to keep an even shape.

9. **Note seasonal light variations:** Make sure plants are getting enough light or shade through the seasons.

10. **Adjust humidity:** Place humidity-loving plants in the bathroom or on a tray of damp pebbles.

CONDITIONS AND ENVIRONMENT

Look after the long-term health of plants and flowers by giving them the light, temperature, humidity, and space they need for optimum growth.

Bright light

In terms of plant health, "full sun" or "bright light" usually refers to an area that gets over twelve hours of direct sunlight a day, often via a south-facing window. Few plants can survive such harsh conditions, which can burn leaves and dry up vital moisture, especially during the strong midday summer sun. Most sun-loving plants, including tropicals, herbs, and succulents, prefer "bright, indirect light" consisting of several hours of direct sun a day, via a west- or east-facing window, farther back in a south-facing room or filtered through sheer curtains.

Low light

"Light shade," preferred by many woodland plants or those with large green leaves, usually occurs as you go deeper into a bright west-facing room, in the corners adjacent to a south-facing window or directly in front of a north-facing one. "Shade" usually occurs at the back of north-facing rooms or those that receive limited or no sun each day, possibly due to neighboring buildings or trees. Don't despair if this is your space—there is a range of shade-loving beauties that will tolerate such conditions, including devil's ivy, some ferns, and low-growing tropicals.

Temperature

If you're growing plants outdoors, it's crucial to factor in elements such as cold, heat, drought, flooding, or wind. Gearing your gardening toward planting for seasonality (page 68) can help, and some plants can be overwintered indoors. Growing plants inside generally provides a more controlled

environment, with the warm, steady "room temperature" ideal for many lush, green tropicals. Watch out for indoor fluctuations in heat or cold, however, from drying radiators or drafty open windows. Some plants also prefer summer outside.

Humidity

Some plants prefer high humidity levels, where the air is saturated with moisture. This includes many tropical rainforest plants, which are ideal for steamy bathrooms. Moderate humidity is the domain of orchids, ferns, some palms, and many foliage plants. Low humidity suits plants such as arid-dwelling cacti and succulents. You can raise humidity by standing plants on a tray of damp pebbles, misting leaves and aerial roots with rainwater, or creating a tropical microclimate by grouping healthy plants together.

Space

Give your plants the space they need for happy, healthy growth. Check the Personal Plant Selector (page 108) for potential height and spread, relative to container planting indoors or outdoors (some specimens will get much bigger than this in the wild!). This can help you choose the right species or cultivars for your garden or home, from huge floor plants or vines to tiny air plants, succulents, or cacti. Don't forget to factor in adequate room for roots or potential flowers or fruits. Additionally, make use of props such as hanging baskets to maximize on limited space.

WATERING

Check the care label or the Personal Plant Selector (page 108) for plant-by-plant watering advice, using the guide below for practical tips.

Top watering

Watering from above is one of the most common methods of watering plants, suitable for most tropical plants and ferns that don't mind getting their foliage wet. Plants need to be in pots with drainage holes at the bottom to prevent waterlogging, and paired with a plant sleeve or drip tray. Pour water from above using a small watering can with a fine rose attachment. Water until the compost feels soaked so the moisture reaches the roots. Angle the watering can's neck into the foliage if you need to target any points. Tip out any excess water in the sleeve or tray.

Bottom watering

Some plants, such as African violets, cape primroses, or orchids that would normally grow upside down, don't like getting their leaves wet or having what is known as "wet feet"—when water pools around stems and roots. Cold water is especially prone to leaving spots on foliage,

while soggy compost can encourage root rot and disease. The solution to this is to water from below. Ensure plants are set in pots with drainage holes at the bottom. Then simply stand the pot in a ¾-inch (2cm) deep tray of water, leave for 20 minutes, remove, and drain.

Misting leaves and aerial roots

As a number of nature notes in the Personal Plant Selector reveal, some plants just love a good misting. Such plants generally prefer high humidity and thrive in conditions similar to their native habitat, in rainforests or by streams. Swiss cheese plants, orchids, calatheas, philodendrons, and many ferns fall into this category. Plants with thin leaves may also appreciate a direct moisture boost, while misting can also help keep leaves clean. To mist, simply aim a fine mister filled with tepid distilled water or rainwater at foliage and aerial roots.

Watering specialty plants

Be aware of plants that have developed special mechanisms to conserve moisture, and water accordingly. Succulents and cacti, for example, have fleshy water-storing stems or leaves. Keep their foliage dry at all times and add a layer of grit or mulch to help water drain away quickly. Water-loving bromeliads, meanwhile, love water so much that they collect it in a cuplike reservoir in the center of the plant. Simply fill the cup with rainwater or distilled water, replenishing when empty. For air plants, soak in a tray of water weekly or mist two or three times a week.

Watering when away

Automatic watering systems need to add sufficient moisture to soil without making it soggy in the process. Most houseplants can survive a weekend without any water, especially if you water periodically anyway; cacti and succulents can go a couple of weeks. If in doubt, use cut-off water bottles with a hole in the lid to drip slowly into soil, a strip of capillary matting with one end in a raised bowl of water and the other end in a pot, or place plants on a piece of capillary matting that also lines a sink. Fill the sink and let the water soak through.

FEEDING

Nutrients can eventually become depleted from a pot or container of soil, so top them up as necessary with a quality feeding routine.

Know your nutrients

Feeding plants makes more sense when you know which nutrients plants need and why. The big three are nitrogen (N), which promotes strong, healthy foliage and is particularly important for leafy houseplants; phosphorus (P), which promotes strong growth and development, starting with the roots; and potassium (K), essential for blooms and fruits, so it is particularly useful for productive crops. Supporting trace elements, only needed in tiny amounts, include boron (B), copper (Cu), iron (Fe), manganese (Mn), molybdenum (Mo), and zinc (Zn).

Listen to your soil

Garden soil can provide an ongoing supply of nutrients but can vary in terms of nutritional balance, texture, and acidity. For best results,

test your soil and choose plants accordingly, adding balancing elements such as sand, grit, or compost if necessary. Container planting gives you more control over the soil, but nutrients will eventually need topping up. Depleted compost can show up as a reduction in soil level, water that drains through too quickly, or crucially, unhappy foliage, flowers, or fruits. Regular feeding in the growing season can help.

Choose the right compost

Get your container plants off to a good start by choosing the right soil mix or compost—use the Personal Plant Selector for a plant-by-plant guide. This includes multipurpose compost, seed compost, specialty compost, and organic potting compost (see Potting and Repotting, page 88). These vary in texture, nutritional balance and delivery, water storage, and core ingredients suitable for a range of purposes.

Choose the right compost for plants, seeds, or edibles, but say no to peat-based products, which deplete valuable natural resources.

Add the right fertilizer

A "balanced" fertilizer delivers an equal 20:20:20 ratio of N:P:K plus a range of trace elements in smaller quantities. It's best to deliver fertilizer in liquid form (for powders, just add water) to reach the roots, diluting and feeding as directed in the Personal Plant Selector. High-potash fertilizer is rich in potassium, ideal for fruits and flowers, while slow-release granular fertilizer is useful for large or woody plants, with nutrients gradually released through watering. Explore organic fertilizers made of seaweed, comfrey, and nettle, which are important for edibles.

Mixing materials and moss

Conditioning the soil to help aerate it, improve drainage, or retain moisture ultimately helps plants access nutrients. Spongy, mineral grains known as vermiculite or perlite soak up then slowly release moisture, ideal for sowing seeds. Gravel or grit can be used at the bottom of a pot or added to soil to increase drainage for cacti, succulents, and other drought-tolerant plants. Horticultural sand is generally mixed with compost to create free-draining conditions, while a layer of sphagnum moss helps sustain a moist environment for water-loving plants.

PRUNING AND PROPAGATION

Prune plants to keep them in healthy, shapely, or blooming condition, and explore propagation techniques to grow or give plants away as gifts.

Pruning plants is easy when you know how, and can be a rewarding meditative activity due to the hands-on approach. And propagation, via stem or leaf cuttings, water, offsets, bulbs, or seeds, is a natural step toward growing your plant family.

The shape of things

Observing plants in the wild and in cultivation has provided a blueprint of relative growth habits for many popular container or houseplant species, but external factors such as light, water, and nutrients can have adverse effects. Something as simple as raising the temperature of a room, or an unseasonal bout of sunshine, can stimulate rapid stem growth or a profusion of leaves or blooms. The natural life cycle of a plant might also lead it to outgrow your garden or home, while pests, diseases, dry air, or low or too harsh light could damage plant parts. This is where pruning comes in. Done well, with the right tools and advice, you can nurture plants back to good health and shape.

Future thinking

If pruning is about sustaining healthy growth in the long term, propagation is about the beginning of a journey in a plant's life. This could be through growing a seed or planting a bulb or propagating houseplants via cuttings, offsets, or in water. However you do it, growing plants from scratch is a supremely nurturing experience and—given a little time, patience, and a few simple techniques—one that can soon become addictive. Spider plants, for example, produce tiny spiderettes on long stolons that root a short distance away from the parent plant in the wild. Place one in a new pot of soil and you are simply mimicking vegetative reproduction in nature. You've also got a new plant for your collection or to give to a friend as a gift.

Ten to try: reasons to prune

Prune plants when necessary to help them retain their shape, promote bushiness, optimize good health, or encourage blooms and fruits.

1. **Remove dead or diseased parts:** This improves the visual effect of a plant and helps prevent further disease.

2. **Remove cracked or broken stems:** Direct energy toward healthy plant parts and minimize risk of disease.

3. **Avoid gangly stems:** Remove awkward growth that wastes energy and negatively affects the shape of a plant.

4. **Avoid rubbing stems:** Stems that rub together can cause abrasion or breaks, which raises the risk of disease.

5. **Brown or discolored leaves:** Remove dead, damaged, or non-variegated leaves; explore the causes of these, where possible.

6. **Keep plants in shape:** Some plants need regular pruning to keep them in shape, others just the occasional trim.

7. **Encourage reflowering:** Removing blooms can help some plants bloom again.

8. **Promote bushiness:** Prune to encourage more vigorous growth and lush foliage—ideal for edible herbs.

9. **Keep plants compact:** Maintain a compact shape to suit space, size, style of plant, or type of garden.

10. **Propagate new plants:** Use healthy cuttings, where appropriate, to propagate new plants.

PRUNING

Combine studied observation with careful, clean cutting to encourage healthy growth, compact or bushy growth, and repeat blooms.

Observe your plants
Observe the plants around you regularly to keep on top of any pruning needs, from straggly stems to dead flowers or leaves. Unhealthy growth can be cut back at any time of the year, but most plants are best pruned in early spring or late winter just before the start of their growth season (see the Personal Plant Selector). When you're ready to prune, go in for a closer inspection. Rotate the plant or walk around larger specimens to identify areas to remove, or areas of new growth such as latent buds where leaves join stems.

Cut mindfully
Use sharp, sterilized secateurs or pruning shears for thicker or woodier stems, or floristry scissors for tender stalks, leaves, or flowers. Make sure all are clean. Be vigilant about removing dead, damaged, or rubbing stems. To tidy up or reshape foliage, cut just above a leaf stem, leaf node, or side stem. To take out a whole stem, remove it at the base. To stop upward growth, take out the leading stem. Take time to stand back and assess the shape as you go. If you notice any obvious holes, prune the surrounding stem tips. Do not cut back more than one-third of a plant.

Promote bushier growth
Promoting bushier growth is useful for shaping or taming container plants or houseplants and increasing the harvest of productive plants such as some herbs and cut flowers. The process involved is sometimes referred to as "pinching out," depending on the plant, whereby the dominant stem or bud is removed to encourage new stems or leaves to emerge from the nodes

below. Try and stagger cuts to help attain varied filled-out growth, trimming some branches or stems back by a quarter, some by half, and others all the way back to the base.

Encourage more blooms

Deadheading flowers stops them from setting seed, telling the plant to try again, thus setting new blooms. This works well with many annual and perennial flowers as well as shrubs. It can also direct energy into improving the general health of foliage and roots. For plants with large flowers, use hand pruners, removing spent top blooms or the whole stem at the base of the plant. Thin or tender stems can be pinched off between fingers, while plants with a profusion of tiny flowers may spring back from an entire plant shearing with a new flush of blooms.

Working with vines

Many healthy vines or climbing plants are rampant growers so may need continuous pruning through the growing season to cut them back to manageable form. As a general rule, remove any dead, damaged, diseased, or unproductive stems; overly tangled stems; and errant stems that are growing away from supports. Also direct the growth of vines using supports such as wires, frames, or trellises. Look up guidelines for your plant first, as requirements vary between species based on climbing habits and also whether there are flowers or fruits involved.

PROPAGATION

Explore a variety of vegetation propagation techniques, alongside growing seeds and bulbs, to help expand or share your plant family.

Stem cuttings in soil
This method is ideal for most soft-stemmed houseplants. In spring or early summer, cut a non-flowering 4- to 6-inch (10–15cm) piece of foliage stem just below the leaf joint. Remove the lower two to three leaves. Dip the end in hormone rooting powder, place the stem into a small pot of cutting compost, firm the soil, and water lightly. Cover with a plastic bag secured with a rubber band. Roots should develop in six to eight weeks. When new shoots appear, transplant into multipurpose compost and set in a bright spot.

Leaf cuttings in soil
Some plants can be propagated by leaf, including begonias, snake plants, and many succulents. For begonias, first cut off a large healthy leaf. Remove a small circular section around the stem. Divide the leaf into sections and slot upright into cutting compost with veins in the

soil. Water, drain, and seal in a plastic bag. When roots and new leaves form, transfer into multipurpose compost and set in a bright spot. For snake plants, use 2-inch (5cm) sections of long leaves. Propagate succulent leaves whole, inserting dried-out cut ends into cactus compost.

Stem cuttings in water

This is an increasingly popular and fun propagation technique, as you can see the roots grow through the glass. Working with plants that have soft, pliable stems, simply remove a non-flowering foliage stem at the base, cutting below the node (bump on the stem) if there is one. Remove the bottom leaves if necessary, to leave a clear 2-inch (5cm) piece of stem. Place the cutting in a glass or jar of water, ensuring any leaves are not submerged. Watch the roots grow until a strong system has developed, then plant in multipurpose compost and then set in a bright spot.

Offsets

For base-growing offsets such as bromeliads, choose a pup that is around one-third the size of the parent plant. Remove the whole plant from its pot, cut off the offset close to the parent, and pull back any papery leaves. Dust the base with hormone rooting powder and insert into a small pot of cactus compost and perlite. Try not to bury the stem. Water and repot when new shoots appear. To propagate cascading offsets from spider plants, for example, set one with a tiny root in a pot of cutting compost near the parent plant. Cut free when it has established its own root system.

Division

This is the practice of separating one plant into several self-supporting ones, by splitting clumps into sections, each with at least one shoot and a root system of its own. Best done in spring or fall, it's suitable for a wide range of container plants, including peace lilies, cast iron plants, snake plants, Boston ferns, and hardy geraniums. Water the parent plant well, remove a little compost from the root ball, and tease apart new shoots. Ensure there are good roots on the original and divided sections. Plant into fresh multipurpose compost, water, and set in a bright spot.

LISTENING

Give plants some extra loving care by learning how to tune in to and address common problems such as pests, diseases, or environmental issues.

Listening to your plants is simply about becoming more aware of the signs and signals that they give off to indicate health and happiness or damage and stress. Combine listening with a solution-based understanding of common problems to help keep them alive and well.

Look and listen

There has been plenty of discussion around the benefits of talking to plants, with some studies indicating that there really is a link between vibrational sounds and increased plant growth. Developing a personal relationship with plants, including meditating with them (page 46), has also been proven to have a positive effect on mental health and well-being. This includes observing plants in order to connect with nature and also listening to their needs through nurturing houseplants or gardening. This could be via something as simple as keeping an eye out for browning leaves or flowers. For the ultimate nurturing relationship, do a regular round of all your plants.

Nature's nuisances

The phenomenon of nature comprises a realm of plants, animals, and other living organisms, some of which interact positively—plants and pollinators, for example—while others engage in a battle for survival. The latter category, for gardeners and houseplant owners, includes a plethora of nature's nuisances, from pests such as spider mites to diseases like powdery mildew. Human neglect can also be an issue. Left unchecked and unresolved, such elements can cause ongoing or even fatal damage to plants. As many problems are quite common, however, there are plenty of ready-made and sustainable solutions out there. By listening to your plants, in terms of prevention and cure, you're already off to a great start.

Ten to try: signs to tune in to

Listen to your plants by looking out for signs of stress such as brown leaf tips, wilting, or a lack of blooms. Find a way to nurture them back to health.

1. **Waterlogging:** This can lead to root rot, fungal diseases, and foliage spots; always use well-draining pots.

2. **Spindly stems:** Often a sign of insufficient light; try moving plants to a brighter position.

3. **Lopsided growth:** Another sign of insufficient light; try rotating plants every few days.

4. **Yellow, red, or pale leaves:** A sign of underfeeding, overwatering, cold drafts, or natural shedding.

5. **Brown leaf tips:** Underwatering, low humidity, high temperatures, or overfeeding could be the cause.

6. **Wilting:** Usually a sign that your plant needs watering but check if waterlogged, root-bound, or subject to pests.

7. **Falling flower buds:** A lack of moisture, soggy soil, extreme temperature, or pests could be the culprit.

8. **No flowers:** Potentially remedied by moving to a brighter spot, feeding, misting, or repotting.

9. **Leaf spots:** Overwatering, underwatering, misting with hard water, or pests or disease could be to blame.

10. **Holes in leaves:** If holes aren't meant to be there, check for pest damage or physical wear and tear.

COMMON PROBLEMS

Gardening is partly about trial and error, and this includes dealing with common problems—pinpointing the issue is halfway to solving it.

Common pests
Small pests such as aphids, mealybugs, spider mites, and scale insects can quickly become numerous, causing frustrating damage to plants. Checking plants regularly—leaves, stems, flowers, and compost—is the best way to prevent an infestation. This is especially important when bringing new plants into your home. Start by picking off insects with your hands using gardening gloves. Many plants can be treated with a homemade insecticide of dilute soap solution or by using sticky traps. Some plants may need discarding to prevent spread.

Common diseases
Overwatering, underwatering, and poor ventilation can all provide an ideal foundation for common plant diseases. Use the Personal Plant Selector (page 108) for optimum care. In the case of powdery fungus, fungal leaf spot, and gray mold, remove affected parts and treat with a fungicide in a ventilated room. Try natural solutions such as neem oil. Downy mildew, sooty mold, rust, virus, root rot, or stem and crown rot have no known chemical cure. Infected parts or sometimes the whole plant may need to be destroyed to stop infection from spreading elsewhere.

Seasonal factors
Outdoor container plants need to be selected with seasonal factors in mind, including changes in weather and light. Weather patterns can also be unpredictable, with unseasonal occurrences such as heat waves, storms, or cold spells potentially causing havoc with the best-laid planting plans. Navigate the elements by choosing tried and tested robust or hardy plants, overwintering tender specimens inside, planting fewer specimens to reduce maintenance, or focusing on indoor container plants instead. Or just enjoy working with nature to do what you can.

Environmental issues

While there is a large element of control over indoor container plants, including species selection, soil type, methods of potting up, position, and everyday and long-term care routines, this can be affected by changes in lifestyle (going on vacation or busy work periods), the seasons (fluctuations in temperature or humidity from heating or open windows), or your home (renovations or changing the usage of a room). Some plants may be extra sensitive to such changes, so be prepared to adjust your care routine to prevent damage, pests, and disease.

Nourishment needs

Many common plant problems are related to the nourishing side of a care routine, with underwatering, overwatering, and a lack of nutrients at the root of many issues. Problems associated with underwatering, such as wilting or brown leaf tips, seem straightforward. But overwatering can cause these issues too, as the roots begin to rot due to excess water. The same is true for overfeeding, where an excess of fertilizer ends up drawing nutrients from a plant's cells. Use the Personal Plant Selector (page 108) to personalize your plant care.

PERSONAL
PLANT
SELECTOR

PERSONAL PLANT SELECTOR

Over 200 plant-by-plant nature notes to help you understand, select, and care for a range of ornamental and edible container plants.

Whether you're looking for the perfect houseplant or thinking of growing herbs or edible crops on your balcony, the Personal Plant Selector can help. It's also a handy reference guide to the ongoing care and maintenance of specimens you are given or already own.

Nature notes

Each entry includes the name, common name, and family of a plant, for easy identification and to help make useful or inspiring connections between "like-minded" specimens. Figures for anticipated spread in terms of plant height and width facilitate choices relating to space, while a general overview of the plant fills in background details on a plant's provenance, cultivated history, ornamental beauty, and potential usage or display. Envisaging a plant in the context of its natural habitat is one of the best ways to understand what kind of care it potentially needs: high humidity and bright, filtered light for a rainforest tropical, or a sunny windowsill for a Mediterranean herb that needs at least six hours of sun.

Special care

Each plant profile continues with basic care information, starting with a planting overview including pot size and soil type. Ideal

position, as determined by light, humidity, ventilation, and seasonality, helps establish where a plant might be best placed in your garden or home. This is followed by specific advice on watering and feeding, two ways to nurture and nourish plants that also help prevent common problems such as pests and disease. Finally, there are common problems to look out for, plus suggested variations to help expand your plant collection or select the perfect plant for your lifestyle, decor, or space. For more details on Happy, Healthy Plants, see page 76.

CONTENTS

Ornamentals

Edibles

ORNAMENTALS

Create the perfect edit of ornamental plants for your garden or home by factoring in elements such as appearance, scent, seasonality, and care.

There are numerous ornamental plants with which to add natural style to your garden or home. Once you've assessed your lifestyle, focus, and space, the following guide will help you narrow things down further in terms of visual, sensory, and practical appeal.

1

Size
The Personal Plant Selector includes plants suitable for a variety of indoor and outdoor spaces. This ranges from large floor plants such as fiddle-leaf figs (page 122) to smaller specimens such as missionary plants (page 136). There are also trailers and climbers (page 158) for growing up walls or in hanging baskets, which are ideal for restricted spaces. Plus shade-tolerant species such as cast iron plants (page 135) or snake plants (page 147) that can survive in darker corners or smaller rooms.

2

Shape
The plant kingdom includes a mind-blowing selection of plants with variously shaped silhouettes, leaves, flowers, fruits, and seeds. Members of the palm family, Arecaceae (page 118), for example, have recognizable characteristics in terms of foliage and style and can be used to create a tropical vibe. Or try grouping contrasting shapes together asymmetrically to create a flowing, organic outline. Using repetition or strong, clean outlines, meanwhile, suggests balance and order.

3

Texture
Texture is about a plant's surface type and how this interacts with light, shadow, and our senses. Use it to create focus or mix things up. Velvety begonia leaves (page 174) appear soft and tactile, while the spiky stems of a bunny ear cactus (page 150) say look but don't touch. Shiny lemon tree leaves (page 208), meanwhile, catch the light, while variously textured dahlias (page 179), succulents (page 144), or ferns (page 114) are perfect for eye-catching container displays.

Color

Color is often used in sensory gardens (page 48), as it has a proven effect on our mood. Green, the overriding color of nature, is a particularly calming shade, with time spent with houseplants or in gardens helping to boost well-being (page 44). Look to variegated foliage to add year-round complementary hues such as red, pink, orange, white, and cream (see Other Foliage, page 122). Flowers (see Other Flowers, page 168) extend the spectrum to yellow, purple, and even blue.

Scent

It's quite possible to design a container garden entirely around scent, from aromatic herbs (page 194) to perfumed shrubs such as gardenia (page 176) to fragrant climbers such as wisteria (page 176) or jasmine (page 165) or seasonal bulbs including hyacinths (page 185) and paperwhites (page 184). Just remember that scent can have a powerful effect on the emotions, so make sure all household members are okay with your plant selections.

Season

Designing for seasonality (page 68) is one of the most inspiring ways to connect with nature. This includes evergreen houseplants, many of which respond to seasons in the wild, but more obviously plants with deciduous foliage or seasonal blooms, fruits, or seeds. Using plants to decorate for events or holidays (page 74) is also fun, from Christmas bulbs such as amaryllis (page 182) to Valentine-style leaves or flowers in the form of philodendrons (page 124) or anthuriums (page 169).

Care

Keep ornamentals looking healthy, happy, and visually appealing by giving them the right care routine. Use the Personal Plant Selector for plant-by-plant advice, plus the guide to Happy, Healthy Plants (page 76) for a general overview on how to help plants thrive and survive. Humidity-loving plants such as calatheas (page 129), bromeliads (page 138), and many rainforest natives love a good mist. Desert-dwelling cacti (page 150) will keep their shape better if you mimic their dry, arid environment.

FERNS

Ferns are a wonderfully varied, largely sculptural, and relatively low-maintenance group of foliage plants. Explore a world of unfurling fronds, vibrant green or variegated leaves, and curious rhizomes with which to style your home inside and out.

BOSTON FERN - *Nephrolepis exaltata*

nontoxic **easy** *care rating*

Also known as: sword fern; boss fern; ladder fern
Family: Rolepidaceae
Grows to: 24 x 24 inches (60 x 60cm)
Needs a humid environment

Native to the shady swamps and forests of South and Central America, the West Indies, Africa, and Polynesia, this cascading, finely divided evergreen fern enjoys a similarly humid and shady environment—perfect for a bathroom. It can also be planted out in a warm temperate, subtropical, or tropical zone, or used as an outdoor pot or hanging basket plant in summer if conditions are stable.

Planting | Choose a pot that is slightly larger than the root ball and has ample drainage holes. Use a 50:50 mix of multipurpose and soil-based compost.

Position | Place in bright but indirect sunshine during fall and winter; move to a semi-shady location in summer. Mature specimens work well on a pedestal.

Watering | Water frequently to prevent the soil from drying out, but avoid waterlogging. Mist regularly and set on a tray of damp pebbles to raise humidity.

Feeding | Fertilize once a month from spring to fall when the plant is actively growing, and every two to three months in winter. Use half-strength balanced liquid fertilizer.

Also try:
Kimberley queen fern (*Nephrolepis obliterata*); fishtail fern (*N. falcata*)

Watch out for:
Avoid touching the leaves as this can cause them to turn brown. If the roots poke out of drainage holes or there's stunted growth, it's time to repot.

STAGHORN FERN - *Platycerium bifurcatum*

nontoxic

medium
care rating

Also known as: common staghorn fern; elkhorn fern
Family: Polypodiaceae
Grows up to: 12 x 36 inches (30 x 90cm)
Best mounted on a board

Staghorn ferns take their name from their uniquely shaped outer leaves, which resemble the horns of a male deer. Native to tropical rainforest areas around the world, the increasingly popular *Platycerium bifurcatum* hails from Australia, where it can be found growing on taller trees. Due to its epiphytic nature, it is usually grown mounted on a piece of wood or in a basket, nourished by a little mound of organic matter underneath.

Planting | Grow in a wire basket lined with sphagnum moss, or affix to a wooden board using moss, nails, and wire. Nourish with bark chips, moss, and orchid compost.

Position | Mirror rainforest conditions by placing staghorn ferns in bright but indirect or diffused light. Avoid direct sun and promote humidity. Indoors is best.

Watering | Water the plant—along with the entire basket or board—once a week in the shower. Allow to dry thoroughly before rehanging. Mist in the interim.

Feeding | Apply a balanced liquid fertilizer monthly from spring to early fall. Reduce to every other month in the dormant winter season.

Also try:
staghorn fern (*Platycerium superbum*); silver elkhorn fern (*P. veitchii*)

Watch out for:
Avoid soaking fronds, as this can cause them to rot.

BIRD'S NEST FERN - *Asplenium nidus*

nontoxic

medium
care rating

Also known as: nest fern
Family: Aspleniaceae
Grows up to: 24 x 16 inches (60 x 40cm)
Follow watering guide carefully

The bird's nest fern is another epiphytic species that's native to tropical areas of Southeast Asia, eastern Australia, Hawaii, Polynesia, and East Africa, and often grows on palm trees. Unlike many other ferns, it has wide, strapped, undivided fronds, which are often crinkled. These fronds roll back as they brown, creating a bird's nest appearance, hence the name. With old fronds kept in check, it makes a beautiful evergreen houseplant.

Planting | Plant in an equal mix of charcoal, loam-based compost, and multipurpose compost. Works well under cover in a consistently moist and protective terrarium.

Position | A perfect fit for warm, humid bathrooms or kitchens with filtered or northern light. Mature plants need space, so consider moving to a larger room or conservatory.

Watering | Keep moist by standing pot in a tray of damp pebbles. Be sure to water around the edge of the central rosette to avoid rot. Mist daily with rainwater or distilled water.

Feeding | Apply a half-strength liquid fertilizer every two weeks from spring to early fall.

Also try:
Japanese bird's nest fern (*Asplenium antiquum* 'Osaka')

Watch out for:
Avoid direct sunlight; avoid hot, dry rooms or cold, drafty ones; repot annually.

DELTA MAIDENHAIR FERN - *Adiantum raddianum*

nontoxic

medium
care rating

Also known as: Venus hair fern
Family: Pteridaceae
Grows up to: 20 x 32 inches (50 x 80cm)
Mist daily to help keep soil moist

Found in the wild on forest floors, rock crevices, riverbanks, and coastal cliffs of tropical America and the West Indies, this popular houseplant is elegant enough for a centerpiece but also works well in a small group. With soft, triangular, fan-shaped or rounded fronds gently cascading from shiny dark leafstalks as fine as human hair, it's delicate but relatively easy to care for with a bit of daily attention. Just don't touch its sensitive leaves.

Planting | Plant in a medium-sized, relatively well-drained container in multipurpose compost. Keep indoors or on a warm balcony. Repot every two years in spring.

Position | Stand in light shade out of direct sunlight and cold drafts. Loves warm, stable, moist, and humid conditions, so it is ideal for a bathroom, kitchen, or terrarium.

Watering | Keep the compost of this water-loving fern moist at all times. Set on a tray of damp pebbles to raise humidity and mist with rainwater daily.

Feeding | Apply a balanced liquid fertilizer to moist soil monthly from spring to fall. Overfeeding can cause more damage than not feeding it at all.

Also try:
variegated maidenhair fern (*Adiantum raddianum* 'Brilliantelse')

Watch out for:
Avoid direct sunshine; ensure the same light intensity from all sides for even growth.

RABBIT'S FOOT FERN - *Humata tyermanii*

nontoxic

medium
care rating

Also known as: spider fern; silver hare's foot fern; bear's paw fern
Family: Davalliaceae
Grows up to: 12 x 20 inches (30 x 50cm)
Proudly display the furry rhizomes

This tender fern native to Fiji (sometimes sold as *Davallia fejeensis*) is usually grown as a houseplant. It works particularly well in dark pots, hanging baskets, or kokedama displays, allowing its furry, rootlike rhizomes to dangle over the sides. The rich green upright triangles of lacy foliage are a lovely contrast to its silvery extensions, while the relatively compact size of this plant makes it ideal for smaller spaces.

Planting | Plant in a 2:1:1 mix of soil-based compost, multipurpose compost, and charcoal. Can grow outside in frost-free summer months or subtropical climates.

Position | Will flourish in a brightly lit spot away from direct sunlight but with high humidity. An ideal fit for kitchens or bathrooms, but keep away from drying radiators.

Watering | Keep compost moist from spring to fall. Mist regularly and place on a tray of damp pebbles. Allow the top of the compost to dry out between waterings in winter.

Feeding | Apply a half-strength liquid fertilizer every two weeks from spring to fall.

Also try:
hare's foot fern (*Davallia canariensis*)

Watch out for:
Yellow fronds due to dry air; slow plant growth due to lack of nutrients; limp fronds from overwatering.

CRETAN BRAKE FERN - *Pteris cretica*

toxic

easy
care rating

Also known as: Cretan brake; ribbon fern; table fern
Family: Pteridaceae
Grows up to: 24 x 24 inches (60 x 60cm)
Best displayed alone

Most *Pteris* species are native to Europe, Asia, and parts of Africa, and are partially connected by their flat, pinnate fronds that may not be instantly recognizable as a fern. *Pteris cretica* has slim, fingerlike fronds atop wiry stems growing from rhizomes in the soil. There are also beautiful variegated forms such as *P. cretica* var. *albolineata*, which displays a white stripe through the center of each leaflet.

Planting | Plant in a 2:1:1 mix of soil-based compost, multipurpose compost, and charcoal. Can grow outside in frost-free summer months or subtropical climates.

Position | Prefers bright, filtered light or partial shade and a humid atmosphere. Avoid dry air and direct sunlight. Place on a balcony, porch, or patio in warmer months.

Watering | From spring to fall, this fern prefers moist but not wet compost. In winter, allow the top of the compost to dry out between waterings. Mist most days.

Feeding | Apply a half-strength balanced liquid fertilizer once a month from spring to early fall. It shouldn't need additional feed in winter.

Also try:
white-striped Cretan brake fern (*Pteris cretica* var. *albolineata*)

Watch out for:
Cut back brown or tatty fronds at the base to encourage new growth; repot every two years in spring.

ASPARAGUS FERN - *Asparagus setaceus*

toxic

easy
care rating

Also known as: asparagus grass; lace fern; ferny asparagus
Family: Asparagaceae
Grows up to: 96 x 18 inches (240 x 45cm)
Ideal for contrasting with strong shapes

Native to the tropical rainforests of southern Africa where it grows in the partial shade of larger trees, this is not a true fern but is often recognized or referred to as one. A climbing plant by nature, it has soft, delicate feathery leaves, sharp thorny stems that help it grip, and will flower in the wild with bell-like blooms. Cultivated as an ornamental plant or houseplant, it is also grown for its foliage, the leaves often used as fillers in floral arrangements.

Planting | Plant in pots in loose, well-drained, slightly acidic potting soil. If you do grow outdoors, avoid planting in the ground as it can become very invasive.

Position | Place in a bathroom for optimum humidity, in moderate shade or soft, bright light. Can also be used to decorate a patio, balcony, or decking in warmer climes.

Watering | Mimic the moist, humid air of its natural habitat with regular misting of the arching stems. If it appears brown and droopy, it may need more water.

Feeding | Feed with half-strength liquid fertilizer once a month in spring and summer.

Also try:
Japanese bird's nest fern (*Asplenium amtiquum* 'Osaka')

Watch out for:
Wear gloves as this plant is mildly toxic; touching this plant can cause browning leaves.

PALMS

Turn your home, balcony, terrace, or garden into a tropical paradise with a little help from the arching or fanned-out fronds of the palm family (Arecaceae). Palmlike plants such as cycads and ponytail palms can also add to the vibe.

PARLOR PALM - *Chamaedorea elegans*

nontoxic

easy
care rating

Also known as: neanthe bella palm; good luck palm
Family: Arecaceae
Grows up to: 48 x 24 inches (120 x 60cm)
Great for beginners and for purifying the air

Native to the rainforests of southern Mexico and Guatemala, this small, elegant, air-purifying palm tree has a stout presence, fountains of bright green feathery foliage, and small yellow flowers on some mature specimens. Its common name stems from its popularity during Victorian times, when it was often displayed in a receiving room or parlor. It's also slow-growing, so it is ideal for making a big impact in a smaller area without taking over.

Planting | Grow several stems together in a large pot in an equal mix of soil-based and multipurpose compost. Repot every two to three years when root-bound.

Position | Cultivate as a houseplant; ideal for compact spaces, but can be grown outdoors in tropical climes. Prefers light shade. Avoid deep shade or bright sun.

Watering | Water in spring and summer whenever the top inch of soil feels dry. Reduce in winter. Can tolerate low humidity, but it is best to mist leaves once a week.

Feeding | Well-potted parlor palms require minimum nutrition. Apply a balanced liquid feed once a month from spring to fall. Do not feed during winter.

Also try:
bamboo plant (*Chamaedorea erumpens*); Hooper's palm (*C. hooperiana*)

Watch out for:
Avoid giving it too much sunlight or water; cut brown fronds off at the base; bring outdoor specimens indoors at first risk of frost.

KENTIA PALM - *Howea forsteriana*

nontoxic

easy
care rating

Also known as: thatch court palm; palm court palm; paradise palm
Family: Arecaceae
Grows up to: 96 x 60 inches (240 x 150cm)
Low-maintenance; doesn't mind shade

Like the parlor palm, the kentia palm—endemic to the tropical beachside forests of Lord Howe Island off the coast of New South Wales in Australia—displays its arching, dark green glossy fronds atop single stems but is taller and more graceful. Its high-ended nature makes it ideal for bringing height and life to a shady corner of a room. Compared to other palms, it also has a relative tolerance to shade, drought, and drafts and is ideal for beginners.

Planting | Plant in a 3:1 mix of soil-based compost and sharp sand, as per its native habitat. Replace top layer of compost in spring. Repot when tightly root-bound.

Position | This versatile palm likes a lot of light but is also fine in medium light or even shade. The tall but compact fronds make it ideal as a floor plant on stairs or in a hallway.

Watering | Water between spring and fall whenever the top layer of soil feels dry. Although relatively drought-tolerant, it prefers moist air, so mist several times a week.

Feeding | Apply a balanced liquid fertilizer every two to four weeks from spring to early fall. No need to feed in winter.

Also try:
sentry palm
(*Howea belmoreana*)

Watch out for: Don't expect this slow-grower to gain height quick; if you want an immediate showstopper, buy one at the desired height.

ARECA PALM - *Dypsis lutescens*

nontoxic

medium
care rating

Also known as: golden cane palm; yellow palm; butterfly palm
Family: Arecaceae
Grows up to: 72 x 36 inches (180 x 90cm)
Has a high NASA air-purifying score

Hailing from Madagascar, where it grows in large thickets in forests and on sand dunes, the areca palm boasts oversized arching fronds with numerous closely arranged leaves atop yellow bamboolike stems that grow in groups at its base. It is sometimes labeled as *Chrysalidocarpus lutescens* or *Areca lutescens*, while areca palm is also a common name for the betel palm (*Areca catechu*), grown for its intoxicating edible nuts.

Planting | Grow indoors in a large (8–12 inch/20–30cm) pot in soil-based compost. Bring outdoors in warmer weather, if desired, to use as a privacy screen. Needs good drainage.

Position | Prefers bright, filtered light but can tolerate full morning sun. Avoid strong afternoon sun, which can scorch leaves. Also avoid placing near drying heaters in winter.

Watering | Allow the top layer of soil to dry out between waterings. Use distilled water or rainwater and mist regularly. Reduce in winter.

Feeding | Requires fertilizer two to three times during growing season. Do not feed in winter.

Also try:
bamboo palm
(*Rhapis excelsa*)

Watch out for: Don't overwater, as soggy soil can cause root rot; bring inside if temperatures drop below 50°F (10°C).

PONYTAIL PALM - *Beaucarnea recurvata*

Also known as: elephant's foot palm
Family: Asparagaceae
Grows up to: 72 x 36 inches (180 x 90cm)
An incredibly tactile child- and pet-friendly plant

nontoxic

easy
care rating

Although this eastern Mexican native looks like a palm due to a bulbous brown water-storing caudex, it is closer to a yucca (a fellow Asparagaceae) than true palm (Arecaceae) family members. Younger specimens can resemble small rocks with a spurt of protruding leaves, while taller mature plants have an elegant, multistemmed, fountainlike appeal. They are slow-growing but can live for decades if treated correctly.

Planting | Grow as a houseplant; also fares well outside in warm climates. Grow in a large pot in a 3:1 mix of soil-based compost and sharp sand.

Position | High on visual impact but slow growing, so ideal for making a statement in a smaller space. Prefers bright light, so windowsills or warm, sheltered balconies work well.

Watering | Water once a week in summer, allowing soil mix to dry out in between. It can store water in its base if you forget. Only water in short sips in winter.

Feeding | Limit feeding to the growth period in spring and summer when it will benefit from half-strength liquid fertilizer once a month. Do not feed in winter.

Also try:
spineless yucca
(*Yucca gigantea* syn.
Y. elephantipes)

Watch out for:
Position so light falls
on the entire plant for
its crown to protrude;
do not cut the leaves.

FISHTAIL PALM - *Caryota mitis*

Also known as: Burmese fishtail palm; clustered fishtail palm
Family: Arecaceae
Grows up to: 96 x 60 inches (240 x 150cm)
Needs very bright light to thrive

nontoxic

hard
care rating

The fishtail palm is so named for its unusual fan-shaped, serrated leaves that resemble a fishtail or fin. Tall and compact but with relatively slow growth, it's initially a great showstopper for spaces that don't allow for spread. However, given the right conditions it can become very large. Native to Asia but also naturalized in Florida, it loves bright light and a warm and humid environment, so is ideal for a very sunny bathroom.

Planting | Grow in soil-based compost in a pot that just fits the root ball. Repot every two to three years and replace top layer of compost every spring.

Position | Loves very bright, filtered light but not direct summer sun. Great for large hallways, atriums, or warm-weather terraces.

Watering | From spring to fall, water when the soil feels dry, then water sparingly in winter. Encourage humidity by standing on a tray of damp pebbles and misting regularly.

Feeding | Apply a balanced fertilizer monthly from spring to fall. Do not feed in winter.

Also try:
bamboo palm
(*Rhapis excelsa*)

Watch out for:
Spotted leaves due to
a lack of magnesium,
manganese, and iron;
can spread fast if
planted outdoors in
tropical climes.

CHINESE FAN PALM - *Livistona chinensis*

nontoxic

easy
care rating

Also known as: fountain palm
Family: Arecaceae
Grows up to: 78 x 60 inches (200 x 150cm)
Use to create an indoor–outdoor tropical vibe

As the name suggests, broad, fan-shaped, slightly drooping foliage is the signature feature of the plant, while tall, slender stems extending from a single upright trunk create a full silhouette when mature. As this plant grows wide, it's best for indoor locations that offer plenty of space. For outdoor landscaping, Chinese fan palms are happiest in a bright subtropical/tropical environment but are also hardy to 32°F (0°C) and don't mind the wind.

Planting | The Chinese fan palm can tolerate clay, loam, or sandy soil, but any well-drained soil will work. Enrich with compost and use a quality potting mix for container plantings.

Position | Locate indoors or outdoors in a spacious spot with at least four hours of bright or filtered sunlight. It works well as a stand-alone plant or grouped as a screen.

Watering | Water so that the soil is kept lightly moist through spring to early fall, increasing in warm, dry weather and reducing in winter. Avoid soggy soil.

Feeding | Feed with a balanced fertilizer once a month during the spring-summer growing season. Use a specialty palm fertilizer to optimize nutrients. Don't overfeed.

Also try:
dwarf fan palm
(*Chamaerops humilis*)

Watch out for: Spines on the interior of the leaf stems, so avoid planting in areas where people might brush against them.

SAGO PALM - *Cycas revoluta*

toxic

easy
care rating

Also known as: king sago; Japanese sago; cycad
Family: Cycadaceae
Grows up to: 24 x 24 inches (60 x 60cm)
A symmetrical choice for doorways

Although not technically a true palm, this ancient plant with its stout, shaggy trunk and featherlike fronded leaves fits right in with the bunch. Native to Japan, its dense symmetrical growing habit and tolerance of mild to colder (frost-free) climates makes it desirable as a landscaping or houseplant for entrances, corridors, or hallways. The common name "sago" nods to its historical use in the production of this starchy, edible staple.

Planting | Grow indoors or outdoors in a large pot in an equal mix of soil, sand, and potting compost. An unglazed terra-cotta pot can help excess soil moisture to evaporate.

Position | Place in a warm, bright location away from full summer sun and drying radiators in winter. Planting directly into the ground can help speed up slow growth.

Watering | Allow the top layer of soil to dry out between waterings. Don't water the crown as this can cause rot. Mist the leaves regularly in summer.

Feeding | Feed a half-strength fertilizer once a month from spring to fall.

Also try:
chestnut dioon
(*Dioon edule*)

Watch out for: Sharp, needlelike leaves, so take care when planting or positioning; repot every three years or when root-bound.

OTHER FOLIAGE

Foliage plants lead with their leaves, from jungly evergreen tropicals and opening and closing prayer plants, to variegated trailers in shades of pink, red, green, and cream. Group "like-minded" plants together for a lush effect and ease of care.

FIDDLE-LEAF FIG - *Ficus lyrata*

toxic

medium
care rating

Also known as: banjo fig
Family: Moraceae
Grows up to: 72 x 48 inches (180 x 120cm)
The ultimate statement plant for a living room

Native to the rainforests of West Africa, the fiddle-leaf is a popular ornamental tree in subtropical/tropical gardens, where it can grow up to 50 feet (15m) tall. It has also become a hugely desirable houseplant thanks to its stately size, but also its unusual fiddle-shaped, distinctively veined glossy leaves that sprout from a treelike trunk. It can be difficult to care for, however, so be prepared to meet all its requirements to help it thrive.

Planting | Choose a large pot that fits the root ball and plant in a 3:1 mix of soil-based compost and perlite. In warm, humid climates, it can thrive outdoors.

Position | Place in a bright location, away from a window but with lots of indirect light. Avoid drafts. Humidity is essential, so keep away from drying heaters in winter.

Watering | Allow the top 2 inches (5cm) of compost to dry out between waterings from spring to fall. Keep just moist in winter. Mist regularly for healthiest growth.

Feeding | Apply a half-strength balanced liquid fertilizer once a month from spring to fall. An NPK ratio of 3:1:2 is ideal for this nitrogen-loving plant.

Also try:
dwarf fiddle-leaf fig (*Ficus lyrata* 'Bambino'); Bengal fig (*F. benghalensis* 'Audrey')

Watch out for:
It is normal for the leaves to drop after transportation and in winter; this can also be down to lack of watering or very dry air.

INDIA RUBBER PLANT - *Ficus elastica*

toxic

easy
care rating

Also known as: rubber tree; rubber bush
Family: Moraceae
Grows up to: 72 x 48 inches (180 x 120cm)
Adds low-maintenance, shiny-leaved drama

Another member of the fig genus, this South and Southeast Asian native has thick roots and broad, glossy, dark green leaves. Although the foliage has a rubbery appearance, it's the white latex running through its veins—once used to make rubber—that led to its common name. The dark green ones are classic beauties, but for bright locations you could also try variegated offerings in shades of red, yellow, cream, and green.

Planting | Plant in a well-draining pot that's big enough to accommodate the root ball, in a mix of soil-based compost and a little perlite.

Position | Place in a bright or lightly shaded room away from direct sun and drafts. Avoid placing near windows. It has good presence in a living room.

Watering | Water when the top 2 inches (5cm) of soil are dry. Reduce watering in winter. Encourage healthy growth by misting thirsty leaves every few days in summer.

Feeding | Apply a half-strength balanced liquid fertilizer every two weeks from spring to fall. Do not feed in winter.

Also try:
variegated rubber plant (*Ficus elastic* 'Robusta')

Watch out for: Scale bugs or mealybugs—wiping down the leaves regularly can help; variegated options need ample sunlight.

WEEPING FIG - *Ficus benjamina*

toxic

medium
care rating

Also known as: Benjamin fig; ficus tree
Family: Moraceae
Grows up to: 10 x 4 feet (3 x 1.2m)
A good choice for purifying the air

Probably the most well-known ornamental fig, used widely in homes, offices, and commercial spaces, this elegant indoor tree has slender arching branches of small, glossy, dark green or variegated, slightly wavy leaves, and can also be grown as a bonsai. Growing up to 60 feet (18m) tall in the wild, indoor specimens are normally pruned to keep them small and often come with braided trunks as added decorative appeal.

Planting | Plant in soil-based compost in a well-draining pot that fits the root ball. Replace the top layer of compost in spring. Prune into shape after summer.

Position | Prefers bright or filtered light but can tolerate shade. Needs space to accommodate its arching stems. An ideal plant for the corner of a room or a patio.

Watering | Allow the top few inches of soil to dry out between watering. Keep just moist in winter. Use tepid rainwater or distilled water and mist leaves in summer.

Feeding | Apply a half-strength fertilizer once a month from spring to fall.

Also try:
variegated weeping fig (*Ficus benjamina* 'Golden King')

Watch out for: Over- or underwatering can cause leaves to drop. Avoid repotting or moving position.

SPLIT LEAF PHILODENDRON - *Thaumatophyllum bipinnatifidum*

toxic

easy
care rating

Also known as: tree philodendron; lacy tree philodendron
Family: Araceae
Grows up to: 72 x 72 inches (180 x 180cm)
Large, lush, and low-maintenance

Native to the rainforests of Argentina, Bolivia, Brazil, and Paraguay, the split-leaf philodendron has deeply divided, long-stalked, dark green leaves that can grow up to 3 feet (1m) long in the wild. Unlike the vining Swiss cheese plant (*Monstera deliciosa*), for which it is often mistaken, its leaves are fully split from the edges (rather than holey) and it has a supportive trunk. There are also variegated options including 'Gold Satin' and 'Lime Fiddle'.

Planting | Choose a well-draining pot that will comfortably hold the root ball of your plant. Plant in a soil-based potting compost with a little perlite.

Position | Bright indirect or filtered light is ideal. Avoid direct midday sun as this can scorch the leaves, and place away from drafts and heat sources in winter.

Watering | Keep soil moist but never waterlogged. Water when the top 2 inches (5cm) of soil feel dry. Increase humidity by misting and placing on a tray of damp pebbles.

Feeding | Apply a half-strength balanced liquid fertilizer every month between spring and fall to avoid leaves yellowing and to boost growth.

Also try:
philodendron xanadu (*Thaumatophyllum xanadu*)

Watch out for:
Prune dead, diseased, or damaged growth as it appears; trim back to just above a node (where the leaf grows).

IMPERIAL GREEN PHILODENDRON - *Philodendron erubescens* 'Imperial Green'

toxic

easy
care rating

Also known as: imperial philodendron
Family: Araceae
Grows up to: 24 x 36 inches (60 x 90cm)
Big glossy leaves add vitality to living spaces

The large, dark green leaves of 'Imperial Green' philodendrons are slightly more paddle-shaped than most heart-shaped philodendron relatives, with a compact, upright-growing (self-heading) form. A cultivar of *Philodendron erubescens*—the blushing philodendron, named for its deep red flowers—the 'Imperial Green' philodendron exudes health and vitality and is a top choice for purifying the air; ideal for busy living spaces or offices.

Planting | Plant in soil-based or loamy potting mix with optional perlite. Place in a well-draining pot that accommodates the root ball with room to grow.

Position | Prefers bright, filtered light but can also handle shade. Keep away from direct sunlight, which can scorch the leaves, and also avoid drafts and drying heat sources.

Watering | Water between spring and summer when the top 2 inches (5cm) of soil feel dry. Reduce in winter. Mist every few days. It is forgiving if you forget.

Feeding | Feed once a month during spring and summer using a half-strength fertilizer.

Also try: red emerald philodendron (*Philodendron erubescens* 'Red Emerald')

Watch out for:
Yellowing leaves often signify overwatering.

BANANA TREE - *Musa acuminata* 'Dwarf Cavendish'

nontoxic

hard
care rating

Also known as: dwarf banana
Family: Musaceae
Grows up to: 10 x 5 feet (3 x 1.5m)
One for the conservatory, or outdoors in summer

Banana trees have very large leaves, grow fast, and prefer a bright, humid environment so will need a large, consistently warm, sunny space indoors or out. Although originally cultivated to produce the now popular, edible 'Dwarf Cavendish' banana, it is unlikely to produce a fruit crop as a houseplant. What you will get are huge, bright green or red-marked leaves that emerge from a series of pseudostems (leaf sheafs) for a tropical vibe.

Planting | This evergreen perennial needs a large container and should be planted in spring or fall in well-drained soil enriched with organic matter.

Position | Likes a lot of bright light and can even tolerate some direct sun. Ideal for warm conservatories. Fragile leaves will grow back, but best to place out of harm's way.

Watering | Let the soil dry out between waterings. Avoid overwatering, but make sure you keep the large leaves well misted as they need a lot of moisture.

Feeding | Feed with balanced liquid fertilizer once a month in spring and summer. Or mix a controlled-release fertilizer into compost when potting.

Also try: stripe-leaved banana (*Musa acuminata* 'Zebrina')

Watch out for: Bring inside over winter; wrap in horticultural fleece or cut down to a foot high and cover in a layer of mulch to stop water from pooling.

SPINELESS YUCCA - *Yucca gigantea* **syn.** *Yucca elephantipes*

toxic

easy
care rating

Also known as: soft-tip yucca
Family: Asparagaeceae
Grows up to: 60 x 30 inches (150 x 75cm)
Striking architectural foliage for a sunny room

Native to hot, arid parts of the Americas and the Caribbean, this large, upright shrub boasts several palmlike trunks growing from near ground level, from which spiraled rosettes of long, arching, swordlike leaves extend. Unlike its relative the Spanish bayonet (*Yucca aloifolia*), spineless yucca leaves do not have sharp leaf tips, making this species a more popular houseplant choice. Yuccas are also easy to propagate by division and pups.

Planting | Choose a well-draining pot that fits the root ball snugly and fill with a mix of two parts soil to one part sand. Repot every two to three years.

Position | One of the few houseplants that loves full summer sun. Place in a bright conservatory or sunny room. Shadier spots can help reduce growth.

Watering | Yuccas are extremely drought-tolerant but benefit from watering in spring and summer when the top few inches of soil are dry. Do not waterlog or mist.

Feeding | Use a half-strength fertilizer monthly through spring and summer.

Also try:
Spanish bayonet (*Yucca aloifolia*)

Watch out for:
If growing too big, cut the trunk down in spring for new foliage to appear. Never sit in a tray of water.

DRAGON PLANT - *Dracaena marginata*

toxic

easy
care rating

Also known as: dragon tree
Family: Asparagaceae
Grows up to: 48 x 36 inches (120 x 90cm)
Ideal for beginners; thrives in lots
of locations

This low-maintenance stalwart produces fountainlike rosettes of swordlike, red-edged leaves. In mature specimens, these emerge from variously sized elegant woody stems, although the overall silhouette remains slim. Brilliantly colored varieties include 'Tricolor' (dark red margins, green leaves, and a central ivory stripe), 'Colorama' (mainly pink with white and green stripes), and 'Bicolor' (red and green stripes).

Planting | Use free-draining potting compost with added grit. Choose a pot that has plenty of room for the extensive root system. Repot every two to three years.

Position | Prefers bright, indirect light but can thrive in shadier spots. Full sun can scorch leaves. Likes high humidity, so a kitchen or bathroom is ideal.

Watering | Let the top few inches of soil dry out between waterings. Do not overwater, and use distilled water or rainwater to avoid discoloration. Mist every few days.

Feeding | Apply a half-strength balanced liquid fertilizer during spring and summer, although dragon plants survive perfectly well without. Do not feed in winter.

Also try:
corn plant
(*Dracaena fragrans*)

Watch out for: Dragon plants are incredibly slow growing, so start with a larger specimen if you want more architectural impact.

LUCKY BAMBOO - *Dracaena sanderiana*

toxic

easy
care rating

Also known as: Chinese water bamboo; friendship bamboo
Family: Asparageceae
Grows up to: 36 x 24 inches (90 x 60cm)
Said to bring good luck and fortune

These near-indestructible plants can survive in vases of water or pots of soil in a variety of light conditions and are said to bring good luck and fortune to those who own them, especially if given as gifts. Originally native to Africa, these bamboolike plants are actually closer to a succulent and are often braided, twisted, or curled into a variety of eye-catching styles prior to purchase.

Planting | Grow in well-drained rich potting soil; can also thrive in a vase of distilled water (at least 1 inch/2.5cm at all times) and pebbles. Change water weekly to avoid algae.

Position | Prefers filtered sunlight but can tolerate part shade. Avoid direct sun and cold or hot drafts. Provide more light if the color begins to fade.

Watering | Water with distilled water. Average humidity is fine.

Feeding | Add a drop of balanced fertilizer monthly for potted plants; apply every other month for those grown in water; if leaves are yellowing, do not feed at all.

Also try:
bamboo palm
(*Chamaedorea seifrizii*)

Watch out for:
Trim down top-heavy offshoots to 2 inches (5cm) of the stem.

AMAZONIAN ELEPHANT EAR - *Alocasia × amazonica*

toxic | medium *care rating*

Also known as: African mask; Amazon elephant ear
Family: Araceae
Grows up to: 48 x 36 inches (120 x 90cm)
Stunning but sensitive; highly toxic

Easily distinguishable by its wavy-edged, dark green, purple (underside), and silver-veined foliage, this tropical Southeast Asian plant is stunning but sensitive, so it requires dedicated care. Stemming from underground rhizomes, it can grow rapidly with new heart- or lance-shaped leaves, doubling in size over the space of a week in the warm summer growing period. Can be grown alone, or it looks great in mixed containers.

Planting | Choose a pot that has adequate space for root growth filled with a potting mix of composted bark, loam, and sand. Can propagate by division in spring or summer.

Position | Place in a warm, humid environment in bright, indirect light. Keep away from cold drafts or heaters. Most specimens are small enough to place on a shelf.

Watering | Keep soil moist with distilled water during the growing season between spring and summer. Set on a tray of damp pebbles and mist leaves every day.

Feeding | Feed with a balanced liquid fertilizer every two to three weeks from spring to early summer. Do not feed in the dormant winter period.

Also try:
alocasia regal shields (*Alocasia* 'Regal Shields')

Watch out for:
Overwatering can lead to fungal infections; remove infected brown- or black-spotted leaves immediately.

ELEPHANT EAR - *Caladium bicolor*

toxic | easy *care rating*

Also known as: heart of Jesus; angel wings
Family: Araceae
Grows up to: 24 x 12 inches (60 x 30cm)
Striking green, white, and pink foliage

The leaves of this elephant ear are similar in style to those of the *Alocasia*—large, wavy-edged, and lance- or heart-shaped with contrasting veining—but *Caladiums* have a smaller growing habit, making them ideal for compact spaces. Choose from numerous variants displaying striking foliage in variegations of green, white, pink, and red, including 'Freida Hemple', 'Little Miss Muffet', 'Pink Beauty', and 'White Christmas'.

Planting | Plant in a well-draining pot of composted bark, loam, and sand. In winter, bring outdoor plants or tubers inside, as they will not survive the cold or frost.

Position | Prefers partial to full shade. Avoid direct sunlight, which can burn the leaves. There are sun-tolerant varieties, including 'Florida Fantasy'.

Watering | Keep soil moist with distilled water during the growing season between spring and summer. Set on a tray of damp pebbles and mist leaves every day.

Feeding | Feed every two to three weeks from spring to early summer.

Also try:
arrowhead vine (*Syngonium* 'Neon Robusta')
Watch out for:
Check the signage, if growing from tubers, to make sure it's the right variegation.

ZEBRA PLANT - *Alocasia zebrina*

toxic

easy
care rating

Also known as: elephant ear; tiger plant
Family: Araceae
Grows up to: 36 x 36 inches (90 x 90cm)
Prized for its arching zebra-striped stems

This species of the *Alocasia* "elephant ear" genus is prized for its zebra-striped stems. Found in the tropical wilds of Southeast Asia, where it grows at the base of much larger trees, its large leaves help to capture as much sun and rain as possible in order to thrive. The broad leaves and striking stems provide a good focal feature in a minimalist room or mixed with other unusual plants to create a bohemian vibe.

Planting | Plant in a well-draining mix of composted bark, loam, and sand, in a pot that allows it to be slightly root-bound. Pot up incrementally as the plant grows in size.

Position | These big, arching leaves like a lot of bright light but not direct sun, which can scorch the leaves. Avoid windows and heaters. Looks striking on a plant stand.

Watering | Water in spring to fall when the top 2 inches (5cm) of soil are dry. Optimize humidity by standing on a tray of damp pebbles and misting leaves regularly.

Feeding | Feed every two weeks in spring to fall with a balanced liquid fertilizer. Do not feed in the dormant winter period.

Also try: Amazonian elephant ear (*Alocasia × amazonica*)

Watch out for:
Dust leaves regularly to keep them clean and maximize growth. Ensure there's enough light to keep stems from reaching out.

ZEBRA PLANT - *Aphelandra squarrosa*

nontoxic

medium
care rating

Also known as: saffron spike zebra
Family: Acanthaceae
Grows up to: 24 x 24 inches (60 x 60cm)
Colorful late summer/fall blooms add zing
to the stripy leaves

Another zebra plant, but this time named for its green- and cream-striped foliage. Native to the rainforests of Brazil, it can become a huge, sprawling shrub in the wild but as a houseplant is usually relatively small and compact, making it ideal for shelves and sideboards. If given optimum light conditions and humidity, it also flowers in late summer/fall, displaying bright yellow-orange leaves with short-lived true flowers inside.

Planting | Plant in a medium-sized pot in soil-based compost. Remove flower stems after blooming and then prune to the bottom set of leaves. Repot in spring.

Position | Prefers bright, natural light. Avoid direct sun, artificial light at night, and deep shade. The striped leaves and colorful flowers can help brighten a sunny corner.

Watering | Keep soil moist through spring to fall. Only water in the dormant winter period when the top of the compost is almost dry. Wipe leaves and mist regularly.

Feeding | Apply a balanced liquid fertilizer once every two weeks between spring and early fall. Do not feed in the dormant period in winter.

Also try: zebra plant
(*Calathea zebrina*)

Watch out for:
Leaf tips can brown
and curl if humidity
is too low or foliage is
exposed to direct sun;
leaf drop may indicate
dry soil or a drafty
position.

ZEBRA PLANT - *Calathea zebrina*

nontoxic

easy
care rating

Also known as: prayer plant
Family: Marantaceae
Grows up to: 24 x 24 inches (60 x 60cm)
A green-striped, low-maintenance beauty

Calatheas are celebrated for their decorative, attention-grabbing, long-stalked ovate foliage that grows from a basal rosette, and the zebrina is no exception. Commonly and botanically named for its distinctive dark and lime green zebra-like striped leaves, made further attractive by their purple undersides, the foliage also closes at night as if in prayer. Native to the rainforest understory, treat it to a bright but shady humid spot.

Planting | Calatheas thrive best in a well-draining mix of soil, potting compost, and perlite. Repot in spring before they get root-bound, usually every two years.

Position | Prefers bright but filtered light. Experiment with lighter and shadier positions to see which bring out the best coloration in the leaves.

Watering | Keep the soil moist but not wet. A well-draining pot is key. Encourage vital humidity by placing on a tray of wet pebbles and misting several times a week.

Feeding | Feed monthly in spring and summer with a half-strength fertilizer.

Also try:
rattlesnake plant
(*Calathea lancifolia*)

Watch out for:
Lack of humidity can
cause brown or curling
leaves; lack of draining
can cause the roots to
rot.

RATTLESNAKE PLANT - *Calathea lancifolia* syn. *Goeppertia insignis*

nontoxic

medium
care rating

Also known as: prayer plant
Family: Marantaceae
Grows up to: 30 x 18 inches (75 x 45cm)
Perfect for low-maintenance pattern-lovers

The rattlesnake plant is similar to *Calathea zebrina* but with narrow, wavy-edged foliage with dark green, snakelike, oval markings on a lime-green base. The underside of these leaves is a deep plum, and is a wonderful feature when leaves begin to close "in prayer" at night, as all calatheas do. This arresting foliage also grows more elongated as the plant matures, but retains a bushy habit, making it ideal as a floor plant or tabletop accent.

Planting | Use a soil-based compost mixed with perlite in a medium-sized, well-draining pot. Replenish the top 2 inches (5cm) of the soil in the spring months.

Position | Calatheas love high humidity and bright, filtered light, so a sunny bathroom is ideal. Keep out of direct sunlight as this can scorch the leaves.

Watering | Water with tepid distilled water or rainwater. Ensure soil stays moist in spring and summer. Reduce watering in winter. Stand on a tray of wet pebbles and mist regularly.

Feeding | Feed with a half-strength balanced liquid fertilizer every two weeks between spring and fall. Do not feed in winter.

Also try:
pinstripe plant
(*Calathea ornata*)

Watch out for: Too much discoloration could indicate overwatering, so make sure the soil is not waterlogged.

PEACOCK PLANT - *Calathea makoyana* syn. *Goeppertia makoyana*

nontoxic

hard
care rating

Also known as: cathedral windows
Family: Marantaceae
Grows up to: 20 x 20 inches (50 x 50cm)
Colorful but slightly fussy

The "peacock" calathea stands out due to its rounded, exquisitely patterned, light-catching foliage showcasing dark green featherlike markings on a pale green-white base. The undersides are a rich pinkish-maroon color, adding a gorgeous splash of warmth as rolled-up leaves emerge. It has a tall, upright, dense growth that makes it perfect for adding color and pattern to semi-shady corners, but can be slightly difficult to care for.

Planting | Place in a well-draining medium pot, in a mix of potting soil and perlite. Repot every one to two years at the start of the growing season.

Position | Place in moderate to low filtered light to help keep the leaves vibrant. High humidity is vital, so a bathroom or kitchen is ideal.

Watering | Water so soil stays moist between spring and fall. Reduce in winter. Place on a tray of wet pebbles, mist frequently, and consider investing in a humidifier.

Feeding | Feed every two weeks between spring and fall.

Also try:
rattlesnake plant
(*Calathea lancifolia*)

Watch out for: Brown or yellow leaves can indicate dry air; keep away from heaters, drafts, and direct sunlight.

STROMANTHE - *Stromanthe sanguinea* 'Triostar'

nontoxic

easy
care rating

Also known as: prayer plant
Family: Marantaceae
Grows up to: 18 x 24 inches (45 x 60cm)
Provide space for striking leaves to expand

Green, pink, red, and cream spear-shaped leaves make this one of the most artistic plants you can find. In the rainforests of South America, this can bring a pop of color to the understory, while at home it can brighten up or add interest to a plain room. Also known as a prayer plant, it curls up its leaves at night and is sometimes labelled as a calathea. The stromanthe is much easier to care for, however, so it is ideal for beginners.

Planting | Plant in a well-draining, relatively shallow pot in an equal mix of multipurpose and soil-based compost. Perlite can help hold moisture.

Position | Loves humidity, so it is ideal for a bathroom. Prefers the dappled light of its native rainforest, so opt for bright, filtered light. Allow space for leaves to spread out.

Watering | Keep compost moist from spring to summer. Reduce watering in winter. Set on a tray of damp pebbles and mist daily to help provide humidity.

Feeding | Feed with a half-strength balanced liquid fertilizer once a month between spring and late fall. Do not feed in winter.

Also try:
Stromanthe thalia
'Magic Star'

Watch out for:
Too much shade can inhibit the sought-after variegation, so reposition if the leaves start going green; avoid direct sunlight as this can burn the leaves.

PRAYER PLANT - *Maranta leuconeura* **var.** *erythroneura*

nontoxic

*easy
care rating*

Also known as: herringbone plant; *Maranta* 'Fascinator'
Family: Marantaceae
Grows up to: 24 x 24 inches (60 x 60cm)
Red-veined foliage folds "in prayer" at night

This clump-forming evergreen is known for its intricately patterned, dark olive oval leaves with a bright green central zone and a distinguishing red midrib and veins. Like many species of its relative the calathea, its leaves have a maroon-red underside bringing additional color, warmth, and interest. Often referred to as a "prayer plant," it closes its leaves at night, pressing together like hands in prayer and unfolding again at dawn.

Planting | Plant in a relatively small, shallow pot of soil-based compost. It is slow growing but will benefit from being repotted every two to three years.

Position | Prefers bright, filtered light. Avoid direct sunlight, which can burn the leaves, and drafts. Thrives best in a warm, humid space such as a bathroom.

Watering | Water so that the soil stays moist in spring until fall. Reduce over winter. Stand on a tray of damp pebbles and mist regularly to provide humidity.

Feeding | Feed with a half-strength balanced liquid fertilizer every two weeks from spring to fall. Do not feed in winter.

Also try: rabbit's foot prayer plant (*Maranta leuconeura* var. *kerchoveana*)

Watch out for: Too much sun exposure can cause washed-out or brown, blotchy leaves; too cool or dry a space may cause leaf drop or a fungal infection.

CROTON - *Codiaeum variegatum*

toxic

hard
care rating

Also known as: garden croton; Joseph's coat
Family: Euphorbiaceae
Grows up to: 60 x 30 inches (150 x 75cm)
A large, colorful, leathery-leaved shrub

Native to the forests and scrublands of Indonesia, Malaysia, Australia, and the western Pacific Ocean islands, this tropical evergreen shrub has large, thick, shiny and leathery leaves in vivid combinations of red, yellow, and green, dependent on the variety. The best-known crotons have multicolored leaves but there are also cultivars with just yellow and green markings, plus a choice of leaf shapes including broad, narrow, lobed, and spiraled.

Planting | Plant in a soil-based compost in a well-draining pot that accommodates the root ball. Repot every two to three years. Can be grown outdoors in warmer climates.

Position | Prefers bright, filtered light, constant warmth, and high humidity. A bright bathroom or warm conservatory is ideal. Avoid direct sunlight and drafts.

Watering | Water with tepid water between spring and fall so the soil stays moist. Allow the top layer of soil to dry out in winter. Set on a tray of damp pebbles and mist daily.

Feeding | Feed with a balanced liquid fertilizer every two weeks from spring to fall. Do not feed in winter. Overfeeding can cause leaves to dull and damage roots.

Also try: spiral croton (*Codiaeum variegatum* 'Spirale')

Watch out for: Crotons grow quite large and bushy but can be trimmed to size; all parts of the plant are toxic, so wear gloves when handling.

NEVER NEVER PLANT - *Ctenanthe burle-marxii*

nontoxic

easy
care rating

Also known as: fishbone prayer plant
Family: Marantaceae
Grows up to: 24 x 18 inches (60 x 45cm)
Low-maintenance, graphic foliage

This tropical rainforest groundcover plant native to Brazil and other parts of Central and South America hails from the same family as species of *Calathea*, *Maranta*, and *Stromanthe*. As well as similar markings—in this case lime green with lighter green fishbone patterns with a deep maroon underside—it also closes its leaves at night and is thus often sold as a prayer plant. A generally undemanding plant, it adds color to plain rooms.

Planting | Plant in a suitably sized pot in a mix of soil-based and multipurpose compost and perlite. Repot every two to three years in spring or if plant becomes root-bound.

Position | Prefers bright, indirect light as per its native environment. Avoid excessive or direct sunlight. Provide medium to high humidity.

Watering | Water so the soil stays moist between spring and fall but dries out between waterings in winter. Stand on a tray of damp pebbles and mist occasionally.

Feeding | Apply fertilizer monthly between spring and fall. Do not feed in winter.

Also try: beautiful ctenanthe (*Ctenanthe burle-marxii* 'Amabilis')

Watch out for: Leaf curling or brown tips in low humidity.

COLEUS - *Plectranthus scutellarioides*

toxic

medium
care rating

Also known as: painted nettle
Family: Lamiaceae
Grows up to: 24 x 12 inches (60 x 30cm)
Displays vivid, sometimes pyschedelic foliage

This bushy, woody evergreen perennial has similar shaped leaves to its mint family relative, the deadnettle (*Lamium* spp.). Also sold under the synonyms *Coleus scutellarioides* and *Solenostemon scutellarioides*, this pretty, variously colored and patterned plant is often grown as an outdoor bedding annual as well as a houseplant. Choose from thousands of cultivars, including 'Wizard', 'Red Velvet', and 'Inky Fingers'.

Planting | Pot indoor plants in an equal mix of soil-based and multipurpose compost. Prune back after winter and repot. Can also grow from seed in spring.

Position | Brings color and variegation to partially shaded summer and fall borders in the garden. Indoors, prefers bright light but not direct sunlight.

Watering | Keep soil moist through spring to fall. Allow the top of the soil to dry out between winter waterings. Do not overwater or mist.

Feeding | This plant is grown for its leaves, not its size or flowers, so does not need much food. Apply a balanced liquid fertilizer every month from spring to fall.

Also try:
Plectranthus scutellarioides 'Wizard Mix'

Watch out for:
Pinch out the stem tips to keep the plant bushy and compact.

WATERMELON PEPEROMIA - *Peperomia argyreia*

nontoxic

easy
care rating

Also known as: watermelon begonia
Family: Piperaceae
Grows up to: 8 x 8 inches (20 x 20cm)
Leaves look like mini watermelons

Native to moist areas of South America, where it is often found growing on rotten wood, this cute, compact plant displays charming oval-round leaves that look like tiny watermelons. Non-showy, greenish flowers can appear in summer but are no match for the striking leaves, which also clean the air. Equally attractive is its cousin, the radiator plant (*Peperomia caperata*), which has red-green corrugated leaves and long, wicklike cream flowers.

Planting | Plant in soil-based potting compost or a mix of soil and perlite in a small pot. Can also be grown outdoors as ground cover. Repot in spring after three years.

Position | Prefers light shade in summer and bright but indirect light in winter. Ideal for the middle of a table or grouped with other plants that share a similar care label.

Watering | Allow top layer of compost to dry out between waterings, keeping it almost dry over winter. Set on a tray of damp pebbles and mist every other day.

Feeding | Feed with balanced liquid fertilizer once a month between spring and fall.

Also try:
red log peperomia
(*P. verticillata*)

Watch out for:
Overwatering, lack of water, or temperature stress can cause the leaves to curl inward, so keep an eye out and adjust care accordingly.

NERVE PLANT - *Fittonia albivenis*

nontoxic

medium
care rating

Also known as: mosaic plant
Family: Acanthaceae
Grows up to: 6 x 8 inches (15 x 20cm)
Small but beautiful with contrasting veined leaves

Small in size but big on impact, the nerve or mosaic plant is a spreading evergreen perennial native to the rainforests of Colombia, Peru, Bolivia, Ecuador, and Brazil. Perfect for terrariums or bottle gardens, hanging baskets or container gardens, the striking green and white or green and red multiveined leaves are eye-catching. Arranging with other small plants that require similar conditions can help you keep on top of care.

Planting | Plant in soil-based compost in a small, well-draining pot. A terrarium is ideal as it provides the constant humidity and diffused light needed to thrive.

Position | The red, yellow, and white cultivars need bright light with some morning and evening sun for intensive leaf coloring. Green forms can take light shade.

Watering | Water so that the compost stays moist. Nerve plants also demand high humidity, so place on a tray of damp pebbles and mist daily. A humidifier can also help.

Feeding | New or recently repotted plants don't need feeding in the first year. Otherwise, apply a half-strength balanced liquid fertilizer once a month from spring to fall.

Also try:
silver-white veins (*Fittonia albivenis* 'Argyroneura')

Watch out for: Avoid direct sunlight as this can cause light burn; overwatering can lead to yellow leaves and root rot.

CAST IRON PLANT - *Aspidistra elatior*

nontoxic

easy
care rating

Also known as: bar-room plant
Family: Asparagaceae
Grows up to: 24 x 24 inches (60 x 60cm)
A resilient, low-maintenance evergreen

The curious common name of this plant refers to its "cast iron" stalwart nature, making it an ideal choice for beginners or those looking for a low-maintenance plant. It has a tolerance of low light and air quality and is native to the forest understories of Japan, where its long, strappy mottled green and light green leaves reach up to the sky. Perfect for shady corners or windowless rooms.

Planting | Plant in a medium-sized pot in an equal mix of soil-based and multipurpose compost. Repot every two to three years. Can be grown outside in shadier spots.

Position | Can survive in a range of light levels, from filtered light to shady spots. Avoid direct sunshine. Ideal for less-visited areas such as offices or basements.

Watering | Try to keep the compost moist between spring and late summer, and reduce watering in winter. Is tolerant of irregular watering. Do not waterlog.

Feeding | Use a half-strength fertilizer monthly from spring to fall. Do not feed in winter.

Also try:
variegated bar-room plant (*Aspidistra elatior* 'Variegata')

Watch out for:
Extreme lack of moisture can cause leaf tips to brown.

MISSIONARY PLANT - *Pilea peperomioides*

nontoxic

easy
care rating

Also known as: Chinese money plant; coin plant; pancake plant; friendship plant
Family: Urticaceae
Grows up to: 12 x 12 inches (30 x 30cm)
Share its minimalist appeal with friends

One of the most popular small-sized houseplants thanks to its pretty coin-shaped, peperomia-like leaves, thin fleshy stalks, and its habit of creating offshoots that can be easily shared with friends. Native to low Himalayan regions of southern China, it is now found ornamenting windowsills and shelves all over the world. Looks lovely coupled with its silver-patterned, easygoing relative the aluminum plant (*Pilea cadierei*).

Planting | Plant in a small, well-draining pot—terra-cotta is ideal—filled with soil-based compost and perlite. Repot every one to two years when root-bound.

Position | Thrives in medium to bright, filtered light. Keep consistently warm and avoid drafts. Looks pretty on a desk, on shelves, near a windowsill, or by a bed.

Watering | Allow the top layer of compost to dry out between waterings in spring and fall. Keep just moist in winter. Will appreciate regular misting of foliage.

Feeding | Feed with a half-strength balanced liquid fertilizer every two weeks from spring to fall. Do not feed in winter.

Also try:
aluminum plant (*Pilea cadierei*); watermelon peperomia (*Peperomia argyreia*)

Watch out for:
Pileas grow toward the light, so can benefit from regular pot rotation to keep an even, rounded shape. Dislikes overwatering.

ZZ PLANT - *Zamioculcas zamiifolia*

toxic

easy
care rating

Also known as: fern arum; Zanzibar gem
Family: Araceae
Grows up to: 30 x 24 inches (75 x 60cm)
A low-maintenance air purifier

Another popular houseplant due to its dark green, waxy leaves, medium growth, stalwart, easygoing nature, and proven ability to remove a range of toxins from the air. Native to tropical Central Africa and the east African coast, the tall, arching, shiny paired leaves grow from thick potatolike rhizomes that store water—good news for those looking for a low-maintenance or drought-tolerant plant. The "ZZ" moniker is also fun.

Planting | Plant in a well-draining mix of two parts soil-based compost to one part sand. Choose a pot that just fits the root ball. Repot every two to three years.

Position | Prefers bright, filtered light but can tolerate shadier spots. Is ideal for an office or grouped together with more feathery or vining foliage plants.

Watering | Water between spring and fall when the top layer of compost feels dry, and reduce in winter. Can tolerate the odd missed watering. Appreciates frequent misting.

Feeding | Feed with a half-strength balanced liquid fertilizer once a month from spring to fall. Do not feed in winter.

Also try:
raven ZZ (*Zamioculcas zamiifolia* 'Raven'); dwarf ZZ (*Z. zamiifolia* 'Zamicro')

Watch out for:
Trim to neaten each spring; it can become deciduous and lose leaves if it dries out.

FALSE CASTOR OIL PLANT - *Fatsia japonica*

toxic

easy
care rating

Also known as: glossy leaf paper plant; fatsia; Japanese aralia
Family: Araliaceae
Grows up to: 72 x 72 inches (180 x 180cm)
Ideal for shady indoor or outdoor spots

Native to Japan, the genus *Fatsia* derives from the Japanese word for "eight," in reference to this shrubby plant's eight leaf lobes. Its large, fanning, hand-shaped leaves thrive in low light conditions, so this is a good plant for shady areas. It also works well as a potted houseplant, planted outdoors—although it can grow quite big—or used as a screening plant for indoor/ outdoor areas such as conservatories and patios.

Planting | Plant indoors in a pot large enough to accommodate the root ball. Use a mix of soil-based and ericaceous compost.

Position | Happy in a range of light levels from full shade to bright sun, but prefers filtered light or light shade. Avoid hot, dry environments in winter.

Watering | Water so that the soil is just moist between spring and fall. Reduce in winter. Do not let it dry out completely.

Feeding | Use a half-strength fertilizer every two weeks from spring to fall.

Also try:
variegated false castor oil plant (*Fatsia japonica* 'Variegata')

Watch out for:
Trim to keep in compact shape; cream umbels can bloom in late summer.

BROMELIADS

Bromeliaceae family plants are known for their strappy colorful or patterned leaves, striking architectural flowers, or—in the case of the pineapple—even their fruits. They're easier to care for than many people think, as long as you get to know their needs.

AECHMEA - *Aechmea* spp.

nontoxic

easy
care rating

Including: silver vase plant; Amazonian zebra plant
Family: Bromeliaceae
Grows up to: 24 x 24 inches (60 x 60cm)
Beautiful blooms, ideal for beginners

Native to Central and South America, popular varieties of this epiphytic bromeliad include the silver-leaved, pink-blooming urn or silver vase plant (*Aechmea fasciata*), the red flower–spiked Amazonian zebra plant (*Aechmea chantinii*), and the red-blue flowering Foster's favorite (*Aechmea fosteriana*). Leaves are thick, fleshy, and artistic, growing in a rosette, while the flowering bracts are stunning and long-lasting enough to be a main feature.

Planting | Grow in a small, well-draining pot in an equal mix of orchid and multipurpose compost. Repot young plants in a slightly bigger container in spring.

Position | Produces oxygen at night rather than during the day, so it is an ideal bedroom companion. Prefers indirect light or moderate shade. Avoid direct sunlight.

Watering | Water "tank" bromeliads (with leaves that form a reservoir to hold water at their bases) such as *Aechmea* by filling the leaf well with rainwater or distilled water every four to eight weeks in spring to fall. Reduce in winter. Mist often.

Feeding | Apply a half-strength balanced liquid fertilizer every two weeks between spring and late summer, by adding to the leaf well. Do not feed in winter.

Also try:
silver vase plant
(*Aechmea fasciata*);
Amazonian zebra plant
(*A. chantinii*)

Watch out for:
Beware of backward-curving spines on the leaves when handling, flagged up by the botanical name, which stems from the Greek word for "spear tip."

ANANAS - *Ananas* spp.

nontoxic

medium
care rating

Including: variegated pineapple
Family: Bromeliaceae
Grows up to: 24 x 36 inches (60 x 90cm)
Deliciously attractive conversation starter

This genus of terrestrial bromeliad includes the false pineapple (*Ananas sagenaria*) and the edible pineapple (*Ananas comosus*), also grown as a houseplant, displaying the same dense rosette of swordlike, spiny green leaves and—if given the right conditions—exquisite pink-purple inflorescences followed by fleshy fruits. The fruit is technically edible, although not sweet like cultivated varieties. A cream- and green-leaved variety brings extra appeal.

Planting | *Ananas* thrives well in an equal mix of orchid and multipurpose compost. Restricting pot size will help contain growth. Repot young plants in early spring.

Position | Needs bright light, moderate humidity, and no drafts. The spiny leaves spread outward, so provide enough room for wide growth.

Watering | Keep barely moist at all times, watering frequently in spring and summer. Set on a tray of damp pebbles and mist daily.

Feeding | Feed with a half-strength balanced liquid fertilizer every two weeks from spring to fall, especially when fruiting. Feed once a month in winter.

Also try:
ornamental pineapple
(*Ananas comosus*
'Corona')

Watch out for:
Pineapple plants flower once and produce a single fruit, after which they die back; they can produce suckers that are capable of fruiting again.

VRIESEA - *Vriesea* spp.

nontoxic

medium
care rating

Including: flaming sword
Family: Bromeliaceae
Grows up to: 24 x 18 inches (60 x 45cm)
Livens up a room with exotic splendor

The *Vriesea* genus includes some of the biggest bromeliads, with most growing as epiphytes on trees. The most well-known houseplant is the flaming sword (*Vriesea splendens*), available in numerous colorways. The green and reddish-brown striped leaves grow in a rosette, creating a central "vase" that needs to be kept moist, while the spiked flowerhead of bright red bracts and tubular green-yellow flowers rises up like a "flaming sword."

Planting | Plant in a small, well-draining pot in an equal mix of orchid and multipurpose compost. Repot young plants up a size in early spring.

Position | Can tolerate a range of light levels but needs bright, filtered light for blooming. Avoid direct sunlight, cold drafts, and drying heaters.

Watering | Mimic native conditions by topping up the central well of leaves with rainwater or distilled water. Water when the top layer of compost feels dry. Mist daily.

Feeding | Feed with a quarter-strength balanced liquid fertilizer or mist with a quarter-strength foliar fertilizer once every two months in spring and summer.

Also try:
flaming sword (*Vriesea splendens*)

Watch out for:
Can take 3–5 years to flower and slowly die back after blooming; however, offsets or pups are easy to propagate.

GUZMANIA - *Guzmania* spp.

nontoxic

medium
care rating

Including: scarlet star
Family: Bromeliaceae
Grows up to: 18 x 18 inches (45 x 45cm)
An uplifting office plant

Native to Ecuador and Colombia where they grow as epiphytes on trees, these striking, large-flowered plants come in numerous colors and shades. Scarlet star (*Guzmania lingulata*) is the most popular, with a star-shaped rosette of flat, shiny green leaves and an eye-catching red, pink, orange, or yellow fleshy flower bract (depending on the variety) with a cluster of true white flowers in its center.

Planting | Pot in a heavy-bottomed, well-draining container in an equal mix of orchid and multipurpose compost. Repot young plants in early spring.

Position | Prefers warm temperatures and bright, filtered sunlight. Avoid direct sun, drafts, and drying heaters. Arrange with other humidity-loving plants.

Watering | Allow compost to dry out between waterings. Refill central leaf cup with rainwater or distilled water every four to five days. Mist leaves, flowers, and roots daily.

Feeding | Feed once a month with a half-strength fertilizer applied to the central cup.

Also try:
scarlet star (*Guzmania lingulata*)

Watch out for: Can succumb to root rot if planted in a potting mix that becomes waterlogged.

BILLBERGIA - *Billbergia* spp.

nontoxic

medium
care rating

Also known as: friendship plant
Family: Bromeliaceae
Grows up to: 24 x 24 inches (60 x 60cm)
A lovely pedestal plant to pass on to friends

Commonly found wild in Brazil, the most popular form of this epiphytic bromeliad, the friendship plant (*Billbergia nutans*), has broad, strappy leaves and beautiful pink flower bracts with pink-blue blooms that flop downward. This growth habit makes it ideal for placing on a plant stand or in a hanging basket. It also produces numerous pups, which are traditionally gifted to loved ones, hence the common name.

Planting | Plant in an equal mix of orchid and multipurpose compost in a small pot. Pot up young plants in early spring.

Position | Thrives in bright, filtered light. Avoid direct sunlight and drying heat. Encourage blooming by placing in a slightly cooler position over fall and winter.

Watering | Keep compost moist and mist daily through spring to fall with rainwater or distilled water. Allow top layer of compost to dry out between waterings in winter.

Feeding | Apply a half-strength balanced liquid fertilizer directly to the leaf cup every month in spring and summer. Do not feed in winter.

Also try:
friendship plant
(*Billbergia nutans*)

Watch out for:
Overwatering causes yellowing leaves or collapsing flowers; underwatering promotes pale leaves or brown leaf patches.

NEOREGELIA - *Neoregelia* spp.

nontoxic

medium
care rating

Also known as: blushing bromeliad
Family: Bromeliaceae
Grows up to: 12 x 24 inches (30 x 60cm)
Fill the central well to water

These beautiful epiphytic plants provide an ideal breeding ground for frogs in the South American rainforest. The most common houseplant species is the blushing bromeliad (*Neoregelia carolinae*), which boasts a slightly flattened rosette of arching straplike leaves, which turn a deep pinkish-red in the central region before a small bloom of non-showy violet flowers appears. Variegated 'Tricolor' has striking yellow and dark green leaves.

Planting | Plant in a small pot in an equal mix of orchid and multipurpose compost. Repot every year in a fresh compost mix.

Position | Prefers bright, filtered light and a humid environment. Makes a good compact plant for the corner of a warm conservatory or bathroom.

Watering | Mimic nature by refilling the central well with rainwater or distilled water every four to six weeks so compost stays moist. Mist leaves every few days.

Feeding | Mist leaves with a half-strength liquid fertilizer monthly. Do not overfeed.

Also try:
blushing bromeliad
(*Neoregelia carolinae*)

Watch out for:
Once flowered it will die back and produce pups. Remove offsets to create new plants.

AIR PLANTS

*Air plants are epiphytic bromeliads of the genus **Tillandsia**, which can survive with the minimum of nutrients, mounted in a pot or on the wall. Choose from numerous species and cultivars, from spidery rosettes to some that only flower for the day.*

TILLANDSIA XEROGRAPHICA - *Tillandsia xerographica*

nontoxic

medium
care rating

Also known as: xerographica
Family: Bromeliaceae
Grows up to: 4 x 18 inches (10 x 45cm)
Ideal for small spaces but does best with
weekly watering

This xerophytic epiphyte is able to survive in the wild with little or zero available water, being native to the dry forests or scrublands of Mexico, Guatemala, and El Salvador. It has a rosette of silvery-gray tapering leaves turning bluish-pink in bright light, which curl downward to form a dense clump. Mature specimens can flower given the right conditions, producing rose-red leaf bracts, yellow-green floral bracts, and violet tubular true flowers.

Planting | Place in or on a suitable container such as a dish, jar, piece of wood, or specially made air plant stand. No need to add soil or compost, just observe watering needs.

Position | This pocket-sized plant is small enough for the leanest spaces. Use to decorate or brighten up walls or shelves. Prefers bright, filtered light. Avoid direct sun.

Watering | Water once a week by placing on a tray of tepid rainwater or distilled water for around 30 minutes. Leave to drain. Avoid wetting flowers. Mist regularly.

Feeding | Invest in a specialty *Tillandsia*, orchid, or *Bromeliad* fertilizer and spray leaves or add fertilizer to irrigation water. A feed once a month at most is fine.

Also try:
There are over 500 species of *Tillandsia* to choose from. Follow the same conditions for all.

Watch out for:
Like many bromeliads, tillandsias die back after flowering but produce offsets; cut back the mother plant to encourage growth, or detach when big enough.

TILLANDSIA IONANTHA - *Tillandsia ionantha*

Also known as: sky plant

A popular tillandsia thanks to its thin, tapering silver-green leaves, which turn shades of pink and red before the appearance of a beautiful violet bloom. There are dozens of available cultivars, all of which are extremely hardy and hard to kill, although regular soakings and mistings are required. Ionanthas love sunlight, so a bright spot is ideal. Common cultivars include 'Guatemala', 'Mexico', 'Rubra', 'Fuego', and 'Peanut'.

TILLANDSIA JUNCEA - *Tillandsia juncea*

Rushlike air plant

A tall, elegant, grassy-looking air plant with thin leaves growing from ovular sheaths, ideal for adding sculptural contrast in a collection of more sprawling tillandsias. It is prone to drying out and turning brown if not watered regularly, so keep an eye on the delicate foliage. Mature plants grow relatively large and can flower, displaying several small spears or a single spike of tiny pink and purple flowers. Looks great in a desktop planter.

TILLANDSIA STRICTA - *Tillandsia stricta*

Upright air plant

This versatile plant survives in the wild on sand dunes as well as trees and comes in a choice of varieties. Some have soft leaves, others are hard, while colors vary from different tones of green to foliage that's almost black. Although mature plants only display true flowers for a day, the beautiful bracts in shades of red, pink, blue, or purple can hold their color for several weeks. Varieties include 'Azure Flame', 'Stiff Purple', 'Black Tips', and 'Black Beauty'.

TILLANDSIA CYANEA - *Tillandsia cyanea*

Pink quill plant

The pink quill plant is so named for its featherlike pink bracts from which purple-blue true flowers emerge—the element that lends it its botanical name. The leaves are long, narrow, dark green, and strappy, holding their beauty after the three-month-long bloom has died down. Eventually the leaves also die back, during which time pups emerge. Leave several offsets in place on the mother plant to promote multiple flowerheads.

SUCCULENTS

These fleshy-leaved plants often hail from dry, desert areas where storing water in stems or foliage is vital to survival. As houseplants, they are a verdant, highly varied group of plants, including spiraling houseleeks, ropelike donkey's tails, and juicy aloe vera.

HOUSELEEK - *Sempervivum* spp.

nontoxic

easy
care rating

Also known as: hen and chicks; live forever
Family: Crassulaceae
Grows up to: 8 x 12 inches (20 x 30cm)
Ideal as a houseplant or for green rooftops

Among the most frost-resistant succulents, houseleeks are suitable for outdoor projects such as green roofs as well as growing as a houseplant. Similar in appearance to the closely related *Echeveria*, they have spiraling leaves and starry flowers that appear on stout stems in summer. Part of their appeal is that there are numerous varieties to collect in shades of green, red, burgundy, and gray, some with a fine covering of hairs.

Planting | Plant in two parts soil-based compost to one part sand in a small breathable terra-cotta or cement pot. Repot when root-bound.

Position | Can tolerate a range of conditions but prefers full sun. Can tolerate frost but not waterlogging. Ideal for green roofs and alpine rockeries.

Watering | Water moderately from spring to fall, allowing the top layer of compost to dry out in between. Water once a month in winter.

Feeding | Can benefit from feeding with a half-strength balanced liquid fertilizer once a month from spring to fall. Do not feed in winter.

Also try:
common houseleek (*Sempervivum tectorum*); cobweb houseleek (*Sempervivum arachnoideum*)

Watch out for:
Can be susceptible to root rot if the soil is soggy, which shows as blackened leaves on the bottom of the rosette.

AEONIUM - *Aeonium* spp.

nontoxic

easy
care rating

Including: tree houseleek
Family: Crassulaceae
Grows up to: 24 x 18 inches (60 x 45cm)
A taller specimen that thrives on neglect

These tall treelike succulents have branched stems topped with rosettes of fleshy leaves, perfect for adding height to a windowsill succulent collection. Most species are native to subtropical hillsides of Madeira, the Canary Islands, and North Africa, where mature plants typically produce long-stalked, small starry flowers in early spring. Perfect grown as a year-round houseplant, there are lots of species with which to form an aeonium collection.

Planting | Plant in a small container filled with cactus compost or establish outside in well-drained soil or a gravel garden. They match well with pelargoniums.

Position | Grow in a pot in a sunny spot outdoors or in bright, filtered light indoors. They can tolerate some direct sun and wind, so are ideal for coastal gardens.

Watering | Water moderately from spring to fall, allowing the top of the compost to dry in between. This mimics downpours in their natural environment.

Feeding | Apply a half-strength balanced liquid fertilizer once a month from winter to late spring. This is the main growing period.

Also try:
pinwheel aeonium
(*Aeonium haworthii*)

Watch out for:
Often go dormant in hot weather, resulting in a tighter inner rosette and outer leaf drop; should recover in cooler weather.

ECHEVERIA - *Echeveria* spp.

nontoxic

easy
care rating

Including: hen and chicks
Family: Crassulaceae
Grows up to: 4 x 12 inches (10 x 30cm)
Tiny but compactly beautiful

With a native range of southern Texas to northwest Argentina, these rosette-forming, tender but tough succulents love a hot, sunny spot, thrive on neglect, and cope well in a drought. Grown primarily for their fleshy, spoon-shaped leaves, mature plants can produce lantern-shaped flowers on tall yellow or red stems if given enough light. Line up a selection of varieties in contrasting shades of blue-green, red, purple, and variegated.

Planting | Grow in a small pot in a mix of three parts soil-based compost to one part sharp sand. Repot every two to three years in spring or when root-bound.

Position | Best grown in bright, filtered light. Avoid direct sun in summer and keep in a cooler but sunny spot in winter. Ideal for a sunny windowsill.

Watering | Allow the top layer of soil to dry out between waterings from spring to fall. Do not water in winter when the plant is dormant.

Feeding | Feed with a half-strength fertilizer two to three times during the growing period.

Also try:
Mexican snowball
(*Echeveria elegans*)

Watch out for:
Mealybugs can be a problem on indoor plants; these pests need to be wiped off immediately.

HAWORTHIA - *Haworthia* spp.

nontoxic

easy
care rating

Including: pearl plant; polka-dotted succulent
Family: Asphodelaceae
Grows up to: 8 x 6 inches (20 x 15cm)
Spiky contrast to rounded specimens

Mostly native to South Africa, haworthias are much spikier than their succulent relatives, the sempervivums and echeverias. The fleshy aloe vera–like green leaves grow in a similar rosette form and, depending on the variety, can sport contrasting white raised stripes or reddish bumps that add textural appeal. Smaller species can be grown in fun containers such as tiny terra-cotta pots or teacups. They can also go outdoors in warmer weather.

Planting | Grow in cactus compost or use one part horticultural grit to two parts soil-based potting compost. Repot every two to three years when root-bound.

Position | Prefers full sun or bright, filtered light but generally does best in sheltered locations outdoors. Group with other succulents on a windowsill or balcony.

Watering | Allow the compost to dry out between waterings in summer, and water sparingly in winter. Never allow water to collect in the rosette.

Feeding | Apply a half-strength balanced liquid fertilizer or a cactus fertilizer once a month from spring to fall. Do not feed in winter.

Also try:
zebra haworthia
(*Haworthia attentuata*)

Watch out for: White or yellow leaves usually point to too much sun; avoid direct sunlight when moving outdoors.

ALOE VERA - *Aloe vera*

toxic

medium
care rating

Also known as: true aloe
Family: Asparagales
Grows up to: 24 x 24 inches (60 x 60cm)
An ornamental and soothing medicinal plant

Originating from the Arabian Peninsula, aloe vera now grows wild in tropical, semi-tropical, and arid climates around the world in gardens. It is also grown as a garden and houseplant both as an ornamental and for the soothing properties of its leaves, the sap of which can cool burns and sunburn (but is toxic to pets). Not to be mistaken for its larger, spikier relative, the American aloe (*Agave americana*), the sap of which is toxic.

Planting | Plant in cactus compost in a pot that just fits the root ball. Repot every two to three years in spring, transferring offsets to new pots to create new plants.

Position | Prefers bright, filtered light. Avoid direct sunlight, shade, and cold drafts. Can be grown outside in subtropical climes or brought outdoors in summer.

Watering | Irrigate this natural water storer between spring and fall when top of compost is dry. Reduce in winter, watering just enough so the leaves stay plump.

Feeding | Feed with a cactus fertilizer two or three times during the growing period.

Also try:
many-leaved aloe (*Aloe polyphylla*)

Watch out for: A leggy growth habit could mean insufficient light; leaves turn brown and soft if overwatered.

AMERICAN ALOE - *Agave americana*

toxic

medium
care rating

Also known as: century plant; blue steel agave
Family: Asparagaceae
Grows up to: 36 x 36 inches (90 x 90cm)
Sculptural; can get large outdoors

Similar in appearance to aloe vera, the fleshy, strappy leaves of this desert plant are typically gray-green in color. However, this plant is often sold in its variegated format (*Agave americana* 'Marginata'), the foliage of which boasts a yellow stripe around its sharp, spiky borders (use caution around children and pets). For those with the ideal climate—hot and arid—it can be grown outdoors, providing outsized sculptural interest.

Planting | To grow indoors, plant in cactus compost in a well-draining pot that will fit the root ball. Planted outdoors in arid, tropical climes, it can grow very large.

Position | Let it bask in full sun or bright, filtered light, whether grown indoors or out. Indoor plants appreciate being placed outdoors during the summer months.

Watering | Water sparingly, letting the compost dry out between waterings. New plants may need more water as they establish. Warm, dry, arid conditions are ideal.

Feeding | Feed with a half-strength balanced liquid fertilizer a few times a year. Overfeeding can cause a salt buildup in the soil.

Also try:
royal agave (*Agave victoriae-reginae*)

Watch out for:
Overwatered or poorly drained plants can suffer root rot; hard, dry brown spots could indicate lack of watering.

SNAKE PLANT - *Sansevieria trifasciata*

toxic

easy
care rating

Also known as: Saint George's sword; viper's bowstring hemp
Family: Asparagaceae
Grows up to: 30 x 12 inches (75 x 30cm)
A robust air purifier ideal for semi-shady spaces

Although now used as an ornamental houseplant, the long, thick fibers of the snake plant were once used to make bowstrings in its native habitat of tropical West Africa. The mottled green and silver, yellow-edged, long, strappy foliage resembles a snake, hence its most well-known common name. While usually chosen as a houseplant for its foliage, the snake plant is also resilient, easy to care for, and good for purifying the air.

Planting | Plant in a pot that will just accommodate the roots in cactus compost. Repot only when tightly root-bound.

Position | Prefers light shade or filtered light. Tolerant of low light levels where they can thrive but will grow more slowly. Avoid direct sun.

Watering | Allow the top of the compost to dry out between waterings from spring to fall. Water once a month in winter. Can withstand irregular waterings.

Feeding | Feed a half-strength fertilizer monthly between spring and fall.

Also try:
twisted snake plant (*Sansevieria trifasciata* 'Twisted Sister')

Watch out for: Root rot can mean overwatering; results in mushy leaves.

AFRICAN MILK TREE - *Euphorbia trigona*

toxic

easy
care rating

Also known as: tender euphorbia; cathedral cactus
Family: Euphorbiaceae
Grows up to: 36 x 24 inches (90 x 60cm)
Attractive cactuslike leaves

A member of the large and diverse *Euphorbia* genus, which is well known for its collection of outdoor border plants, this striking houseplant has statuesque dark green stems and fingerlike leaves. Often mistaken for a cactus, along with its relatives the pencil cactus (*Euphorbia tirucalli*) and pincushion euphorbia (*Euphorbia enopla*), it looks fantastic as a focal point in minimalist rooms and is a great slow-growing, low-maintenance option.

Planting | Plant in a pot that fits the root ball in either cactus compost or two parts soil-based compost and one part horticultural grit. Repot every two to three years.

Position | Loves to sit in bright, direct light, ideally in full sun. Prefers warm environments away from drafts. A great way to add architectural interest to rooms.

Watering | Relatively drought-tolerant, allow the compost to dry out between waterings from spring to fall. Hold back from watering in winter.

Feeding | Feed with a half-strength balanced liquid fertilizer from spring to fall. No need to feed in winter.

Also try:
pincushion euphorbia (*Euphorbia enopla*)

Watch out for:
Gets its name from the milky sap within its stems, which can be toxic to small children and pets, so keep out of reach.

BURRO'S TAIL - *Sedum morganianum*

nontoxic

medium
care rating

Also known as: donkey's tail
Family: Crassulaceae
Grows up to: 4 x 12 inches (10 x 30cm)
Unique ropelike stems

A truly unique specimen, great as a focal point, the donkey's tail gets its name from its long, hanging, ropelike extensions made up of tiny, teardrop-shaped blue-green fleshy leaves. These leaf lengths grow slowly but can trail up to 48 inches (120cm) long over several years if given the right conditions and handled with care. In the wild or in tropical gardens, plants can bloom with red, yellow, or white flowers, but this is rare in houseplants.

Planting | Plant in a small breathable container in cactus compost or a mix of two parts soil-based compost and one part horticultural grit. Repot only when root-bound.

Position | Thrives best in warm, bright, filtered light. A sunny windowsill that boasts several hours of sunlight a day is ideal. Outdoors, opt for morning sun.

Watering | Donkey's tail is relatively drought-resistant, so less is more. Let the soil dry out completely between waterings in spring and summer. Reduce watering in winter.

Feeding | Feed a half-strength fertilizer once a month from spring to fall.

Also try:
moonstones (*Pachyphytum oviferum*)

Watch out for:
Can be delicate when handled; if leaves fall off, let them scale over, then use to grow new plants.

JADE PLANT - *Crassula ovata*

toxic

easy
care rating

Also known as: money tree; lucky plant
Family: Crassulaceae
Grows up to: 36 x 36 inches (90 x 90cm)
Considered lucky in many Asian cultures

Native to South Africa and Mozambique, the jade plant is one of the most well known and popular houseplants, thanks to its thick, shiny, jade-colored leaves, bonsai-like silhouette, and easy-care habit—it really is hard to kill this one! As it can handle a range of light levels and some neglect, it is ideal for shadier spots. Considered lucky in many Asian cultures, it will bring a feel-good factor into your home. It can also be grown as a bonsai.

Planting | Plant in a small pot in a mix of three parts sand and one part sharp sand. Wear gloves while handling, as the sap is toxic.

Position | Jade plants can tolerate shadier spots but thrive best if given four to six hours of bright sunlight a day with some shade in the afternoon.

Watering | Allow the top layer of compost to dry out between waterings from spring to fall. Water just enough to keep leaves fleshy in winter.

Feeding | Apply a half-strength balanced liquid fertilizer several times during the growing season from spring to fall. Do not feed in winter.

Also try:
red dwarf jade plant
(*Crassula ovata*
'Crosby's Compact')

Watch out for:
Overwatering can
cause root rot and leaf
fall; leaves can also
turn slightly red or
yellow if exposed to too
much direct sunlight.

CACTI

These spiky succulents store water mainly in their thickened or bulbous stems, while the spines are actually modified leaves that help deter herbivores and prevent water loss. Available in a diverse array of shapes and sizes, some with flowers, they make highly collectible houseplants.

BUNNY EAR CACTUS - *Opuntia microdasys*

nontoxic

easy
care rating

Also known as: prickly pear; polka-dot cactus; angel's wings
Family: Cactaceae
Grows up to: 12 x 18 inches (30 x 45cm)
An elegant, fun, and sculptural form

The bunny ear cactus looks like it is comprised of a stack of broad, spiky leaves (use caution around children and pets), but each pair of these oval pads are actually flattened stems dotted with bristlelike glochids. Despite the furry bunny-ear appearance, do not be tempted to touch, as these barbed spines can really get stuck in. This cactus flowers in summer with attractive yellow blooms, but this is rare in houseplants. Grow it for the architectural form and the cute name.

Planting | Plant in cactus compost or an equal mix of soil-based compost, sand, and perlite in a well-draining, breathable pot that will accommodate the roots.

Position | Mimic its native habitat in arid regions of Mexico by placing in a warm, sunny spot in summer and a cooler position in winter. Avoid too much direct sun.

Watering | Water weekly from spring to early fall, letting the compost go dry in between waterings. Water once or twice in winter.

Feeding | Feed with a cactus fertilizer every two months between spring and fall. Do not feed in winter. Moving plants outdoors in summer can accelerate growth.

Also try:
eastern prickly pear (*Opuntia humifusa*); old man's whiskers (*O. aciculata*)

Watch out for:
If one of the bunny ears is knocked off, use it to propagate a new plant. Simply tuck it into cactus compost and it should form roots.

OLD LADY CACTUS - *Mammillaria hahniana*

nontoxic

easy
care rating

Also known as: powder puff cactus
Family: Cactaceae
Grows up to: 10 x 20 inches (25 x 50cm)
Short and squat with a crowning glory

Although not from the same genus as the old man cactus (*Cephalocereus senilis*), this cactus does have some features in common, notably a columnar growth habit and dense, bristly white hairs and fine spines (use caution around children and pets). The old man cactus grows tall with red, yellow, or white flowers that rarely appear; the old lady is squat and often bought for its crown of bright pink-purple funnel-shaped flowers followed by small red fruits.

Planting | Wear protective gloves. Plant in a small, well-drained, breathable pot filled with cactus compost or an equal mix of soil-based compost, sand, and perlite.

Position | Loves warm, bright light. A windowsill that gets morning sun is ideal. Avoid direct sun. Move to a cooler position in winter. Fares well outdoors in tropical climes.

Watering | Water once a week from spring to early fall; let the compost go dry in between. Reduce to watering once a month in winter to encourage dormancy and flowering.

Feeding | Feed with a cactus fertilizer every month in spring and summer. Do not feed in winter. Moving plants outdoors in summer can accelerate growth.

Also try:
old man cactus
(*Cephalocereus senilis*)

Watch out for:
Prolonged dampness can cause root rot; if moving outdoors, choose a dry, sheltered spot.

PERUVIAN APPLE CACTUS - *Cereus repandus*

nontoxic

medium
care rating

Also known as: hedge cactus; columnar cactus; column cactus
Family: Cactaceae
Grows up to: 36 x 6 inches (90 x 15cm)
Tall and stately

Cereus cacti derive their name from the Greek and Latin for "candle," and generally have a treelike columnar growth with four to ten well-defined ribs lined with stout spines (use caution around children and pets). Most commonly found is the Peruvian apple cactus, which has cylindrical blue-green stems and gray thorns. It can grow to heights of over 100 feet (30m) in the wild, so stick with young, suppressed specimens as houseplants.

Planting | Wear gloves. Plant in a medium, heavy, well-draining and breathable pot filled with cactus compost or an equal mix of soil-based compost, sand, and perlite.

Position | Needs at least four to six hours of bright sun per day; by a window or in a conservatory that gets morning sun is ideal. Move to a cooler spot in winter.

Watering | Water in the spring/summer growth period when the very top layer of compost is dry. Water once or twice in winter when dormant.

Feeding | Use a cactus fertilizer monthly in summer. Place outdoors in a sheltered spot.

Also try:
spiraled column cactus (*Cereus forbesii* 'Spiralis')

Watch out for:
Rotate the pot a quarter turn every week or two; do not allow to stand in water.

MOON CACTUS - *Gymnocalycium mihanovichii*

nontoxic

easy
care rating

Also known as: ruby ball; red cap; hibotan cactus
Family: Cactaceae
Grows up to: 4 x 2 inches (10 x 5cm)
Add a pop of color to your cacti

This curious cactus is not one but two cacti grafted together, where the green stem of a *Hylocereus* cactus (usually a dragon fruit cactus) provides a pedestal for a moon cactus (*Gymnocalycium mihanovichii*). The most popular mounted stems are mutated moon cacti that are tipped with small spines (use caution around children and pets) and completely lack the green pigment chlorophyll, exposing their bright red, yellow, or orange color.

Planting | Plant in a small, breathable, well-drained pot, or in a dish garden using cactus compost or an equal mix of soil-based compost, sand, and perlite.

Position | Set in full sunlight in a warm, dry spot with low humidity—a sunny windowsill is ideal. Group together with other cacti and succulents with the same needs.

Watering | Let the compost dry out between waterings in spring and summer. Water deeply each time and watch the plant plump up. Reduce watering in winter.

Feeding | Feed with cactus fertilizer once a week during spring and summer and once a month in winter. Feeding provides both cacti with nutrients and can boost color.

Also try:
pincushion cactus (*Mammillaria polythele*)

Watch out for:
Do not overwater as this can cause root rot; if the host cactus dies, so will the grafted moon cactus.

CHRISTMAS CACTUS - *Schlumbergera* x *bridgesii*

nontoxic

easy
care rating

Also known as: holiday cactus
Family: Cactaceae
Grows up to: 18 x 18 inches (45 x 45cm)
A lovely winter-flowering pedestal plant

With its flat, segmented stems, with sharp spines (use caution around children and pets) and bright pink flowers that open up around Christmastime—or midwinter depending on where you are in the world—this attractive plant could be mistaken for a flowering succulent. It has a trailing habit, making it ideal for hanging baskets or plant pedestals, and it makes a fun plant, bestowing uplifting blooms well into the new year.

Planting | Plant in a well-draining pot in cactus compost or three parts soil-based compost to one part leaf mold and one part horticultural grit. Try in a hanging basket.

Position | This epiphyte cactus grows wild on trees in jungle-type woodlands and prefers partial shade or filtered sun and a humid environment. A bright bathroom is ideal.

Watering | Keep compost moist but not wet in spring and summer. Reduce watering after flowering. Stand on a tray of damp pebbles and mist daily with distilled water.

Feeding | Benefits from using a fertilizer during the growing season.

Also try:
Christmas cactus (*Schlumbergera* × *buckleyi*)

Watch out for:
After flowering, a rest is needed; reduce watering and move to a cooler place.

FOREST CACTUS - *Rhipsalis boliviana*

toxic

easy
care rating

Also known as: Bolivian forest cactus
Family: Cactaceae
Grows up to: 40 x 12 inches (100 x 30cm)
The perfect trailer for a jungly rainforest vibe

Native to the Bolivian jungle, this epiphytic spine-free trailing cactus, made up of a mass of flattened, succulent-like stems with spines (use caution around children and pets), makes a great style statement cascading from a shelf, pedestal, or hanging basket. It's a fast grower, so make sure you have enough space below for it to trail down. Given the right conditions, including enough indirect bright light, it can produce pink or white flowers.

Planting | Plant in a well-draining, medium-sized pot or hanging basket in cactus compost or an equal mix of soil-based compost, sand, and perlite. Repot every one to two years.

Position | Prefers a warm, bright, or partially shaded spot with indirect sunlight. In the warmer months, expose it to some fresh air by opening a window or door.

Watering | Let the soil dry out between waterings from spring to fall. When watering, soak completely, mimicking rainfall. Do not water in winter.

Feeding | This fast-growing plant does well on its own but can benefit from a boosting feed with cactus fertilizer once a month in summer.

Also try:
chain cactus (*Rhipsalis paradoxa*); mistletoe cactus (*Rapsalis baccifera*)

Watch out for: Avoid humid rooms such as bathrooms or steamy kitchens and never let it sit in a tray of water.

FISHBONE CACTUS - *Epiphyllum anguliger* syn. *Disocactus anguliger*

nontoxic

easy
care rating

Also known as: zig zag cactus; rick rack cactus
Family: Cactaceae
Grows up to: 24 x 24 inches (60 x 60cm)
Highly scented flowers bloom for just one night

What drove this pretty forest cactus to create its leaves in the style of large, flat, zigzagging fishbones, we may never know. Found dangling from the branches of large trees in Mexican rainforests, the trailing tendrils tend to grow as long as allowed and have small but sharp spines (use caution around children and pets). For added drama, it also blooms in fall, producing scented white-yellow blooms, which mature into edible kiwilike fruits in the wild.

Planting | Plant in a well-draining pot in cactus compost or an equal mix of soil-based compost, sand, and perlite. Choose a heavy pot to stop it from toppling over.

Position | Thrives best in bright, filtered light away from direct sun. A sunny room, away from a window, is ideal. A stylish choice for a focal point on a table or sideboard.

Watering | Allow the soil to dry out between waterings in spring and summer. Water lightly in fall and winter. Do not allow to stand in water.

Feeding | Encourage optimum health and growth by feeding with cactus fertilizer monthly.

Also try:
rick rack cactus (*Selenicereus anthonyanus*)

Watch out for: The flowers only bloom after dark and for one night only; if you see a bud appearing, launch a vigil.

ORCHIDS

The ancient and diverse orchid family includes a wide range of alluringly lipped flowering plants, bringing exotic beauty to your home. From moth orchids to dancing ladies to the sublime slipper orchid, it's hard not to get addicted.

MOTH ORCHID - *Phalaenopsis* spp.

nontoxic

easy
care rating

Also known as: phalaenopsis orchid; miniature moth orchid
Family: Orchidaceae
Grows up to: 36 x 24 inches (90 x 60cm)
Long-lasting, year-round blooms

Native to parts of Asia and Australia and numbering sixty true *Phalaenopsis* species, moth orchids have wide base leaves and long-lasting flowers on arching single stems that bloom year-round. Showy but undemanding, there are numerous hybrids of at least one *Phalaenopsis* ancestor that boast a range of colored and patterned flower forms, including miniature versions. Most are sold unnamed unless bought from a specialty orchid supplier.

Planting | Moth orchids are epiphytic and thrive best in a small amount of orchid compost in a transparent pot to help keep aerial roots exposed to light. A slip pot can be added.

Position | Prefers warmth all year round with light shade in summer, moving to a brighter spot in winter. Avoid direct sun, drafts, and temperature fluctuations.

Watering | Water with distilled water every five to seven days in spring and summer. Reduce in winter. Do not let roots dry out, but avoid splashing leaves. Mist occasionally.

Feeding | Feed with orchid fertilizer when watering. Avoid salt buildup by eliminating feed every fourth watering. Reduce feeding to once a month in winter.

Also try:
moth orchid hybrids (*Phalaenopsis* hybrids including miniatures)

Watch out for:
Moth orchid flowers last for around three months. When blooms fade, cut the flower stalk back to just above the second node; a new side shoot may grow.

SLIPPER ORCHID - *Paphiopedilum* spp.

nontoxic

easy
care rating

Also known as: lady slipper orchid
Family: Orchidaceae
Grows up to: 12 x 8 inches (30 x 20cm)
Elegant, slipperlike flowers

Slipper orchids are mainly terrestrial plants with alluring flowers that have a slipperlike lip or pouch at the base. The broad green or mottled leaves fan out at the base, while the long-lasting flowers—mainly blooming from winter to early summer—come in various colors and markings depending on the species or named hybrid. One of the most elegant is *Paphiopedilum* 'Maudiae', with a large green-striped white flower and variegated leaves.

Planting | This ground-dwelling orchid can be planted in an opaque pot in orchid compost or a mix of four parts finely composted bark and one part perlite.

Position | Prefers a shady or low-filtered light position in summer and a brighter position in winter. Avoid direct sunlight. Mottled-leaf varieties need more warmth.

Watering | Keep compost moist between spring and fall with rain or distilled water. Reduce watering in winter but avoid dry soil. Set on a tray of damp pebbles. Do not mist.

Feeding | Feed with an orchid fertilizer every two weeks from spring to fall, reducing the amount in winter by diluting the strength to half.

Also try:
Paphiopedilum 'Maudiae'

Watch out for:
Repot annually after flowering but do not bury new growth.

BOAT ORCHID - *Cymbidium* spp. and hybrids

toxic

easy
care rating

Also known as: cymbidium orchid
Family: Orchidaceae
Grows up to: 48 x 30 inches (120 x 75cm)
Showy blooms in winter

Boat orchids are semi-terrestrial by habit, sending thin roots into the soil and flowering in late fall through to spring, making them an ideal plant to help brighten up a room through winter. The apple-green leaves are long and strappy, while sprays of large blooms rise up on flower spikes that can last from one to three months. Choose from numerous hybrids, including tall-growing "standards" and smaller miniatures.

Planting | *Cymbidium* orchids do not have aerial roots and thus can be planted in an opaque pot. Use orchid compost or a mix of composted bark, perlite, and charcoal.

Position | Works well in cooler climates. Prefers filtered sunlight all year round with morning sun and afternoon shade. Avoid direct sunlight as this can burn the plant.

Watering | Water every week during spring and fall. Reduce to every two weeks in winter but don't let the soil dry out. Use rainwater or distilled water. Mist every few days.

Feeding | Feed with a weak orchid fertilizer every two weeks in summer.

Also try:
red column cymbidium (*Cymbidium erythrostylum*)

Watch out for:
Place in a sheltered spot for a drop in temperature at night, needed for flower buds to form.

NOBLE DENDROBIUM - *Dendrobium nobile* hybrids

nontoxic

easy
care rating

Also known as: nobile rock orchid
Family: Orchidaceae
Grows up to: 24 x 18 inches (60 x 45cm)
Multistemmed with showy blooms

This stunning, multistemmed bloomer is a popular, relatively easy-care houseplant and is also grown as a cut flower. Although branching in nature and sporting pseudobulbs like its relative the *Oncidium*, the flower spikes grow upward, displaying multiple showy blooms and short, strappy, semi-deciduous fleshy leaves. Flowers are variegated, usually in shades of white, pink, or purple, and typically bloom through winter for many weeks.

Planting | Constrict the roots in a snug, opaque pot of orchid compost or a similar mix of six parts composted bark to one part each of perlite and charcoal.

Position | Prefers a warm, bright position. Avoid direct summer sun and cold drafts. A change of temperature at night helps blooming, so place outside in summer.

Watering | Water one to two times a week with tepid rainwater or distilled water in spring and summer, when soil feels dry. Mist roots in winter to keep pseudobulbs wet.

Feeding | Feed with an orchid fertilizer or half-strength balanced liquid fertilizer through spring and summer. Reduce by half at the end of summer. Do not feed in winter.

Also try:
white noble
dendrobium
(*Dendrobium nobile*
'Star Class Apollon')

Watch out for:
Overwatering can lead
to rot and cause plants
to wilt or yellow. Repot
every year.

DANCING LADY ORCHID - *Oncidium* spp. and hybrids

nontoxic

easy
care rating

Also known as: spray orchid; butterfly orchid;
dancing doll
Family: Orchidaceae
Grows up to: 24 x 24 inches (60 x 60cm)
A dainty creeping orchid, also ideal for floristry

A popular floristry orchid and houseplant for its dainty spray of multiple winged blooms, appearing like dancing ladies or butterflies; most flower in fall to winter, often with yellow or golden tones. These mainly epiphytic orchids are also sympodial in nature—with a creeping, branching habit as opposed to upward-growing, single-stemmed monopodial orchids—with visible pseudobulbs that help them store water.

Planting | Plant in a snug-fitting, well-draining opaque pot in orchid compost. Oncidiums can also be mounted using sphagnum moss and fishing wire to secure.

Position | The most popular oncidiums are warm orchids from the subtropics, which do not like the cold. Grow in bright light away from drafts.

Watering | Water weekly from spring to fall with rainwater or distilled water when top of compost is dry. Mist regularly, avoiding wetting leaves. Mounts need more water.

Feeding | Feed with a quarter-strength orchid fertilizer every few waterings.

Also try:
white-lipped oncidium
(*Oncidium leucochilum*)

Watch out for:
Can withstand drought,
although wrinkled
pseudobulbs indicate a
need for water.

VANDA ORCHID - *Vanda* spp. and hybrids

nontoxic

medium
care rating

Also known as: V. orchid
Family: Orchidaceae
Grows up to: 48 x 24 inches (120 x 60cm)
Bold colorful blooms with large roots

Vanda orchids are monopodial, which means that they grow from a single stem with roots emerging from the bottom. The flowers are imposing, colorful, and often patterned, stemming from a distinctive ladder of alternate green leaves. The roots are something of a feature, often becoming too large and curtainlike for their pots. For this reason, they are commonly grown in clear vases or slatted baskets and require precise conditions.

Planting | Accommodate roots in a large clear vase or slatted basket. These epiphytic plants naturally grow on rock with little soil. No potting compost is required.

Position | Prefers bright light but not direct sunlight, high humidy but not stuffy air, and regular drenching. A well-ventilated conservatory or bathroom is ideal.

Watering | Water once or even twice a day by plunging roots into rainwater or distilled water for 15 minutes. Water weekly in winter. Mist a few times a day.

Feeding | These thirsty plants are also heavy feeders. For ease, mist with a ready-mixed orchid fertilizer once a week. Feed every two months in cool weather or winter.

Also try:
Sander's vanda
(*Vanda sanderiana*)

Watch out for:
Too little light causes deep green leaves, spindly growth, and weak flowers. Mealybugs and aphids can also be a problem.

PANSY ORCHID - *Miltoniopsis* spp. and hybrids

nontoxic

easy
care rating

Also known as: Colombian orchid
Family: Orchidaceae
Grows up to: 24 x 24 inches (60 x 60cm)
Compact with fragrant, pansylike flowers

Pansy orchids are the common name for *Miltoniopsis* orchids (cool-growing, hailing mainly from the highlands of Colombia) and *Miltonia* orchids (native to warmer regions of central and southern Brazil). Both have masklike flowers that resemble pansies, but *Miltoniopsis* orchids have clusters of flat pseudobulbs and are more usually found as houseplants. A popular type is 'Herr Alexandre', with fragrant white blooms and a purple and yellow eye.

Planting | Plant in a clear pot in specialty orchid compost, or in six parts composted bark and one part each of perlite and charcoal. Repot if growth starts to suffer.

Position | Prefers bright, filtered light away from direct sunshine and drafts. A shady spot in summer moving to a bright windowsill in winter is ideal.

Watering | Soak soil every one to two days with rainwater or distilled water. Allow to drain. Reduce to every two to three weeks in winter. Set on a tray of damp pebbles and mist daily.

Feeding | Feed with orchid fertilizer every two weeks. Flush to remove buildup of harmful salts.

Also try:
pansy orchid
(*Miltoniopsis* 'Herr Alexandre')

Watch out for: A sign of underwatering is wrinkled leaves. Check for root rot, which can also cause this symptom.

TRAILERS AND CLIMBERS

Introducing plants that grow by climbing or rambling up walls, winding around supports, or cascading over the edges of pots, hanging baskets, shelves, or plant pedestals is a great way to green up or add blooms to your home, balcony, or outside space.

SWISS CHEESE PLANT - *Monstera deliciosa*

toxic

easy
care rating

Also known as: fruit salad plant; Mexican breadfruit
Family: Araceae
Grows up to: 26 x 8 feet (8 x 2.5m)
Loved for its large holey leaves

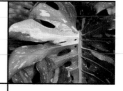

Often sold with its stems tied to a mossy pole, this hugely popular climbing plant has large, glossy, heart-shaped leaves that are fully or partly split like holey cheese, hence its common name. Native to the south of Mexico and Panama but naturalized elsewhere, in the wild it grows by attaching itself to a host tree, producing a delicious cornlike fruit that tastes of pineapple.

Planting | Grow in a large pot in three parts soil-based compost to one part sand. Replace top layer of compost annually in spring or repot every two to three years.

Position | Prefers bright, filtered light. Can thrive in light shade but needs some sun to produce the fenestrate (holey) leaves. Can be trained up a wall with some support.

Watering | Water between spring and fall when the top layer of compost feels dry. Reduce watering slightly in winter. Set on a tray of damp pebbles and mist every other day.

Feeding | Help it grow big, strong, and holey by feeding with a half-strength balanced liquid fertilizer once a month from spring to fall. Do not feed in winter.

Also try:
variegated Swiss cheese plant (*Monstera deliciosa* 'Variegata')

Watch out for:
Smaller plants can be sold without leaf holes. This is because the windows develop as the plant matures. Keep it happy and healthy by dusting leaves.

HEART LEAF - *Philodendron scandens* syn. *Philodendron hederaceum*

toxic

easy
care rating

Also known as: sweetheart plant
Family: Araceae
Grows up to: 60 x 60 inches (150 x 150cm)
Create a wall of lush heart-shaped leaves

Native to Central America and the Caribbean, this evergreen climber is so named for its heart-shaped leaves. Although commonly sold entwined around a mossy pole where it keeps a compact shape, it is often trained up wires to create a jungly green wall, or grown in a hanging basket with the stems trailing down. Lush and easy to care for, this is a must-have houseplant.

Planting | Grow in a large pot of two parts soil-based compost to one part perlite. Repot when specimens become root-bound to encourage growth.

Position | Thrives best in filtered sun or light shade. Can tolerate shadier spots, but this can inhibit growth or produce faded leaves. Trail up furniture or a wall.

Watering | Water from spring to fall so that the compost stays moist. Water in winter when the top of the compost feels dry. Mist every few days.

Feeding | Feed with a balanced liquid fertilizer once a month between spring and fall. Do not feed in winter. Benefits from flushing with distilled water every so often to remove salts.

Also try:
variegated heart leaf (*Philodendron scandens* syn. *Philodendron hederaceum* 'Brasil')

Watch out for:
Attach another mossy pole to the top and let it keep climbing if it is getting big.

ARROWHEAD VINE - *Syngonium podophyllum*

toxic

easy
care rating

Also known as: goosefoot plant; nephthytis; five-fingers
Family: Araceae
Grows up to: 36 x 24 inches (90 x 60cm)
Comes in variations of green, white, and pink

Usually sold as a compact houseplant in its infant form, its naturally vining habit needs to be trimmed to keep it in shape. It can also be grown as a climber or used to trail along a countertop. Commonly named for the arrowhead silhouette of the young leaves, the foliage morphs into a five-pronged goosefoot shape as it matures. Choose from numerous variegated cultivars.

Planting | Plant in a medium, well-draining pot in soil-based compost. A breathable terracotta pot that wicks away moisture is ideal.

Position | Prefers bright, filtered light. Avoid direct sun. Greener varieties need more shade, while variegated cultivars need a brighter spot to promote good color.

Watering | Allow the top layer of compost to dry out between waterings from spring to fall. Reduce watering in winter. Set on a tray of damp pebbles and mist leaves regularly.

Feeding | Feed with a half-strength balanced liquid fertilizer every two weeks from spring to fall. Do not feed in winter.

Also try:
variegated arrowhead vine (*Syngonium podophyllum* 'White Butterfly')

Watch out for:
Repot yearly for vigorous growth. Pinch leaves for bushier growth.

DEVIL'S IVY - *Epipremnum aureum*

 toxic

 easy
care rating

Also known as: golden pothos; ivy arum;
money plant
Family: Araceae
Grows up to: 72 x 72 inches (180 x 180cm)
Trail from shelves or hanging baskets

So named because it can grow even when kept in the dark and seems to be impossible to kill, devil's ivy is thus a fantastic plant for beginners or those looking for a low-maintenance specimen. Native to French Polynesia but naturalized in many tropical countries, it clings onto trees using small roots. Left to its own devices in such climates it can be invasive, but as a houseplant it is a lush, green, or variegated trailing addition to a shelf or mantelpiece.

Planting | Plant in a medium, well-draining pot that just fits the root ball in soil-based compost. To grow as a climber, tie stems to a moss pole or grow along wires.

Position | Thrives in a range of light levels from bright light to low shade. For most vigorous growth choose a brighter spot, avoiding direct sun.

Watering | Water so that the compost stays moist between spring and fall. In winter, water when the top of the compost is dry. Mist occasionally.

Feeding | Feed with a balanced liquid fertilizer monthly from spring to fall to encourage growth. Do not feed in winter.

Also try:
variegated devil's ivy
(*Epipremnum aureum*
'N' Joy')

Watch out for:
Trailing stems can
sometimes be a bit
leafless, so snip off to
encourage new growth.

HOYA - *Hoya* spp.

 nontoxic

 easy
care rating

Also known as: wax flower; wax vine
Family: Apocynaceae
Grows up to: 13 x 13 feet (4 x 4m)
Lush leaves and clusters of fragrant waxy flowers

This shrubby evergreen climber boasts typically succulent leaves and sweetly fragrant, waxy clusters of white or pink star-shaped flowers with a dark pink or maroon center. Popular species include *Hoya carnosa*, from which numerous cultivars have been developed over 200 years, and the more compact *Hoya lanceolata* subsp. *bella*. In the wild they can grow to great lengths, so try training up a wall, but can also be kept shrublike.

Planting | Find a pot that accommodates the root ball and plant in an equal mix of orchid compost, multipurpose compost, and perlite. Repot when root-bound.

Position | Prefers a warm, bright room in the house or a heated conservatory. Shade from direct sun to avoid leaf burn. Can be trained along wires or a hoop.

Watering | Keep the compost moist between spring and fall. Water when the top of the compost is dry in winter. Set on a tray of damp pebbles and mist when not in bloom.

Feeding | Feed a half-strength, high-potash fertilizer every two weeks in spring and summer.

Also try:
variegated hoya (*Hoya
carnosa* 'Variegata')

Watch out for:
Do not move the plant
when flower buds are
forming, or remove the
flower stalks as they
may reflower.

SILVER INCH PLANT - *Tradescantia zebrina*

toxic

easy
care rating

Also known as: spiderwort
Family: Commelinaceae
Grows up to: 6 x 24 inches (15 x 60cm)
Petite silver, green, and purple striped leaves

Found wild in tropical wetlands and rainforests around the world, the fast-growing inch plant can create dense mats. As a houseplant, the three-toned zebra-striped leaves are its standout feature, perfect for tumbling over the sides of hanging baskets, shelves, or mantelpieces. Leaves emerge purple before developing silver and dark green stripes on their topside. Easy to propagate from a small section, it's an ideal plant to pass on.

Planting | Plant in a medium pot in a mix of three parts soil-based compost, one part sharp sand, and one part perlite. Repot when root-bound or every two to three years.

Position | Prefers bright, filtered light away from drafts, heat sources, and direct sun. Variegation tends to be better in a bright position.

Watering | Water from spring to fall when the top layer of compost feels dry. Reduce in winter. Mist the leaves every few days, avoiding the flowers.

Feeding | For optimum growth and health, feed with a balanced liquid fertilizer once a month from spring to early fall. Do not feed in winter.

Also try:
Tradescantia zebrina
'Purpusii'

Watch out for:
Be careful if planting outdoors as it can become invasive and only needs a small amount of stem to propagate.

SPIDER PLANT - *Chlorophytum comosum*

nontoxic

easy
care rating

Also known as: spider ivy; ribbon plant
Family: Asparagaceae
Grows up to: 12 x 24 inches (30 x 60cm)
A classic hanging basket or pedestal plant

Native to tropical and southern Africa, spider plants became so ubiquitous as houseplants during the 1970s that they ended up with something of a boring reputation. Viewed through a fresh lens, there is good reason for their popularity—their long, light green and mid-green striped leaves produce cute clonelike plantlets on dangling stems. There are several variegated cultivars and even a covetable curly version.

Planting | Plant in an equal mix of soil-based and multipurpose compost, in a pot that accommodates the root ball.

Position | Prefers bright, indirect light. Can tolerate lower light levels but growth may be inhibited. Ideal on a pedestal or in a hanging basket in any room.

Watering | Water so that the compost stays moist between spring and fall. Allow the top layer of compost to dry out between winter waterings. Can tolerate drought.

Feeding | Feed a half-strength balanced fertilizer every few weeks from spring to fall.

Also try:
curly spider plant
(*Chlorophytum comosum* 'Bonnie')

Watch out for:
If you want to pass spider plants on, make sure your mother plant is in a bright spot.

CREEPING FIG - *Ficus pumila*

toxic

*easy
care rating*

Also known as: climbing fig
Family: Moraceae
Grows up to: 36 x 36 inches (90 x 90cm)
Good as ground cover or a green wall

This tropical ivylike native of East Asia behaves like a liana (a long-stemmed woody vine) in the wild, scrambling up trees by way of a latex substance produced by its aerial roots. In landscaping it is often used to create indoor or outdoor ground cover, green walls, or screens, although it cannot withstand frost. Most commonly it is used as a dainty, trailing houseplant, its small, round green or variegated leaves cascading from hanging baskets or pedestals.

Planting | Plant in a medium pot or hanging basket filled with soil-based compost. Can be planted outdoors in warmer, frost-free climates but will colonize the space.

Position | Prefers filtered sun, light shade, and high humidity. Can survive lower light levels. Good for green walls or ground cover in mixed containers.

Watering | Water between spring and fall so that the soil is kept moist but not soggy. Let the soil dry out a little between winter waterings. Mist every day in hot weather.

Feeding | Feed with a balanced liquid fertilizer every month in spring and summer to boost growth rate. Decrease to every other month in winter.

Also try:
variegated creeping fig (*Ficus pumila* 'Snowflake'); curly creeping fig (*F. pumila* 'Curly')

Watch out for:
Creeping figs only last a few years in their pots; they can, however, be easily propagated through stem cuttings.

STRING OF HEARTS - *Ceropegia woodii*

nontoxic

easy
care rating

Also known as: hearts entangled; rosary vine; sweetheart vine
Family: Apocynaceae
Grows up to: 4 x 40 inches (10 x 100cm)
The daintiest, heart-leaved trailing plant

A perfect houseplant for a hanging basket, high shelf, or mantelpiece, it is much loved for its long, delicate trailing stems of tiny, heart-shaped gray-green leaves. Added attraction comes from the blushing pink-purple of the underside of the leaves, while curious long pink and purple tubular flowers followed by needlelike seedpods may appear if given the right conditions. Can also be grown outside in tropical climes.

Planting | This semi-succulent plant does well in cactus compost in a small pot or hanging basket. Repot only when root-bound.

Position | Prefers bright light but can survive in lower light levels, although this may affect coloration. Enjoys raised humidity levels, so it is ideal for a bright bathroom.

Watering | Let the top layer of compost dry out between waterings in spring and summer. Reduce in winter so compost is almost dry, making it ideal for hanging baskets.

Feeding | Feed with a half-strength balanced liquid fertilizer once a month in spring and summer. Do not feed in winter.

Also try:
variegated string of hearts (*Ceropegia woodii* 'Marlies Variegata')

Watch out for:
Vines can be trimmed if they get too straggly. Take time unwinding if they arrive coiled up.

STRING OF PEARLS - *Senecio rowleyanus*

toxic

easy
care rating

Also known as: string of beads; string of peas
Family: Asteraceae
Grows up to: 20 x 8 inches (50 x 20cm)
A stylish contender for a high shelf

This curious daisy family member is native to drier parts of southwest Africa where it grows as a creeping perennial succulent vine. In the wild, the "strings of pearls" trail on the ground, often in the shade of other plants and rocks, rooting to form dense mats. As a houseplant it makes a stylish trailing plant (use caution around children and pets) that, thanks to its fleshy, water-storing, pealike beads, can survive periods of drought.

Planting | This plant's succulent nature thrives in a well-draining pot of cactus compost or a mix of three parts soil-based compost to one part sharp sand.

Position | Suits a combination of bright morning sunlight followed by softer filtered light or light shade in the afternoon. Avoid humid areas.

Watering | Keep soil lightly moist between spring and fall. Reduce watering in winter but do not let the soil dry out.

Feeding | Feed with a half-strength fertilizer every two weeks from spring to fall.

Also try:
variegated string of pearls (*Senecio rowleyanus* 'Variegata')

Watch out for:
Flattened leaves could indicate that it is not getting enough water.

LIPSTICK PLANT - *Aeschynanthus pulcher*

nontoxic

medium
care rating

Also known as: red bugle vine
Family: Gesneriaceae
Grows up to: 8 x 28 inches (20 x 70cm)
Boasts gorgeous red blooms

Prized for its bright red tubular flowers that resemble lipstick emerging from a darker tube (the sepals), this epiphytic climber also boasts attractive succulent-like evergreen leaves. Native to tropical regions of Southeast Asia, where it can be found growing in tree branches or rocks, the vinelike habit is ideal for hanging baskets, tall containers, or plant pedestals. Although summer flowering, the blooms can appear year-round.

Planting | Prefers a well-draining pot that just fits the root ball, and an aerated mix of four parts compost, one part sand, and one part perlite. Repot when tightly root-bound.

Position | Bright but filtered light and a warm environment is ideal. Avoid direct sun as this can scorch the leaves, but give enough light to promote flowering.

Watering | Water from spring to fall with tepid rainwater or distilled water when the top of the compost feels dry. Reduce in winter. Mist every other day.

Feeding | Feed with a half-strength balanced liquid fertilizer once a month during the growing season of spring and summer.

Also try:
curly lipstick plant
(*Aeschynanthus pulcher*
'Curly')

Watch out for:
Poor drainage, damp leaves, or soggy compost can lead to fungal problems, leaf drop, or root rot.

STEPHANOTIS - *Stephanotis floribunda*

nontoxic

medium
care rating

Also known as: Madagascar jasmine; bridal wreath
Family: Apocynaceae
Grows up to: 10 x 10 feet (3 x 3m)
A long-flowering fragrant climber

Large, glossy, leathery leaves and clusters of highly scented, jasminelike, waxy white flowers make this lovely plant an ideal cut flower candidate for a wedding bouquet. It is also popular grown indoors, as a large conservatory climber or a compact houseplant often trained over a hoop. In bloom it will fill a room with sensual fragrance for weeks and can be moved outside during the summer months.

Planting | Plant in soil-based compost in a pot that just fits the root ball. Repot every two to three years or renew the top layer of soil in spring.

Position | Prefers bright, filtered light. Avoid direct sun. Keep plants cool in summer when they can be moved outside if frost-free. Ideal for a warm conservatory.

Watering | Water in spring and summer so the soil stays moist. Allow the top layer of soil to dry out in winter. Stand on a tray of damp pebbles and mist daily in summer.

Feeding | Feed every two weeks from spring to early fall with a high-potassium liquid feed.

Also try:
variegated stephanotis
(*Stephanotis floribunda*
'Variegata')

Watch out for:
Limit pruning to early spring. A lack of flowering could be due to low humidity.

JASMINE - *Jasminum* spp.

nontoxic

easy
care rating

Including: common jasmine; Chinese scented jasmine
Family: Oleaceae
Grows up to: 26 x 8 feet (8 x 2.5m)
Fills room with a heady evening fragrance

Native to central Asia, common jasmine (*Jasminum officinale*) has been cultivated for thousands of years as both an ornamental and medicinal plant. The white star-shaped blooms, growing in clusters between twining stems of small pointed leaves, are especially fragrant in the evening. Chinese scented jasmine (*Jasminum polyanthum*) looks the same but is more suitable as a houseplant, often trained over a hoop or up a trellis.

Planting | Grow in soil-based compost in a pot that fits the root ball. Common jasmine can be planted outside, while Chinese scented jasmine is best as a houseplant.

Position | Either specimen can be grown up a trellis or an obelisk to tame the vigorous, twining habit into shape. Thrives best in morning sun with afternoon shade.

Watering | For indoor specimens, water in spring and summer so the soil stays moist. Allow the top layer of soil to dry out in winter. Don't waterlog.

Feeding | Feed potted jasmine with a balanced liquid fertilizer during the growing season in spring and summer. Do not feed in winter.

Also try:
variegated jasmine (*Jasminum officinale* 'Argenteovariegatum')

Watch out for: Chinese scented jasmine can be moved outside in summer but should be brought inside in temperatures below 50°F (10°C).

STAR JASMINE - *Trachelospermum jasminoides*

nontoxic

easy
care rating

Also known as: Chinese star jasmine
Family: Apocynaceae
Grows up to: 20 x 28 feet (6 x 9m)
Gorgeous glassy leaves and scented flowers

This evergreen, woody liana (long-stemmed, woody vine) native to eastern and southeastern Asia is similar in appearance to stephanotis but is more compact with smaller leaves and flowers. Although it prefers bright sunlight, it can also be grown in some shade, making it ideal for a sheltered balcony, terrace, or conservatory. Flowering time is from mid- to late summer when it exudes a wonderful scent. Suitable for gardens or indoor-outdoor spaces.

Planting | Plant in the ground or in a large pot using soil-based or multipurpose compost. Mix some sand into the soil to help with drainage.

Position | Thrives in a range of light levels from full sun to dappled shade. Some shelter is ideal, away from cold, drying winds or drafts.

Watering | Water so that the soil is moist from spring to early fall. Reduce in winter, allowing the surface of the compost to dry out between waterings.

Feeding | Feed with fertilizer monthly through the growing season.

Also try:
variegated star jasmine (*Trachelospermum jasminoides* 'Variegata')

Watch out for:
Tie young shoots in place until the plant is established.

PASSIONFLOWER - *Passiflora* spp.

nontoxic

medium
care rating

Including: blue passionflower;
red passionflower
Family: Passifloraceae
Grows up to: 10 x 3 feet (3 x 0.9m)
Exquisite showy flowers; ideal for balconies

Passionflowers are some of the most beautiful vining plants, displaying showy flowers with a distinctive central corona. The most common is the frost-hardy blue passionflower (*Passiflora caerulea*), which can survive mild temperate climates; the purple passionflower (*Passiflora incarnata*) is fully hardy but still prefers a sheltered spot; while the red passionflower (*Passiflora racemosa*) is tender and suited to a conservatory or bright room.

Planting | Grow indoor specimens in a well-draining pot that just fits the root ball. Use soil-based compost. Cut back growing tips after planting to encourage branching.

Position | Full sun or dappled shade is ideal. Avoid direct sunlight and shelter from cold, drying winds. Grow red passionflowers indoors in a warm, bright spot.

Watering | Keep compost moist in spring and summer and mist indoor plants daily. Reduce in winter, allowing the soil to dry out between waterings.

Feeding | From mid-spring to summer, feed with a balanced liquid fertilizer every two weeks. Do not feed in winter. Excessive feeding can lead to rapid foliage growth at the expense of flowers.

Also try:
blue passionflower
(*Passiflora caerulea*);
purple passionflower
(*P. incarnata*)

Watch out for:
Passionflowers benefit
from fan-training
rather than being left
alone to scramble.

BOUGAINVILLEA - *Bougainvillea* spp.

toxic

medium
care rating

Also known as: paper flower
Family: Nyctaginaceae
Grows up to: 26 x 5 feet (8 x 1.5m)
Brighten a conservatory or terrace with
these exotic blooms

This vigorous tropical climber is most often seen growing up walls and houses in warmer climes. However, in milder climates it can be grown indoors in a large pot and brought into the garden in summer until the first frost. The actual flower is small and white but is surrounded by colorful sepal-like bracts in shades of pink, magenta, purple, red, orange, white, or yellow. Can be grown as a bonsai, but prune in late winter or early spring.

Planting | Grow in a large pot in well-draining soil-based compost. If growing outside or in a conservatory, train up a trellis or wall. Use a cane to support smaller specimens.

Position | Bougainvilleas love a bright spot, although they may need shading from direct sunlight under glass. Consider rotating plants to ensure even light.

Watering | Keep soil moist during spring, summer, and fall. Reduce in winter, letting the top layer of compost dry out between soakings.

Feeding | Feed weekly from spring to early fall with a half-strength balanced liquid fertilizer. Do not feed in winter. Indoor plants especially appreciate a nutritional boost.

Also try:
bougainvillea 'Mrs Butt' (*Bougainvillea × buttiana*)

Watch out for:
Too much aggressive pruning can inhibit the color of the blooms. Prune in the fall after flowering.

IVY - *Hedera* spp.

toxic

easy
care rating

Including: English ivy; Japanese ivy
Family: Araliaceae
Grows up to: 26 x 5 feet (8 x 1.5m)
Pretty in mixed containers or window boxes

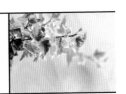

Ivy is a well-known plant in the wild, in gardens, and as a foliage plant in floral designs, but it can also be grown as a houseplant. There are numerous interesting varieties and cultivars, including English ivy (*Hedera helix*), its gold and green variegated relative ivy 'Goldchild' (*Hedera helix* 'Goldchild'), and white-veined Japanese ivy (*Hedera rhombea*), all of which look pretty trailing from a hanging basket, in a small pot, or given the run of a balcony wall.

Planting | Plant outside in soil or indoors in soil-based compost. Train up a wall or keep compact in a small pot, hanging basket, or a mixed container.

Position | Ivy needs bright light to flourish, although variegated types can thrive in filtered light. Low light levels can lead to leggy, sickly plants.

Watering | Let the top layer of compost dry out between waterings in spring and summer. Reduce watering in winter. Avoid standing in water.

Feeding | Benefits from balanced liquid fertilizer monthly during the growing season.

Also try:
Japanese ivy (*Hedera rhombea*)

Watch out for:
Wash dust and pests from the leaves regularly by hosing them down with a shower.

OTHER FLOWERS

Seasonal or year-round bloomers are a great way to add living color and interest to indoor or outdoor spaces, from small, vibrant African violets and fragrant gardenias, to collectible auriculas and shrubby classics such as the mophead hydrangea.

PEACE LILY - *Spathiphyllum wallisii*

toxic

easy
care rating

Also known as: white sails; spathe flower
Family: Araceae
Grows up to: 24 x 24 inches (60 x 60cm)
Said to be air- and aura-purifying, bringing peace

Native to tropical forests of South and Central America, the peace lily is an elegant and easy-care must-have for beginners or plant collectors. Leaves are dark green, glossy, and arching, forming a clump at the base. The distinctive flowers, from which the plant gets its botanical name, appear as a spike of small yellow flowers clustered within a tear-shaped white spathe, which fades to a pale green as the spring blooming season progresses.

Planting | Plant in a medium, well-draining pot in an equal mix of soil-based and multipurpose compost. Repot only when root-bound.

Position | Can survive a range of light levels but prefers bright, indirect light, which aids blooming. Avoid direct sun and drying heaters. A bright, humid bathroom is ideal.

Watering | Keep compost moist from spring to fall. Allow the top layer of compost to dry out between winter waterings. Set on a tray of damp pebbles and mist regularly.

Feeding | Benefits from feeding with a balanced liquid fertilizer every two weeks during spring, summer, and fall. Do not feed in winter.

Also try:
large peace lily (*Spathiphyllum wallisii* 'Mauna Loa' or 'Sensation')

Watch out for: Brown or yellow leaves can indicate either under- or overwatering, or a buildup of minerals from tap water. Switch to distilled water and monitor.

TAIL FLOWER - *Anthurium andraeanum*

toxic

easy
care rating

Also known as: flamingo flower; flamingo lily
Family: Araceae
Grows up to: 18 x 12 inches (45 x 30cm)
Make a feature of its exotic, head-turning blooms

Glossy, arrow-shaped leaves provide the perfect backdrop for this striking houseplant's enticing waxy flowers. In shades of white, pink, red, and wine, each bloom comprises a long spadix of flowers extending from a large heart-shaped spathe. Native to rainforests of South America and the Caribbean where it grows in or under large trees, it prefers similarly warm, humid, dappled conditions but is relatively easy to care for.

Planting | Plant in a medium pot in an equal mix of soil-based and multipurpose compost, keeping the root ball just above the surface. Use moss to keep moisture in.

Position | Prefers bright, filtered light and a consistently warm, humid environment. Avoid direct sun and cold drafts. A sunny bathroom is ideal.

Watering | Allow the top layer of soil to dry out between waterings. Keep moist but do not allow to stand in water. Set on a tray of damp pebbles and mist every few days.

Feeding | Encourage blooming by feeding with a half-strength balanced liquid fertilizer every two weeks through spring and summer. Do not feed in winter.

Also try:
dark leaved and flowered tail flower (*Anthurium andraeanum* 'Black Love')

Watch out for:
Overwatering can cause root rot, which appears as brown leaves or mushy roots.

POINSETTIA - *Euphorbia pulcherrima*

toxic

easy
care rating

Also known as: Mexican flame flower; Christmas Eve flower
Family: Euphorbiaceae
Grows up to: 24 x 12 inches (60 x 30cm)
A red and green Christmas classic

Although best known as a popular Christmas houseplant, this bright red and green plant is actually native to mid-elevation rainforests of Mexico, Guatemala, and other regions of Central America. It is possible to keep it as a year-round houseplant, but the showy bracts need 14 hours of darkness for 6–8 weeks before winter "blooming" and abundant sunlight during the day in order to turn a vibrant color.

Planting | If repotting, plant in a medium pot in a mix of three parts soil-based compost to one part horticultural grit. Repot in spring.

Position | Help bracts stay colorful by placing in bright, filtered light. Keep in a warm environment away from direct sunlight and cold drafts.

Watering | Water when the surface of the compost feels dry. Overwatering can cause root rot. Encourage humidity by misting regularly.

Feeding | Appreciates feeding monthly with a low-nitrogen, high-potassium fertilizer.

Also try:
variegated poinsettia (*Euphorbia pulcherrima* 'Silverstar')

Watch out for:
Be careful when transporting as cold winter temperatures can damage foliage.

ROSE OF CHINA - *Hibiscus rosa-sinensis*

toxic

 easy
care rating

Also known as: Chinese hibiscus; China rose
Family: Malvaceae
Grows up to: 36 x 72 inches (90 x 180cm)
Trumpet-shaped flowers for indoors or out

A relative of *Hibiscus sabdariffa*, from which a popular red-colored herbal infusion is made, the rose of China has similarly lush foliage and trumpet-shaped flowers. It generally blooms in summer, in shades of white, red, yellow, or orange (depending on the cultivar), with a deep red at the throat, although it can flower at other times of the year and can be grown outside in warmer climates in borders or large pots, or kept pruned as a houseplant.

Planting | Plant in a large pot filled with an equal mix of soil-based and multipurpose compost. Replace the top layer of compost each year and repot every two to three years.

Position | Prefers a warm spot and bright light away from direct sun and drafts. Keep houseplants pruned as they can get tall, or grow taller specimens outside.

Watering | Keep compost moist through spring and summer, allowing the top layer of soil to dry out between winter waterings. Mist leaves regularly.

Feeding | Feeding every two weeks from spring through to fall with a balanced liquid fertilizer can help promote blooms. Do not feed in winter.

Also try:
variegated rose of China (*Hibiscus rosa-sinensis* 'Cooperi')

Watch out for:
Choose a pot that slightly constricts the roots.

ETERNAL FLAME - *Goeppertia crocata* syn. *Calathea crocata* 'Tassmania'

nontoxic

easy
care rating

Also known as: saffron-colored calathea
Family: Marantaceae
Grows up to: 24 x 24 inches (60 x 60cm)
Flame-colored flowers to brighten a room

Although the eternal flame can be grown for its foliage—dark, metallic green, broadly oval leaves with burgundy undersides and an overall wrinkled appearance—it is most prized for its long-lasting orange flowers that arise from within on tall stems like glowing flames. The flowers (actually orange bracts that house true flowers) last for around three months, while the leaves close at night in common with other "prayer plants."

Planting | Plant in a medium, well-draining pot in soil-based compost. Repot every two to three years when root-bound.

Position | Prefers a warm, stable temperature, a humid environment, and bright, filtered light away from direct sun or drafts. A sunny bathroom is ideal.

Watering | Keep compost lightly moist all year round. Promote humidity by standing the pot on a tray of damp pebbles and misting daily with tepid water.

Feeding | Feed with a liquid fertilizer monthly from spring to early fall.

Also try:
bird of paradise (*Strelitzia reginae*)

Watch out for:
Withering leaves can be a result of too much calcium in the water, dry air, or underwatering.

BIRD OF PARADISE - *Strelitzia reginae*

toxic	**hard** *care rating*	**Also known as:** crane flower **Family:** Strelitziaceae **Grows up to:** 36 x 24 inches (90 x 60cm) Blooms like an exotic bird

It's not hard to see how this plant got its common name, thanks to the bright orange and blue-purple flowers that arise like the feathers of a tropical bird from a beaklike spathe. This sculptural feature, sitting perpendicular to the stem, provides a rest for pollinating sunbirds to sit on in the wild. Often supplied as cut flowers, the blooms can also be enjoyed as part of an attractive houseplant, although it can take three years for a specimen to flower.

Planting | Grow in a large pot filled with three parts soil-based compost and one part horticultural grit. Replace the top layer of compost every year.

Position | Prefers humidity and bright, full sun year-round and an aerated position in summer. At least six hours of direct morning sun is ideal to encourage blooming.

Watering | Water so compost stays moist during spring and summer. Allow the top layer of soil to dry out between winter waterings. Set on a tray of damp pebbles and mist daily.

Feeding | Feed with a balanced liquid fertilizer every two weeks from spring to fall. Do not feed during the dormant period in winter.

Also try:
giant white bird of paradise (*Strelitzia nicolai*)

Watch out for:
Browning leaves and non-flowering specimens are signs that conditions are not right. Try increasing humidity and light.

GERBERA DAISY - *Gerbera jamesonii*

nontoxic	**hard** *care rating*	**Also known as:** barberton daisy; African daisy **Family:** Asteraceae **Grows up to:** 24 x 24 inches (60 x 60cm) A summer of tall, daisylike blooms

Sometimes called African daisy—a name also commonly applied to species of *Osteospermum*—this lovely plant has large, bright green, slightly lobed leaves and tall stems of daisylike blooms in shades of orange, red, yellow, and pink. Gerberas are popular cut flowers but, given the right conditions, also make lovely summer-blooming or repeat-flowering houseplants. Look out for hardier cultivars to grow outside in temperate climes.

Planting | Plant in a small pot in an equal mix of soil-based and multipurpose compost. Repot when root-bound. Overwinter outdoor specimens inside.

Position | Prefers a bright, well-ventilated but sheltered spot with morning sun. Bright light is required for repeat blooming, but avoid direct afternoon sun.

Watering | Keep the compost just moist in spring and summer, allowing the top layer of compost to dry out between waterings. Reduce in winter and cooler zones.

Feeding | Apply a high-potash fertilizer every two weeks from spring to late summer.

Also try:
hardier gerbera (*Gerbera jamesonii* 'Garvinea Sweet Glow')

Watch out for: Avoid very humid areas such as bathrooms as this can encourage fungus growth.

AFRICAN VIOLET - *Streptocarpus* sect. *Saintpaulia* cultivars

nontoxic **medium**
care rating

Also known as: saintpaulia
Family: Gesneriaceae
Grows up to: 4 x 8 inches (10 x 20cm)
Pretty but fickle; perfect for a windowsill

African violets are a windowsill favorite thanks to their diminutive size and pretty, all-year blooms. Although violet by name, they are available in flowering shades of purple, pink, red, and white, some with frilly, ruffled, or double petals. The extensive list of cultivars also includes specimens with variously shaped fuzzy leaves, so there's lots of scope to create a diverse collection. Not to be confused with true violets (*Viola* spp.), which are edible.

Planting | Plant in a small pot in a mix of two parts soil-based compost to one part multipurpose compost. Repot only when tightly root-bound.

Position | Prefers bright, filtered light away from drafts. Avoid direct sunlight but move to a sunny windowsill in winter. Ideal for a warm, humid kitchen.

Watering | Watering from above can cause the leaves to rot. Instead, water from below by placing on a saucer of water. Drain thoroughly. Set on a tray of damp pebbles.

Feeding | Apply a half-strength liquid balanced fertilizer or a specialty African violet fertilizer monthly from spring to late summer. Do not feed in winter.

Also try:
African violet (*Saintpaulia ionantha*); 'Blue Boy' (*S.* 'Top Dark Blue')

Watch out for:
Raising African violets is all about balance. Too stuffy, cold, wet, or dry can result in leaf or bloom damage, but the challenge is part of the appeal.

CAPE PRIMROSE - *Streptocarpus* hybrids

nontoxic

medium
care rating

Also known as: streps
Family: Gesneriaceae
Grows up to: 24 x 24 inches (60 x 60cm)
Comes in a huge assortment of colors

A close relative of the African violet but much easier to care for, the cape primrose displays a rosette of large, wrinkled, lance-shaped leaves and tall stems of five-lobed flowers of white, pink, blue, purple, or red (depending on the cultivar), often adorned with nectar guidelines. Originating from woodlands, rocky slopes, and grasslands in southern Africa, they do well in partial shade, bringing blooming color from spring through fall.

Planting | Plant outdoors in a pot of humus-rich, well-draining soil. Overwinter inside in temperate climates. Plant indoors in a small pot in multipurpose compost.

Position | Prefers a partially shady spot with sun for half the day between spring and fall. In winter, move to a sunny windowsill that gets direct sun most of the day.

Watering | Allow the top layer of compost to dry out before spring and summer waterings. Reduce waterings in winter. Water by placing in a tray of water for 20 minutes; drain well.

Feeding | Benefits from a high-potash fertilizer once a month from spring to fall. Do not feed in winter. Remove dead flowerheads to encourage further blooms.

Also try: cape primrose 'Albatross' (*Streptocarpus* 'Albatross')

Watch out for: Avoid excessive heat and sun; prone to root rot, so place in a well-draining terra-cotta pot high in the soil.

AURICULA - *Primula auricula* and *Primula hirsuta* hybrids

toxic

medium
care rating

Also known as: mountain cowslip; bear's ear
Family: Primulaceae
Grows up to: 20 x 20 inches (50 x 50cm)
Collect a theater of cultivars

A relative of the primula, these jewel-like, spring-flowering alpine plants are traditionally displayed in rows of individual pots called "theaters." The leaves appear as low-growing rosettes of semi-evergreen or powdery foliage, while the bold, circular flowers stand tall and proud on upright stems. True to their native habitat, they need cool outdoor conditions to grow, although a theater can provide shelter from extreme conditions.

Planting | Auriculas look wonderful planted separately in well-draining terra-cotta pots. Use a mix of three parts soil-based compost to one part grit to aid drainage.

Position | Prefers humidity and bright, full sun year-round and an aerated position in summer. At least six hours of direct morning sun is ideal to encourage blooming.

Watering | Growing in pots helps maintain vital drainage. Water from spring to fall so the soil is just moist, watering directly into the soil and avoiding the leaves. Reduce in winter.

Feeding | Feed nitrogen fertilizer in spring, then weekly watering with tomato fertilizer.

Also try: *Primula auricula* 'Winifred'

Watch out for: Vine weevils, which can nibble the foliage or the roots; if you can tug a plant out easily, it may be infected.

PAINTED LEAF BEGONIA - *Begonia* spp.

toxic

medium
care rating

Including: rex begonia; fancy leaf begonia; king begonia
Family: Begoniaceae
Grows up to: 36 x 18 inches (90 x 45cm)
A perfect pairing of leaf and flower

Painted leaf begonias are mainly grown indoors for their decorative patterned foliage, which comes in a variety of styles, including polka dot (*Begonia maculata*), swirling green and silver (*Begonia* 'Escargot'), and red-leaved (*Begonia* 'Rubra'). The flowers are not as showy or colorful as bedding plant begonias, such as cultivars of *Begonia* × *tuberhybrida* or *Begonia boliviensis*, but are usually tall, white, and elegant.

Planting | Painted leaf begonias prefer a pot that just constricts the root ball. Plant in an equal mix of soil-based and multipurpose compost. Repot when root-bound.

Position | Prefers bright, filtered sun or light shade. Avoid direct sun, heaters, and cold drafts. Can be grown under glass in a frost-free environment.

Watering | Keep compost moist from spring to fall, allowing the top layer to dry out between waterings in winter. Stand on a tray of damp pebbles but do not mist.

Feeding | Apply a high-nitrogen fertilizer every two weeks from spring to fall. Specimens with larger flowers benefit from switching to a high-potash feed when in bud.

Also try:
painted leaf begonia (*Begonia rex*); trailing begonia 'Million Kisses' (*Begonia* 'Million Kisses')

Watch out for:
Rex begonias require the perfect balance of water, light, and temperature; crisping leaves could indicate a lack of water or too much sun.

KALANCHOE - *Kalanchoe* spp.

toxic

Including: flaming Katy;
flower dust plant
Family: Crassulaceae
Grows up to: 18 x 18 inches (45 x 45cm)
Fleshy leaves and long-flowering blooms

easy
care rating

Mainly native to Madagascar and tropical Africa, these succulent flowering plants have simple or pinnately lobed foliage and tubular or bell-shaped four-lobed flowers. Popular species include flaming Katy (*Kalanchoe blossfeldiana*), which has round fleshy leaves and long-flowering red, pink, or white blooms, and the flower dust plant (*Kalanchoe pumila*), displaying silvery serrated-edged leaves and small, starry pink flowers.

Planting | Plant in a medium-sized pot in cactus compost or two parts soil-based compost to one part horticultural grit. Repot one size larger each year.

Position | Prefers bright, filtered light in a well-ventilated room. Can be brought outdoors in warm summer temperatures, but overwinter in case of frost.

Watering | Water in spring and summer from the base when the compost feels dry. Drain well and avoid wetting leaves. Keep compost almost dry in fall and winter.

Feeding | Benefits from a half-strength balanced liquid fertilizer every month in spring and summer. Do not feed in winter.

Also try:
flower dust plant
(*Kalanchoe pumila*);
panda plant (*Kalanchoe tomentosa*)

Watch out for: Powdery mildew may occur if placed in too humid an environment; move to a bright, dry spot.

JERUSALEM CHERRY - *Solanum pseudocapsicum*

toxic

Also known as: Christmas cherry;
Madeira winter cherry
Family: Solanaceae
Grows up to: 18 x 24 inches (45 x 60cm)
Starry flowers mature into cherry red fruits

easy
care rating

Although mainly grown for its abundance of red, orange, and golden tomatolike winter fruits—plants are often used in festive Christmas decorations, hence its other common name—this compact plant also displays wavy-edged dark green leaves and starry white summer flowers. It can be grown as a sheltered container or patio plant in summer, as well as a year-round houseplant. Just don't be tempted to eat the inedible, toxic fruits.

Planting | Plant in a small pot of equal parts soil-based and multipurpose compost. Cut back the stems of shriveled fruits to encourage bushy, compact growth.

Position | Prefers bright or filtered light from fall to spring, a spell outdoors after the frosts, and a cool bright space in summer.

Watering | Water so that the soil stays just moist between spring and midwinter. After fruiting, allow the top layer of compost to dry out between waterings.

Feeding | Use fertilizer monthly from spring. Do not feed again until after fruits have shriveled.

Also try:
variegated Jerusalem cherry (*Solanum pseudocapsicum* 'Variegatum')

Watch out for: Give the plant a gentle shake to distribute pollen.

GARDENIA - *Gardenia jasminoides*

toxic

hard
care rating

Also known as: cape jasmine
Family: Rubiaceae
Grows up to: 24 x 24 inches (60 x 60cm)
Fill your home with sweet summer scent

One of over 100 species of *Gardenia*, the cape jasmine is found wild in parts of South and Southeast Asia, where it can grow into a large, dense shrub. As a houseplant it stays relatively small and compact, with beautifully glossy dark green leaves and huge, loosely funneled white flowers. Renowned for its sweet, woody yet feminine fragrance, this is a great choice for naturally scenting the home during the blooming season of summer and fall.

Planting | Can be grown outside in acid soil in a well-draining, frost-free, sheltered site or warmer climes. Or plant in a large, well-draining pot in ericaceous compost.

Position | Prefers bright, filtered light, out of direct sun and drafts. Keep summer temperatures warm by day and cooler at night. Move to a sunny spot in winter.

Watering | Keep compost moist between spring and fall with tepid rainwater or distilled water. Allow the top of the soil to dry out between winter waterings. Mist leaves regularly.

Feeding | Apply a half-strength balanced liquid fertilizer for acid-loving plants every two weeks during spring and late summer. Do not feed in fall or winter.

Also try:
dwarf variety
(*Gardenia jasminoides*
'Buttons' or 'Crown
Jewel')

Watch out for: Check
for pests and make sure
your plant is getting the
right balance of water,
fertilizer, and warmth.

WISTERIA - *Wisteria* spp.

toxic

hard
care rating

Including: Chinese wisteria;
Japanese wisteria
Family: Fabaceae
Grows up to: 20 x 10 feet (6 x 3m)
A fragrant beauty for sunny patios and balconies

Wisteria is known for its twining stems and cascades of fragrant purple or white flowers in late spring, most commonly used to adorn walls, fences, and pergolas. Although it thrives best directly in soil, it is possible to grow wisteria in a large container, ideal for a sunny balcony or patio. Flowering may be less abundant, but even one bloom can bring a whole lot of joy. For those up for the challenge, it can also be grown as a bonsai.

Planting | Plant outdoor specimens between fall and spring in fertile, well-drained soil. Or grow in a large container of soil-based compost, trained up a support.

Position | Wisterias are hardy and vigorous and do best with some training and support. Wires, a trellis, a pergola, or an arch are all ideal. Place in full sun or light shade.

Watering | Keep well watered, especially if grown in light or sandy soil, when newly planted, and in dry or hot periods.

Feeding | Feed border-grown wisteria in early spring with rose or flowering shrub fertilizer.

Also try:
Chinese wisteria
(*Wisteria sinensis*)

Watch out for:
Shorten excessive
growth in late summer;
shorten new shoots in
late winter.

INDIAN AZALEA - *Rhododendron simsii*

toxic

hard
care rating

Also known as: florist's azalea; greenhouse azalea
Family: Ericaceae
Grows up to: 18 x 18 inches (45 x 45cm)
Pretty buds and long-lasting blooms

Azaleas are spring-flowering shrubs in the genus *Rhododendron*, the hardiest of which are often planted as large ornamental garden shrubs. The Indian azalea is one of the less hardy "greenhouse azalea" species, which can be grown indoors and sports glossy dark green leaves, clusters of single or double often ruffled flowers in shades of pink, red, white, or bicolored, and lovely opening buds. Some azaleas can also be grown as bonsai.

Planting | Source plants when just in bud. Grow in a medium pot of ericaceous compost. Repot every two to three years in spring when root-bound.

Position | Prefers light shade in spring when in flower, full shade in summer, when it can be placed outside, and a sunny but cool spot in winter to encourage blooming.

Watering | Keep compost moist from spring to fall using rainwater or distilled water. Reduce watering over winter but never let it dry out completely.

Feeding | Feed monthly from spring to fall with a balanced liquid fertilizer suitable for acid-loving plants. Do not feed in winter.

Also try:
Satsuki azalea bonsai
(*Rhododendron indicum*)

Watch out for: Can be difficult to get Indian azaleas to rebloom; help the process by cutting back straggly growth in spring.

CAMELLIA - *Camellia* spp.

nontoxic

hard
care rating

Including: Japanese camellia; tea plant
Family: Theaceae
Grows up to: 13 x 10 feet (4 x 3m)
Ideal for a cool conservatory

Normally grown outdoors, camellias also make stunning indoor plants for conservatories where temperatures stay low enough for them to bloom. They will not fare well in hot homes. Some cultivars that work well indoors include fall camellia (*Camellia sasanqua*), which flowers just after it is brought in for winter; opulently blooming Japanese camellia (*Camellia japonica*); and the tea plant (*Camellia sinensis*).

Planting | Plant outdoor camellias in fall and potted camellias in spring, in acid soil or soil-based ericaceous compost. Homemade leaf mold can help raise acidity.

Position | Prefers cool, frost-free temperatures in partial shade away from direct sunlight. Ideal for conservatories, but protect from afternoon sun.

Watering | Water with rainwater or distilled water. Keep soil moist between spring and early fall, increasing in warm temperatures. Reduce watering in winter.

Feeding | Feed after blooming using a balanced liquid fertilizer for acid-loving plants.

Also try:
fall camellia (*Camellia sasanqua*)

Watch out for:
Deadhead blooms regularly as they begin to turn brown. This does not promote reflowering.

ANGEL'S TRUMPET - *Brugmansia* x *candida*

toxic

hard
care rating

Also known as: datura
Family: Solanaceae
Grows up to: 48 x 36 inches (120 x 90cm)
Showy, trumpet-shaped, fragrant flowers

This showstopping plant with large, scented, trumpet-shaped flowers in shades of yellow, white, or pink, dangling from a branching canopy of dark green leaves, is guaranteed to turn heads. Ideal grown indoors in a large, bright room or a sunny conservatory, it can also be planted outdoors in subtropical or tropical climes as a woody shrub or small tree.

Planting | Indoor plants should be grown in a large container of soil-based compost. Repot every two to three years. All parts are toxic, so wear gloves to protect hands.

Position | Place in a sunny spot but away from direct sunlight. It needs a cool room in winter; an unheated conservatory is ideal.

Watering | Water so that the compost stays moist between spring and early fall. Increase watering if temperatures get warmer. Reduce in winter so compost is just moist.

Feeding | Feed monthly with a balanced liquid fertilizer in spring, switching to a high-potash fertilizer in summer. Do not feed in winter.

Also try:
white flowers
(*Brugmansia* 'Betty Marshall')

Watch out for: Trim stems after flowering to keep it compact but don't prune too hard; keep away from children and pets.

FLOWERING MAPLE - *Abutilon* x *hybridum*

nontoxic

easy
care rating

Also known as: parlor maple; Chinese lantern
Family: Malvaceae
Grows up to: 36 x 24 inches (90 x 60cm)
Long-lasting hollyhock-like blooms

Commonly known as a flowering maple thanks to its maplelike leaves, this mallow family plant is more closely related to hollyhock (*Alcea rosea*) and hibiscus (*Hibiscus* spp.). Blooming from midsummer until late fall, it has long-lasting bell-shaped flowers in shades of red, yellow, pink, and white (depending on the cultivar). The foliage is either dark green or variegated green and gold.

Planting | Plant in a large container in an equal mix of soil-based and multipurpose compost. Pinch out tips in spring for a more compact plant. Repot every two years.

Position | Can be grown in outdoor containers or indoors as a houseplant. Prefers bright light, but avoid direct sunlight. Move to a cooler position in winter.

Watering | Keep compost moist from spring to fall. Allow the top layer of compost to dry out between winter waterings.

Feeding | Fertilize every two weeks in spring and fall, and use a high-potash feed in summer.

Also try:
trailing abutilon
(*Abutilon megapotamicum*), suitable for bonsai

Watch out for:
Can be sensitive to temperature changes; avoid repositioning.

MOPHEAD HYDRANGEA - *Hydrangea macrophylla*

toxic

medium
care rating

Also known as: French hydrangea; lacecap hydrangea
Family: Hydrangeaceae
Grows up to: 36 x 36 inches (90 x 90cm)
Huge flowerheads; lovely indoors and out

If you're thinking of planting a hydrangea outside, there are lots of different species and cultivars to choose from, including the mophead and lacecap (*Hydrangea macrophylla*), the cone-shaped panicle (*Hydrangea paniculata*), and the smooth (*Hydrangea arborescens*). The compact mophead is the most suited to growing as an indoor houseplant, available in a range of colors.

Planting | Plant in a medium or large pot (depending on the specimen) in soil-based compost. If you want to keep the flowers blue, pot in ericaceous compost.

Position | Place in bright, filtered light in a cool room in spring; on a table in a hallway away from drying heaters is ideal. Move outdoors or into a shed in winter.

Watering | Keep compost moist between spring and fall, and just moist in winter. Use rainwater or distilled water for blue varieties, which need more acidic soil.

Feeding | Apply a half-strength balanced liquid fertilizer every two weeks in spring and summer. Do not feed in winter.

Also try: compact blue mophead (*Hydrangea macrophylla* 'Little Blue')

Watch out for: Pruning can help keep plants compact; cut off one-third of old stems after blooms fade for a fuller plant.

DAHLIA - *Dahlia* spp. and cultivars

nontoxic

medium
care rating

Including: single-flowered, waterlily, cactus, and ball dahlias
Family: Asteraceae
Grows up to: 60 x 36 inches (150 x 90cm)
Hugely varied flowerheads

Largely native to upland and mountainous areas of Mexico, dahlias were grown as a food crop by the Aztecs—all parts of the plant are edible, including the nutritious tubers—but are now largely grown for their exquisite, brightly colored flowers, with over 50,000 cultivars to choose from. If grown outdoors, include some single-flowered varieties as they attract the pollinators.

Planting | Grow from seed (½ inch/1.25cm deep) in late winter, or tuber (1 inch/2.5cm deep) in early spring, in a large container of well-draining potting mix with added compost.

Position | Start dahlias off indoors or in a greenhouse in a sunny spot. Bring outside after all risk of frost, or keep in a bright spot indoors. Give them space to spread out.

Watering | Water regularly as roots establish, allowing the top layer of soil to dry out between waterings. Water well in dry and hot weather by soaking fully once a week.

Feeding | Use high-potassium tomato feed weekly in containers; every two weeks in borders.

Also try: dinnerplate dahlia (*Dahlia* 'Cafe au Lait')

Watch out for: Tubers will not survive the frost; store them somewhere dry over winter.

BULBS

Bulbous plants survive by storing food during dormancy in the form of bulbs, corms, tuberous roots, tubers, or rhizomes. Ideal for containers, try layering or planting successively so you have an ongoing array of beautiful blooms through the year.

CALLA LILY - *Zantedeschia* spp.

toxic

easy
care rating

Also known as: arum lily
Family: Araceae
Grows up to: 24 x 24 inches (60 x 60cm)
Choose from variously colored spathes

The best-known and hardiest calla lily (*Zantedeschia aethiopica*) is most often found outdoors, where it can grow large clusters of lush green leaves with tall stems of white spathes in summer and fall. More colorful, tender types, such as the golden (*Zantedeschia elliottiana*) and pink (*Zantedeschia rehmannii*) calla lilies, and those with purple, dark red, or black spathes or spotted leaves make stunning houseplants.

Planting | Indoor varieties fare best in a wide pot filled with multipurpose compost, with the rhizome—eyes facing up— just visible at the surface.

Position | Tender indoor specimens prefer a warm, bright, frost-free environment. They can be moved outdoors in summer, but overwinter plants or rhizomes inside.

Watering | These riverbank plants need their compost to be kept moist during spring and summer. Reduce watering so that it stays almost dry in winter.

Feeding | Benefits from feeding every two weeks with a balanced liquid fertilizer from spring until the blooms begin to fade. Do not feed in winter.

Also try:
white flowers (*Zantedeschia* 'Ice Dancer'); red and gold (*Z.* 'Fire Dancer')

Watch out for:
A sticky substance on the underside of leaves can indicate the presence of aphids; monitor plants regularly and wipe off any visible pests and secretions.

CYCLAMEN - *Cyclamen* spp.

toxic

easy
care rating

Also known as: sowbread
Family: Primulaceae
Grows up to: 4 x 4 inches (10 x 10cm)
A heartwarming early bloomer

Early blooming cyclamens add a welcome burst of color from fall to spring. Small-flowered florist forms of Persian cyclamen (*Cyclamen persicum*) come in shades of white, crimson, and magenta, some with marbled leaves, and are ideal for windowsills and tablescaping. Purple cyclamen (*Cyclamen purpurascens*), ivy-leaved cyclamen (*Cyclamen hederifolium*), and eastern sowbread (*Cyclamen coum*) make perfect woodland plants.

Planting | Plant tubers 4–6 inches (10–15cm) apart, 1 inch (2.5cm) deep in early fall. Repot indoor plants in an equal mix of soil-based compost and horticultural grit.

Position | Tender indoor specimens prefer bright indirect or filtered sunlight. Too much heat can encourage dormancy. Hardier specimens grow well in light shade.

Watering | Keep soil just moist but be careful not to waterlog. Water once a week by soaking in a tray of water. Drain well. Avoid getting water on leaves.

Feeding | Feed every two weeks with a diluted balanced liquid fertilizer while in full leaf. Do not feed during the dormant summer period.

Also try:
florist's cyclamen
(*Cyclamen persicum*)

Watch out for:
Cyclamens die down in summer, then regrow quickly in fall; don't be alarmed if plants temporarily die back.

FALSE SHAMROCK - *Oxalis triangularis*

toxic

medium
care rating

Also known as: oxalis; purple shamrock; wood sorrel
Family: Oxalidaceae
Grows up to: 12 x 12 inches (30 x 30cm)
Butterfly wing leaves and starry flowers

This popular indoor plant has delicate, triangular, green, purple, or variegated leaves that fold up at night like butterfly wings, and long-lasting sprays of small, starry pink or white flowers that bloom through spring and summer. Native to parts of South America and naturalized in North America and East India, it grows from corms, going through a period of dormancy each year, but will revive if left alone somewhere cool.

Planting | Plant oxalis bulbs in fall, three to five per medium, well-draining pot. Plant 2 inches (5cm) deep in an equal mix of soil-based compost and horticultural grit.

Position | In-leaf plants require a lightly shaded spot, away from direct sun, from spring to fall. Move to a cool room in winter, keeping away from frost and drafts.

Watering | Let the top layer of compost go dry between waterings from spring to fall. Do not water during the dormant period from fall to winter.

Feeding | Feed monthly with fertilizer from spring to late summer.

Also try:
wood sorrel (outdoors)
(*Oxalis acetosella*)

Watch out for:
Leave alone when plants die back in winter; when new shoots appear, start watering and feeding again.

AMARYLLIS - *Hippeastrum* spp.

toxic

easy
care rating

Also known as: knight's star
Family: Amaryllidaceae
Grows up to: 24 x 12 inches (60 x 30cm)
A handsome festive bloomer

This stunning winter to early spring blooming plant boasts long, strappy leaves and trumpet-shaped flowers, the large bulbs often given as a holiday gift. Although part of the Amaryllidaceae family, the plants commonly referred to as amaryllis are actually from the genus *Hippeastrum*. Choose from numerous cultivars in plain or patterned shades of red, pink, orange, and white, as single-flowered, double-flowered, jumbo, or miniature.

Planting | Plant in late fall or winter in a pot that is just bigger than the bulb. Set the bulb one-third above the surface, using multipurpose compost.

Position | Place in a bright, warm spot. The leaves and then flowers should appear after six to eight weeks. Move to a cooler spot when buds appear to extend blooming.

Watering | Water sparingly while waiting for the first leaves to appear. Increase watering while flowering so the compost stays moist. Do not water after flowering.

Feeding | After flowering, feed with a balanced liquid fertilizer until the foliage dies down in late summer. Do not feed during the dormant period.

Also try:
bright red (*Hippeastrum* 'Monaco'); narrow-petaled (*H.* 'Sumatra')

Watch out for:
For annual blooms, let bulbs die out after flowering. Lift, repot, and place in a cool, dark place for two months, then move somewhere bright and resume care.

NATAL LILY - *Clivia miniata*

toxic

medium
care rating

Also known as: bush lily
Family: Amaryllidaceae
Grows up to: 18 x 12 inches (45 x 30cm)
Fills a room with sweet citrussy scent

A shade-loving woodland plant from South Africa, the long, strappy green leaves arch elegantly outward as if making way for the tall stems of clustered orange, yellow, or apricot blooms. Not only do these flowers bring lovely spring color, some can also fill a room with a sweet, earthy, slightly citrussy scent. Although natal lilies can be taken outside in summer in temperate climates, this should only be done after the last bloom.

Planting | Plant in an equal mix of soil-based and multipurpose compost in a medium pot, allowing the neck of the rhizome to rest above the surface.

Position | Prefers bright, filtered light and warmth from early spring to fall. Needs a cooler, shady spot through winter. Can be grown outside in warmer climates.

Watering | Avoid overwatering by allowing the top of the compost to dry out between waterings from spring to fall. Keep soil almost dry in winter.

Feeding | Feed monthly between spring and early fall with a half-strength balanced liquid fertilizer. Do not feed in winter.

Also try:
green-tip forest lily
(*Clivia nobilis*)

Watch out for:
Restrict roots to encourage flowering, and avoid repotting into a larger vessel. If grown outside, bring indoors before frost.

SIAM TULIP - *Curcuma alismatifolia*

toxic

medium
care rating

Also known as: summer tulip;
lotus ginger
Family: Zingiberaceae
Grows up to: 24 x 24 inches (60 x 60cm)
An exotic "summer tulip"

Native to Thailand and Cambodia, this rhizomatous plant is a member of the ginger family and can grow as a relatively large clumping shrub in the wild. Also known as the summer tulip, it blooms from late spring to late summer in shades of pink, red, violet, and brown (depending on the cultivar). The tuliplike "blooms" are actually colored bracts with true flowers inside, which rise from an upright clump of lush dark green leaves.

Planting | Create a well-draining environment by lining a medium pot with gravel. Add bulb fiber compost and plant the rhizome 3 inches (7.5cm) below the surface in spring.

Position | Place in bright light but out of direct sun. Thrives in high humidity—a warm, steamy bathroom or kitchen is ideal.

Watering | Keep compost moist during spring and summer. Set on a tray of damp pebbles and mist regularly. Reduce to almost dry soil in fall and winter.

Feeding | Feed with a balanced liquid fertilizer every two weeks from spring to late summer.

Also try:
white flowers (*Curcuma alismatifolia* 'Siam Shadow')

Watch out for:
To aid reblooming, cut off spent flower stems and dying leaves after flowering.

NARCISSUS - *Narcissus* spp.

toxic

easy
care rating

Including: daffodil; paperwhite
Family: Amaryllidaceae
Grows up to: 16 x 4 inches (40 x 10cm)
Beautiful trumpet-shaped flowers

Six petal-like sepals around a cup- or trumpet-shaped corona are the defining features of the *Narcissus* genus, which boasts around fifty species. Native to the meadows and woods of southern Europe and North Africa, there are now numerous single-, double-, and umbel-flowered hybrids and cultivars in shades of white, cream, yellow, and orange. Highly scented paperwhite narcissi (*Narcissus papyraceus*) are particularly popular as winter holiday plants.

Planting | Line a deep, wide pot with gravel. Top with bulb fiber compost or two parts soil to one part grit. Plant bulbs in fall, pointed end up, with tips just above the surface.

Position | Place on a bright, sunny windowsill in an unheated room. Narcissi can also be planted outdoors, ideally in groups of bulbs that almost touch.

Watering | Water after planting and keep compost just moist through winter. When leaves and flowers appear, water every other day. Do not water after dying down.

Feeding | Feed every two weeks with a balanced liquid fertilizer after flowering, while the leaves are dying down. Do not feed during the dormant period.

Also try:
paperwhite (*Narcissus papyraceus* 'Ziva' or *Narcissus tazetta*)

Watch out for: They have long roots and need a pot that ideally provides for around 12 inches (30cm) of growth.

SNOWDROP - *Galanthus* spp.

toxic

easy
care rating

Including: common snowdrop; greater snowdrop
Family: Amaryllidaceae
Grows up to: 8 x 3 inches (20 x 7.5cm)
Collect a theater of snowdrops

Each tiny bulb of this winter-flowering favorite produces two bright green leaves and a single flower stem. The white pendulous blooms are formed of two whorls, the delicate yet tough flowers known to push up even through snow, hence the common name. Of the twenty *Galanthus* species, there are numerous collectible cultivars of various shapes, sizes, and green markings, increasingly displayed as a theater of specimens.

Planting | Plant snowdrops "in the green" (just after flowering) in early spring or as dry bulbs in late fall in a well-draining mix of two parts soil to one part grit.

Position | Thrives in light to moderate shade, although the greater snowdrop (*Galanthus elwesii*) prefers full sun to light shade. Position bulbs 2 inches (5cm) deep and apart.

Watering | Water well after planting and keep compost moist until flowering ends. Place on a saucer to allow any excess water to seep out. Drain thoroughly.

Feeding | Feed every two weeks with fertilizer after flowering, while the leaves are dying down.

Also try:
common snowdrop (*Galanthus nivalis*)

Watch out for: Snowdrops can be grown indoors but suffer if grown in soil that dries out or if they get too hot.

HYACINTH - *Hyacinthus orientalis*

toxic

Also known as: common hyacinth; garden hyacinth
Family: Asparagaceae
Grows up to: 10 x 8 inches (25 x 20cm)
Fill your home with heady fragrance

easy
care rating

This classic spring-flowering perennial can also be forced to bloom earlier in winter, making it a popular festive holiday plant as well. Native to parts of the eastern Mediterranean and southwestern Asia, it has been cultivated for hundreds of years, resulting in numerous varieties in shades of blue, pink, purple, white, and apricot. Not only are the spikes of tubular flowers beautiful to look at, they also emit a heady fragrance.

Planting | Plant bulbs in fall, pointed end up so they are just showing above the surface, in a pot of bulb fiber compost or two parts soil-based compost to one part sharp grit.

Position | Place pots somewhere cool or outside in winter. For large flowers and straight stems, allow some full sun as the shoots emerge in spring.

Watering | Water after planting and leave to drain. Keep compost just moist through winter, increasing to consistently moist as leaves and blooms appear.

Feeding | To aid reblooming next year, feed with a liquid seaweed fertilizer every two weeks when the leaves are dying down. Do not feed during the dormant period.

Also try: (*Hyacinth orientalis* 'Delft Blue'); apricot (*H. orientalis* 'Gipsy Queen')

Watch out for: Force blooms to flower early by placing the pot in a dark bag outside. Move to a sunny position inside after 6–8 weeks.

GRAPE HYACINTH - *Muscari* spp.

nontoxic

Also known as: muscari
Family: Asparagaceae
Grows up to: 8 x 4 inches (20 x 10cm)
Perfect in containers of shade-loving plants

easy
care rating

Although part of the same plant family, grape hyacinths are not closely related to the common hyacinth by genus. They do have a certain hyacinth quality about them, however, each tiny bulb producing dainty blue, white, or purple cones of fragrant flowers. Like hyacinths, these early spring favorites are also easy to force, bringing welcome color in winter or for festive holidays. The foliage is lush and grasslike, adding to their wild charm.

Planting | Plant bulbs pointed end up, leaving just the tips exposed, in a small pot of multipurpose compost. Plant bulbs close but not touching to create a clump.

Position | First place in a sheltered spot outside, then move indoors when about to flower. After blooming, place in the shade outside. Blooms can also be forced.

Watering | Water bulbs directly after planting by soaking and draining. Then keep the compost almost dry through winter. Keep the compost moist while flowering.

Feeding | Feed a balanced liquid fertilizer every two weeks after flowering.

Also try: cobalt blue (*Muscari armeniacum*)

Watch out for: Ensure excellent drainage and don't allow outdoor specimens to sit in water over winter as this can cause root rot.

CROCUS - *Crocus* spp.

toxic

easy
care rating

Including: early crocus; snow crocus; fall crocus
Family: Iridaceae
Grows up to: 6 x 4 inches (15 x 10cm)
A joyful harbinger of spring

Native to eastern Europe, crocuses are some of the most joyful harbingers of spring, flowering in shades of purple, yellow, white, and blue depending on the species or cultivar. Favorites include the easily naturalizing woodland crocus (*Crocus tommasinianus*) and the snow crocus (*Crocus chrysanthus*). There are also fall-flowering species, including the edible saffron crocus (*Crocus sativus*).

Planting | Plant corms, pointed side up, in fall. Plant in pots, borders, or grass to a depth of about three times their size. Improve drainage by adding grit to the soil.

Position | Grow outdoors in an open, sunny spot. Indoor pots should first be kept in a cold, dark place for 12–15 weeks, then moved somewhere warm and bright.

Watering | Water bulbs thoroughly once planted, then let the surface of the compost become dry between waterings. Overwatering can cause corms to rot.

Feeding | Crocuses don't need feeding but can benefit from a little bone meal or a dressing of rich compost in fall and early spring.

Also try:
woodland crocus (*Crocus tommasinianus*)

Watch out for:
Leaves need to be left to die back naturally in order to produce new blooms the following year.

IRIS - *Iris* spp.

toxic

easy
care rating

Including: bearded iris; miniature iris
Family: Iridaceae
Grows up to: 6 x 4 inches (15 x 10cm)
Choose miniature varieties for pots

The iris is one of the most elegant flowers, taking its genus and common name from the Greek goddess of the rainbow. All irises have three inner petals that stand upright and three outer petals called falls, but there are hundreds of colorful species and cultivars ranging in size. One of the best to grow in containers or indoors is the early miniature iris (*Iris reticulata*), grown in large groups in a single pot or layered with other bulbs.

Planting | Plant bulbs, pointed side up, in late fall in a well-draining pot of soil-based compost and sand. Plant 2 inches (5cm) deep and ½ inch (1cm) apart.

Position | Set indoor pots in a bright, sunny, warm position. Find a sheltered space for outdoor pots. Flowers take about 12 weeks to bloom.

Watering | Place on a tray and water after planting, draining any excess away. Then water when the compost feels dry. Reduce waterings once the leaves die back.

Feeding | Feed a balanced liquid fertilizer or top dressing of rich compost in fall and in spring.

Also try:
bearded iris (*Iris germanica*)

Watch out for: Irises do not like standing water as it can rot the bulbs or rhizomes, so ensure that beds and pots have good drainage.

TULIP - *Tulipa* spp.

toxic

easy
care rating

Including: early, mid-season, and late
Family: Liliaceae
Grows up to: 10 x 8 inches (25 x 20cm)
Create drifts of collectible cultivars

Originally native to southern Europe and central Asia, tulips have been widely cultivated for centuries and have become naturalized around the world. There are now thousands of cultivars, from the single-stemmed, cup-shaped earlies, to the most opulent parrot, double, fringed, or Rembrandt varieties. Taller, heavy-headed tulips do well in outdoor borders, while smaller, low-growing types such as *Tulipa humilis* can be grown indoors.

Planting | Grow in a well-draining pot filled with soil-based compost and sand. Plant in late fall, pointed side up, 2 inches (5cm) deep so tips are exposed and ½ inch (1cm) apart.

Position | First place pot in a cool, frost-free spot. When plants start to sprout, move them to a sunny spot indoors or a sunny, sheltered spot outdoors.

Watering | Soak thoroughly after planting, letting any excess water drain away. Water indoor container tulips when the top layer of compost feels dry.

Feeding | After planting bulbs, top dress with a diluted balanced liquid fertilizer, avoiding the planting hole. Water well to disperse through the soil.

Also try:
low-growing tulip
(*Tulipa humilis*);
single-flowered
(*T.* 'Red Revival')

Watch out for: For
successive flowering,
layer the earliest-
flowering bulbs
8 inches (20cm) deep,
the second-earliest
6 inches (15cm) deep,
and the last just below
the surface.

BONSAI

Created using special techniques that train specimens such as figs, firs, and flowering cherries into miniature form, these charming plants are a good way to make a stylized statement in a smaller space and introduce a Zen or Japanese vibe.

FICUS GINSENG - *Ficus microcarpa*

toxic

medium
care rating

Also known as: Chinese banyan
Family: Moraceae
Grows up to: 40 x 20 inches (100 x 50cm); size as trained
A swollen trunk and glossy green leaves

One of the most popular indoor tree species for bonsai beginners, the ficus ginseng (*Ficus microcarpa*) has amazing swollen roots that stand above the pot, and a mass of short-stemmed, glossy, smooth, deep green oval leaves. It can also be found growing to its natural size as an ornamental street tree in parts of Asia, North Africa, and the Americas. The name "ficus ginseng" is also applied to its relative, *Ficus retusa*, which has slightly longer leaves.

Planting | Plant in a high-quality, free-draining bonsai soil made from beads of dried loam that encourage small feeder roots. Repot every two to three years or when root-bound.

Position | Provide a good amount of light by placing on a bright windowsill or growing under plant lamps. Place outside in the summer months in a warm, sunny spot.

Watering | Water when the soil gets slightly dry, increasing in warm climates. Mist daily but do not drench as this can cause fungal issues.

Feeding | Feed with a specialty bonsai feed or a half-strength balanced liquid fertilizer twice a week in summer and once a month in winter.

Also try:
weeping fig
(*Ficus benjamina*)

Watch out for:
Dry air and a lack of light can weaken the plant, resulting in leaf drop. Use plant lamps and mist frequently to help aid recovery.

SWEET PLUM - *Sagaretia theezans*

 toxic

 medium
care rating

Also known as: Chinese sweet plum; mock buckthorn
Family: Rhamnaceae
Grows up to: 24 x 18 inches (60 x 45cm);
size as trained
The prettiest blooming bonsai

Native to China, this pretty bonsai specimen has stunning rusty red to glossy green foliage and small yellowish-white flowers, giving way to blue plum-shaped fruits and reddish flaky bark. The trunk is slow-growing, so specimens are often pre-grown in fields in order to provide a stout trunk. Evergreen in warmer climates and deciduous in colder temperate zones, they symbolize protection, creativity, and new life—an ideal gift for newborns.

Planting | Plant in a high-quality, free-draining bonsai soil made from beads of dried loam that encourage small feeder roots. Repot every two to three years or when root-bound.

Position | Prefers a bright spot with lots of natural daylight, but avoid direct afternoon or summer sun. Move outside in warm summers but return inside before frosts.

Watering | Water when the soil feels slightly dry by standing briefly in water or drenching from above so the root ball is evenly wet. Drain well. Mist in dry conditions.

Feeding | Feed with a specialty bonsai feed or a half-strength balanced liquid fertilizer twice a week in summer and once a month in winter.

Also try:
pomegranate
(*Punica granatum*)

Watch out for: Trim fast-growing summer shoots to keep them from looking straggly and encourage a compact canopy and healthy budding.

CHINESE ELM - *Ulmus parvifolia*

 toxic

 medium
care rating

Also known as: lacebark elm
Family: Ulmaceae
Grows up to: 12 x 8 inches (30 x 20cm);
size as trained
Ancient-looking with serrated leaves

Indigenous to China and Southeast Asia, this majestic, hardy tree grows to heights of 80 feet (24m) in its natural habitat, with fine branches of small, leathery, single-toothed leaves. As a bonsai it can appear ancient and weathered thanks to its rugged, flaky bark of mottled gray, rust, tan, and red. It's also an ideal specimen thanks to a high tolerance of pruning and a wide range of temperatures, light, and humidity conditions.

Planting | Plant in a high-quality, free-draining bonsai soil made from beads of dried loam that encourage small feeder roots. Repot every two to three years or when root-bound.

Position | Chinese elms thrive in full sun or partial shade and can be left outdoors year-round in temperate climates. In warmer climates, move this plant to a cool spot in winter.

Watering | Water thoroughly when the top layer of soil feels dry, ensuring that the entire root mass is watered. Mist as necessary in hot, dry environments.

Feeding | Feed with bonsai feed or half-strength fertilizer once a week in spring and summer.

Also try: Japanese elm
(*Zelkova serrata*)

Watch out for: Curling or dry, crispy leaves indicate underwatering. Water by dunking the whole pot in a bowl of water and then leaving outside to drain.

GINKGO - *Ginkgo biloba*

toxic

medium
care rating

Also known as: maidenhair tree; fountain of youth
Family: Ginkgoaceae
Grows up to: 16 x 10 inches (40 x 25cm);
size as trained
Keep this living fossil outdoors

As the only living species in its genus, this robust living fossil tree—often grown in temples or as a street tree to help combat pollution, and even surviving the atomic bomb in Hiroshima—makes a symbolic as well as beautiful bonsai, suitable for growing outside. Leaves are uniquely fan-shaped, turning from green to golden in fall, while the small, unpleasant-smelling fruits are rare in this diminutive form. As a gift it symbolizes longevity.

Planting | Plant in a high-quality, free-draining bonsai soil or standard, well-draining soil-based compost. Repot young plants annually, mature specimens every two to five years.

Position | Place outside all year round in a sunny position or semi-shade for younger specimens. It can withstand frost, but protect the root ball of pot-grown specimens.

Watering | Water so that the soil stays moist during periods of growth in spring and summer. Reduce in winter so that the soil is almost dry.

Feeding | Feed with a bonsai fertilizer or half-strength balanced liquid fertilizer from spring until the leaves turn yellow in fall. Do not feed in winter.

Also try:
ficus ginseng (*Ficus microcarpa*)

Watch out for:
It is incredibly resilient and rarely suffers from pests or fungal diseases; ensure it is watered well but not overlogged.

CHINESE JUNIPER - *Juniperus chinensis*

toxic

medium
care rating

Also known as: juniper
Family: Cupressaceae
Grows up to: 28 x 20 inches (70 x 50cm);
size as trained
Can be displayed with stripped bark

This evergreen coniferous bonsai has dark green needles, small, blue-black, berrylike cones, and a gnarled, twisted trunk. It can be crafted into a variety of styles, including upright formal, slanting, semi-cascade, and full cascade with contrasting exposed deadwood. Native to China, Japan, Korea, and other parts of East Asia, it forms a small tree or large bush in the wild, popular cultivars for bonsai including the dwarf, vase-shaped 'Shimpaku'.

Planting | Plant in a high-quality, free-draining bonsai soil or standard, well-draining soil-based compost. Repot young trees every two years, older ones less frequently.

Position | Place outdoors year-round in a bright location with lots of sunlight. Protect during periods of extreme cold or frost. Do not bring indoors.

Watering | Let the top layer of soil dry out between waterings. Do not overwater. Mist regularly, especially after repotting.

Feeding | Feed a half-strength balanced liquid fertilizer weekly during the growing season.

Also try:
Japanese black pine (*Pinus thunbergii*)

Watch out for:
Cut long shoots that stick out at the base during the growing season to develop foliage pads.

JAPANESE MAPLE - *Acer palmatum*

nontoxic

medium
care rating

Also known as: palmate maple
Family: Sapindaceae
Grows up to: 40 x 10 inches (100 x 25cm);
size as trained
A lovely colorful tree for courtyards

One of the most colorful bonsai trees, the Japanese maple boasts five-pointed, hand-shaped foliage that changes color throughout the year from fresh green or bronze in spring, to bright green in summer, to bright crimson in fall. In winter, the leaves drop to reveal the beautiful gray bark and silhouette. Native to Japan, China, and Korea, there are several varieties, including the red-leaved 'Deshojo' and 'Seigen'. Ideal for courtyards.

Planting | Plant in a high-quality, free-draining bonsai soil mixed with pumice and lava rock. Repot every two years as the strong roots grow quickly and need pruning.

Position | Place outside in bright, filtered light, avoiding direct sun, which can cause leaves to scorch. Although frost-hardy, it will need to be protected in extreme cold.

Watering | Water daily with rainwater or distilled water during the growing season, increasing to several times a day on hotter days. Avoid drought but do not waterlog.

Feeding | Feed every two to three weeks in early spring with a high-nitrogen fertilizer. Then feed every two weeks with a half-strength balanced liquid fertilizer until fall.

Also try: Japanese flowering cherry (*Prunus serrulata*)

Watch out for: Pinch out new shoots in early spring when one or two pairs of leaves have formed to retain the desired shape; treat aphids with dish soap.

DWARF JADE - *Portulacaria afra*

toxic

medium
care rating

Also known as: miniature jade
Family: Didiereaceae
Grows up to: 12 x 12 inches (30 x 30cm);
size as trained
Symbolizes good luck and prosperity

Native to dry regions of South Africa, the dwarf jade is a soft, fleshy, woody tree with a thick, craggy trunk, fine branch structure, and green, oval-shaped padded leaves. Similar in appearance to the jade plant (*Crassula ovata*) but with smaller leaves, both plants are suitable for bonsai and require similar easy-care conditions, including a warm, sunny position indoors. As gifts, jade plants symbolize good luck and prosperity.

Planting | Plant in a high-quality, free-draining bonsai soil. Repot every two years in spring, being careful not to water for a week after repotting to allow damaged roots to dry.

Position | Grow in a warm, sunny spot indoors in temperate zones. If your plant is receiving enough bright light, it will develop red tips on the leaves.

Watering | Allow the top layer of soil to dry out slightly between waterings. Reduce watering in winter, especially if kept in a cooler spot.

Feeding | Feed monthly from spring to fall with a half-strength balanced liquid fertilizer.

Also try: jade plant (*Crassula ovata*)

Watch out for: Prune regularly to force it to grow branches on the lower trunk. Be cautious if wiring as this can easily damage the soft trunk.

EDIBLES

Growing your own herbs, spices, fruits, and vegetables can be incredibly rewarding, not just in terms of a potential crop but also because of how beautiful and vital many of these plants can be. Use the following guide to narrow down preferences in terms of use, aroma, looks, and taste.

1

Uses

Many herbs and spices have been around for thousands of years. Properties suitable for nourishing, healing, and styling have been documented since antiquity, from calming lavender (page 207) and pungent oregano (page 195), to pretty-flowered dill (page 199). All of these can be grown indoors as well as in pots or raised beds in the garden. A surprisingly wide range of nutritious fruits and vegetables can also be grown in containers or indoors, from microgreens (page 213) to spring onions and celery (page 215).

2

Flavor

Choosing what to plant based on flavor is of huge importance if your main focus is on cooking. Fill sunny windowsills with basil (page 194), rosemary (page 196), and thyme (page 196). Try growing your own ginger (page 204), which also makes a beautiful houseplant, or chili (page 214), choosing from mild and hot cultivars, which can be grown in pots year-round. It's even possible to grow your own black pepper (page 205), although this might be a more bountiful conversation than crop.

3

Aroma

Smell and taste are closely linked, with just the mere hint of a delicious aroma creating an appetite for the food to come. Weave such scents into your garden or home as well as your cooking, from invigorating rosemary (page 196), wonderful in soups, stews, and casseroles, to citrus-fresh cilantro (page 198), ideal for salads, sauces, and garnishes. Fragrant herbs are also lovely in drinks (see The Cocktail Garden, page 58) including lemon verbena (page 201), mint (page 195), and tarragon (page 200).

4

Color

Color stimulates the senses, warms the emotions, and adds style to food and drinks. Celebrate different shades of green herbs. Grow bright blue borage flowers or purple violas or violets (page 203) to freeze in ice or decorate cocktails. Choose from variously hued cultivars of heritage tomatoes (page 213) to create an interesting salad, plus add variety in an edible garden. Or try growing red and green cut-and-come-again lettuce leaves (page 212) or bright orange calendulas (page 202). All in all, a whole rainbow of goodness.

5

Season

Plan your edible container garden to produce a succession of crops through the year, many of which can be grown in pots or containers indoors or on terraces or balconies. Fresh salads and radishes in spring; edible flowers and sweet, juicy fruits such as strawberries and raspberries in summer; squashes and pumpkins—which can also be used to decorate your home—in fall; and kale and Swiss chard in winter. Use herbs to add another layer of seasonality.

6

Harvest

While you may not produce a huge harvest from growing fruits or vegetables in containers or pots, what you can do is ensure that everything you grow is of the very best quality. Even a few home-grown alpine strawberries (page 210) now and again can make the difference in a breakfast bowl or pudding. Some container crops do keep on giving, however, including different types of microgreens (page 213) and a wide variety of evergreen, semi-evergreen, and cut-and-come again herbs.

7

Care

Growing your own herbs, fruits, and vegetables can require quite specific plant care, from the need for organic potting soil, to the timing of planting seeds or potting up outside, to nutrient-boosting feeding regimes. Pay due diligence to such requirements using the Personal Plant Selector as a guide. Enjoy getting acquainted with nature's life cycles while nurturing leaves, flowers, fruits, and seeds, and with them, a growing connection to what we know as food.

HERBS AND SPICES

Herbs and spices, from basil, oregano, and lavender to ginger and turmeric, are some of the most rewarding plants to grow at home, providing instant access to aromatic, flavorsome, or healing stems, leaves, flowers, seeds, and even roots.

BASIL - *Ocimum basilicum*

nontoxic

easy
care rating

Also known as: sweet basil; common basil
Family: Lamiaceae
Grows up to: 20 x 20 inches (50 x 50cm)
The perfect herb for a sunny windowsill

This aromatic annual or biennial tender herb has bright green, broadly ovate leaves and spikes of tubular white or pink-tinged flowers in late summer if left to bloom. The leaves and flowers are edible and often used in Mediterranean cooking, on pasta or pizza, or in salads. Grow on the kitchen windowsill to provide a continuous supply of fresh leaves, pinching out to actively promote new growth. Experiment with different varieties.

Planting | Grow as an annual in a medium, well-draining container of organic potting soil. Can be grown from seed indoors in early spring or outdoors in summer.

Position | If grown indoors, place on a sunny windowsill, where it may even survive the winter. Outdoors, place in a sunny, sheltered position when all risk of frost is gone.

Watering | Water freely in summer in the morning. Do not waterlog. Reduce watering during winter for overwintering plants.

Feeding | Feed indoor plants monthly from spring to fall with a half-strength balanced liquid or organic fertilizer. Feed outdoor plants every two weeks.

Also try:
Thai basil
(*Ocimum basilicum* var. *thyrsiflora*); lemon basil
(*Ocimum × africanum*)

Watch out for:
Pinch out flowerheads as they appear to ensure continued leaf growth, and cut back after flowering. Check regularly for aphids and mildew.

OREGANO - *Origanum vulgare*

 nontoxic

 easy *care rating*

Also known as: wild marjoram; herb of joy
Family: Lamiaceae
Grows up to: 3.2 x 3.2 feet (1 x 1m)
Try Greek or golden varieties

This heat-loving "herb of joy," used in Mediterranean and Mexican cooking and as a medicinal herb, can be grown indoors or out, alone or with herbs that like the same conditions. Often confused with its close relative marjoram (*Origanum majorana*) due to similar oval-shaped leaves, square stems, and whorled flower spikes, oregano's scent and flavor is much more pungent, camphorous, and bitter, and the flowers a deeper pinky purple.

Planting | Sow in early spring or plant in late spring and summer in organic potting soil. Move seedlings outside only when all risk of frost has passed.

Position | Grow indoors in small terra-cotta pots or in boxes by a bright window with plenty of morning sun. Grow outdoors in summer in a sunny, sheltered spot.

Watering | Let the top layer of soil dry out between waterings. Water regularly but do not waterlog. Oregano can cope with periods of drought.

Feeding | Feed with a half-strength balanced liquid or organic fertilizer or fortify with compost. Some fertilizers can change the taste of herbs, so you can experiment.

Also try: golden oregano (*Origanum vulgare* 'Aureum')

Watch out for: Cut back when unruly; should reduce the need for repotting. Indoor plants may need to be replaced after six months.

MINT - *Mentha* spp.

 nontoxic

 easy *care rating*

Including: peppermint; spearmint
Family: Lamiaceae
Grows up to: 3.2 x 3.2 feet (1 x 1m)
Ideal for making fresh mint tea

This uplifting herb grows in almost every part of the world as one of over twenty different species. This includes spearmint/garden mint (*Mentha spicata*), apple/pineapple mint (*Mentha suaveolens*), peppermint (*Mentha × piperita*), and pennyroyal (*Mentha pulegium*). All are easily grown inside or out, providing a source of fresh or dried mint for culinary purposes, tea, or well-being.

Planting | Plant young specimens in medium-sized pots of organic potting soil in spring. Pots help to contain spreading. Rotate pots every few days for even growth.

Position | Mint prefers bright, indirect light. It will die back fully outdoors in winter but only a little indoors if given warmth and light. Dry or freeze leaves for later use.

Watering | Water well after planting. Water regularly to keep the soil moist, but don't waterlog. Cuttings can also be grown in a water-filled glass or bottle for use inside.

Feeding | Mint is exceptionally vigorous and doesn't need help with growth.

Also try: spearmint/garden mint (*Mentha spicata*)

Watch out for: Rejuvenate congested clumps by removing the root ball, splitting in half, and repotting.

ROSEMARY - *Salvia rosmarinus*

nontoxic

easy
care rating

Including: upright rosemary;
prostrate rosemary
Family: Lamiaceae
Grows up to: 60 x 60 inches (150 x 150cm)
Drought-tolerant but needs lots of sun

Native to the coastal dry scrub and rocky hillsides of the Mediterranean, this aromatic herb was formerly part of the now-defunct genus *Rosmarinus*, which means "dew of the sea." A woody shrub with panicles of blue-purple tubular, lipped flowers, just a few sprigs can instantly add depth to a stew, casserole, or roast. It can also be grown as an anti-inflammatory, antibacterial medicinal herb, and used in hair tonics, bath oils, teas, and cleaning products.

Planting | Plant outdoors in well-drained soil in a sunny, sheltered position. Grow indoor plants in an equal mix of soil-based and cactus compost.

Position | Rosemary needs six to eight hours of direct sunshine, so a sunny patio or windowsill is ideal. Indoor plants may need the help of a bright fluorescent light to really thrive.

Watering | Make sure any pots have good drainage. Water when the top of the soil feels dry, or more in hot weather. Do not waterlog or let dry out completely.

Feeding | Feed plants in containers with a half-strength balanced liquid or organic fertilizer after flowering is finished. Expose new plants to sunlight before bringing indoors.

Also try:
semi-prostrate rosemary (*Salvia rosmarinus* 'Prostratus')

Watch out for:
Place outdoor pots on feet and apply a thick mulch around plants in the ground for protection from cold.

THYME - *Thymus* spp.

nontoxic

easy
care rating

Including: common thyme;
lemon thyme
Family: Lamiaceae
Grows up to: 20 x 20 inches (50 x 50cm)
Grow to add to a bouquet garni

This tiny-leaved, warmly pungent herb has been cultivated since ancient times. A key component of the flavoring herb mix bouquet garni, along with parsley and bay leaf, and delicious in roasts, biscuits, cakes, breads, and vinegars, it also contains naturally antibacterial and antiseptic thymol, which can be used to soothe the throat in the form of syrup or tea. The nectar-rich pink, purple, or white flowers are also great for the bees.

Planting | Grow indoors in a well-draining equal mix of soil-based and cactus compost in a breathable terra-cotta pot. Grow outdoors in three parts soil to one part sand.

Position | Thyme needs a lot of light. A windowsill or sunny patio with six to eight hours of direct sun is ideal. For shady indoor spots, fluorescent grow lights can help.

Watering | Water when the top layer of soil is dry, then saturate. Do not allow to become waterlogged. It can survive periods of drought.

Feeding | Thyme prefers nutrient-poor soil and is often better planted alone.

Also try:
lemon variegated thyme (*Thymus* 'Lemon Variegated')

Watch out for:
If thyme begins to flower, this is not a sign that it is bolting. You can eat the flowers, too.

SAGE - *Salvia officinalis*

nontoxic

easy
care rating

Also known as: garden sage;
common sage; culinary sage
Family: Lamiaceae
Grows up to: 3.2 x 3.2 feet (1 x 1m)
Steep the pungent leaves in vinegar or oil

A woody shrub with soft, hairy, gray-green leaves, blue-purple flowers, and a warm minty-floral aroma and taste can be grown as an attractive border plant or contained in a pot. Delicious in roasts and stuffing, it can also be used medicinally as a tea, in vinegar, or as a sore throat gargle. Grown outside, it can sprawl and grow quite large, but in a pot it stays relatively contained, where it can be harvested all year round.

Planting | Grow indoors in a well-draining equal mix of soil-based and cactus compost in a breathable terra-cotta pot. Grow outdoors in three parts soil to one part sand.

Position | Sage also likes a lot of sun. A sunny windowsill or patio with at least six to eight hours of direct sunlight is ideal. Or supplement indoors with fluorescent grow lights.

Watering | Wait until the top of the soil feels dry before watering. Increase watering during hot weather but do not waterlog. Sage can survive periods of drought.

Feeding | Can benefit from feeding with a half-strength balanced liquid or organic fertilizer every two weeks during the summer growing season.

Also try:
purple sage
(*Salvia officinalis*
'Purpurascens')

Watch out for: Pruning plants after flowering helps to maintain an attractive shape and encourages lots of healthy new growth.

CHERVIL - *Anthriscus cerefolium*

nontoxic

easy
care rating

Also known as: common chervil; French parsley; gourmet's parsley
Family: Apiaceae
Grows up to: 20 x 20 inches (50 x 50cm)
Flavorsome leaves

Easily confused with potentially toxic members of the carrot family such as hemlock (*Conium maculatum*), it's therefore a good idea to grow your own. The feathery, parsleylike leaves have a mild, sweet aniseed flavor, while the delicate umbels of tiny white flowers mature into long-beaked fruits. A traditional ingredient of the French herb mix fines herbes, it is often used to add color and flavor to sauces, fish, or eggs.

Planting | Sow seed directly into organic potting compost through spring and summer. Thin out so seedlings are 6 inches (15cm) apart or grow in separate pots.

Position | Grow in a cool, part-shady spot indoors or out. Plants will run to seed if subjected to high indoor temperatures or dry, sunny weather. Can survive winter under a cloche.

Watering | Water plants regularly, especially during hot, dry summers. Keep soil moist but do not waterlog as this can rot seeds or roots.

Feeding | Feed with a high-nitrogen fertilizer when seedlings are three to four weeks old to boost leaf growth. Create a continuous supply by sowing a succession of seeds.

Also try:
curly chervil
(*Anthriscus cerefolium*
'Crispum')

Watch out for:
Can grow quite tall, so clip the tops regularly for bushier growth and a continuous supply of leaves.

CILANTRO - *Coriandrum sativum*

nontoxic

easy
care rating

Also known as: coriander
Family: Apiaceae
Grows up to: 20 x 20 inches (50 x 50cm)
Delicious citrusy leaves and earthy seeds

Thought to be native to the eastern Mediterranean and Pakistan, cilantro has been cultivated around the world for thousands of years. Historically grown as a cooling, digestive medicinal herb, the round, earthy brown seeds and citrusy parsleylike leaves are a key ingredient of many Asian, Middle Eastern, and South American cuisines. Plants can be treated as a cut-and-come-again crop or allowed to bolt for harvesting seeds.

Planting | Grow indoors in a well-draining equal mix of soil-based and cactus compost in a breathable terra-cotta pot. Grow outdoors in three parts soil to one part sand.

Position | Prefers bright, filtered light with some shade in the height of summer. Partial shade can also help combat bolting, although it will weaken indoor plants.

Watering | Water when the top layer of soil feels dry. Then soak thoroughly until the water comes through the drainage holes. Increase watering during warm summer months.

Feeding | Feed a half-strength fertilizer through the growing season of spring and summer.

Also try:
lemon coriander
(*Coriandrum sativum*
'Lemon')

Watch out for:
Can become spindly; pinch out at the tips to force bushier growth.

PARSLEY - *Petroselinum crispum*

nontoxic   **easy**
care rating

Also known as: curly parsley; ache
Family: Apiaceae
Grows up to: 18 x 18 inches (45 x 45cm)
Choose from flat-leaved and curly varieties

Native to just a very small area of the Balkans, this vitamin- and mineral-rich herb has been cultivated since ancient times for its leaves, seeds, and roots. The species type has curly green leaves, traditionally used as a retro garnish, while more cultivated types such as French (*Petroselinum crispum* 'French') or Italian (*Petroselinum crispum* var. *neapolitanum*) have flat leaves that work better in dishes such as Middle Eastern tabbouleh.

Planting | Grow as an annual, succession sowing through spring and summer each year. Use a breathable pot and well-draining organic potting soil.

Position | Place in a bright spot indoors or out. Outdoor plants can tolerate partial shade. Indoor plants can get spindly, so sow successively or move outside in summer.

Watering | Water when the top layer of soil feels dry, soaking until it runs through the drainage holes. Keep soil moist but don't waterlog as this can cause root rot.

Feeding | Parsley is a heavy feeder and will appreciate a monthly feed of an organic liquid fertilizer such as seaweed.

Also try:
flat-leaved French parsley (*Petroselinum crispum* 'French')

Watch out for:
Harvest stems from the outside of the plant, as this will encourage more growth.

DILL - *Anethum graveolens*

nontoxic   **easy**
care rating

Also known as: Anet
Family: Apiaceae
Grows up to: 20 x 20 inches (50 x 50cm)
A lovely accompaniment for fish

Similar in appearance to fennel (*Foeniculum vulgare*), dill's feathery blue-green leaves and flat umbels of tiny yellow flowers also have a sweet aniseed scent and taste. Widely used in Eurasia and Scandinavia to flavor food or pickles, this cool-season herb can also be grown as a pollinator-friendly ornamental dotted among other shrubs and flowering plants. It's also ideal as a companion plant for cucumbers.

Planting | Sow seed from spring to early summer in organic potting soil. Choose a well-draining container at least 12 inches (30cm) deep to accommodate the long tap root.

Position | Thin plants out to 12 inches (30cm) apart, or up to two plants per medium pot. Grow in a sunny spot with at least six hours of sunlight, or supplement with grow lights.

Watering | Allow the top layer of soil to dry out between waterings. Soak thoroughly, then drain. Water freely in dry conditions to inhibit bolting.

Feeding | For indoor or container dill, apply a half-strength balanced liquid fertilizer monthly.

Also try:
dwarf dill (*Anethum graveolens* 'Fernleaf')

Watch out for:
Can become tall and leggy; stake plants for additional support or pinch tops to encourage growth.

TARRAGON - *Artemisia dracunculus*

nontoxic

easy
care rating

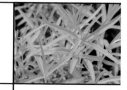

Also known as: estragon
Family: Asteraceae
Grows up to: 40 x 20 inches (100 x 50cm)
Use to flavor sauces, vinegar, and as a digestive

Found wild in parts of Eurasia and North America, this lance-leaved, rarely flowering, anise-flavored plant is also cultivated around the world as a culinary herb. The most popular is French or true tarragon (*Artemisia dracunculus* var. *sativa*) used in béarnaise sauce, fines herbes, infused in white wine vinegar, and as a digestive. Russian tarragon (*Artemisia dracunculus* var. *inodora*) has a more subtle flavor.

Planting | Plant indoors in a well-draining equal mix of soil-based and cactus compost in a breathable terra-cotta pot. Grow outdoors in three parts soil to one part sand.

Position | Grow outdoors in a sunny, sheltered spot, overwintering in a greenhouse or porch. Grow indoors in a bright spot with at least six hours of sunlight.

Watering | Water when the top layer of compost feels dry. Soak, then drain well. Increase watering in hot conditions.

Feeding | Tarragon doesn't require any fertilizer to thrive, plus it could affect the delicate taste—ensure lots of organic compost is dug in before planting instead.

Also try:
French or true tarragon (*Artemisia dracunculus* var. *sativa*)

Watch out for:
Pinch out flowers for a constant supply of leaves.

CHIVE - *Allium schoenoprasum*

nontoxic

easy
care rating

Also known as: common chive; allium
Family: Amaryllidaceae
Grows up to: 20 x 4 inches (50 x 10cm)
Snip with scissors for an oniony garnish

A close relative of onions, garlic, shallots, leeks, scallions, and ornamental alliums, chives are bulb-forming perennials with long, hollow scapes (the stems), grasslike leaves, and a small inflorescence of star-shaped pale purple petals. Native to temperate areas of Europe, Asia, and North America, all parts of the plant are edible, with just a few snips of the stems providing a mild onionlike flavor or garnish to a range of hot and cold dishes.

Planting | Plant indoors in a well-draining equal mix of soil-based and cactus compost in a breathable terra-cotta pot. Grow outdoors in three parts soil to one part sand.

Position | Grow outdoors in full sun. Grow indoors in a bright, sunny spot with at least six to eight hours of direct sunlight. Rotate the pot for even growth.

Watering | Let the soil dry out between waterings. Then soak thoroughly and allow to drain. Chives also enjoy a bit of humidity, so lightly mist between waterings.

Feeding | Feed a half-strength balanced fertilizer every two weeks from spring to fall.

Also try:
garlic chive (*Allium tuberosum*)

Watch out for:
Snip off flowers to encourage new leaves. Late summer, cut leaves down to just above soil level.

LEMON VERBENA - *Aloysia citrodora*

nontoxic

easy
care rating

Also known as: lemon bee bush
Family: Verbenaceae
Grows up to: 24 x 24 inches (60 x 60cm)
Grow a steady source of lemon-flavored tea

Native to parts of South America, this perennial shrub or subshrub can grow quite large in the wild, reaching 10 feet (3m) tall. Grown in a pot, it rarely exceeds 24 inches (60cm), but what it lacks in height it makes up for in the most delicious lemon sherbet scent and taste. The bruised leaves can be used to flavor roasts, marinades, salad dressings, jams, or puddings, and are also used to make herbal tea.

Planting | Grow in free-draining soil outdoors or soil-based compost indoors, in a breathable, well-draining pot. In tropical climes it can be grown as a shrub.

Position | Place in full sun outdoors or in at least six hours of bright daylight indoors. Supplement with grow lamps if necessary to prevent leggy growth or leaf drop.

Watering | Water regularly between spring and fall so that the soil stays moist. Do not waterlog. Plants overwintering indoors can be kept on the dry side.

Feeding | Feed in spring with a half-strength balanced liquid or organic fertilizer. Watering with compost tea can also keep plants productive.

Also try:
lemon balm (*Melissa officinalis*)

Watch out for:
Potted plants moving indoors for winter may lose all or some of their leaves. Repot in spring with fresh compost.

CALENDULA - *Calendula officinalis*

nontoxic

easy
care rating

Also known as: common marigold; golds
Family: Asteraceae
Grows up to: 20 x 20 inches (50 x 50cm)
Brightens up windowsills or patios

This bright orange, sunny-flowered plant adds a welcome burst of summer and fall color to gardens, patios, balconies, or windowsills. It has myriad uses as a medicinal and culinary herb, from the key ingredient in skin-soothing balms to an edible flower in salads or spring rolls. It's also super easy to grow and a rewarding beginner plant for children or those new to gardening. There are also lots of sunset-colored varieties to try.

Planting | Grow from seed in light, free-draining soil or well-draining organic potting soil. Ensure pots have adequate drainage as calendulas hate soggy feet.

Position | Calendulas prefer full sun indoors or out, but can thrive in partial shade. Indoors, a sunny windowsill is ideal. It also works well in mixed containers.

Watering | Keep just moist by letting the soil dry out between waterings. Soak well, then allow to drain. Increase watering during hot spells but don't waterlog.

Feeding | Can benefit from the occasional use of a half-strength balanced fertilizer.

Also try: *Calendula officinalis* 'Indian Prince'

Watch out for: Sow by seed, as seedlings do not transfer well. Deadhead regularly to prolong flowering.

CORNFLOWER - *Centaurea cyanus*

nontoxic

easy
care rating

Also known as: bachelor's button
Family: Asteraceae
Grows up to: 40 x 40 inches (100 x 100cm)
The prettiest blue edible flower

This pretty annual grassland wildflower and herb once grew freely in the wild. Today it has been marginalized by monoculture farming practices but is thankfully increasingly grown on verges, in wildflower meadows, and as a garden ornamental or herb. The bright blue, slightly frilly petaled flowers are also edible and can be used in salads or baking, or used to make a natural dye. It is also traditionally used as an eye-soothing herb.

Planting | Grow from seed in fall or spring in borders, raised beds, or in pots of well-drained or sandy soil. If germinating indoors, move seedlings outside in spring.

Position | Prefers full sun but can tolerate some shade. Plant toward the back of a bed in drifts as they grow quite tall, or use dwarf species for pots or window boxes.

Watering | Water regularly but only when the top layer of soil feels dry. Soak well, then allow to drain. Increase watering during hot spells but don't waterlog.

Feeding | Cornflowers prefer poor soil, as they do in the wild, so no fertilizer is required. They prefer a neutral to slightly alkaline soil.

Also try:
blue cornflower
(*Centaurea cyanus*
'Blue Boy')

Watch out for:
Stalks can easily
become floppy or
flattened by the wind
or rain, so stake while
young.

VIOLA - *Viola* spp.

nontoxic

easy
care rating

Including: viola heartsease; sweet violet
Family: Violaceae
Grows up to: 10 x 10 inches (25 x 25cm)
A lovely garnish for cakes or ice cubes

The *Viola* genus contains around 500 different low-growing species of tiny, five-petaled flowers and simple or lobed leaves. Many are grown as ornamentals, such as larger flowered pansies (*Viola x wittrockiana*), but some also have well-known medicinal and edible properties, including the purple, yellow, and cream viola heartsease (*Viola tricolor*) and the deliciously fragranced, deep purple sweet violet (*Viola odorata*).

Planting | Grow as an annual, biennial, or short-lived evergreen perennial in a border or pot. Plant or sow in moderately fertile soil or soil-based compost.

Position | Prefers full sun or partial shade, but avoid hot summer sun. Perfect for containers with other cool-season plants, on a sunny windowsill, or to edge paths.

Watering | Water regularly but only when the top layer of soil feels dry. Soak well and allow to drain. Increase watering during hot spells but don't waterlog.

Feeding | Feed with a slow-release or balanced fertilizer in the spring and late summer.

Also try:
horned violet (*Viola
cornuta*)

Watch out for:
Deadhead faded flowers
by pinching off blooms
at the base of the
flower stem to promote
blooming.

GINGER - *Zingiber officinale*

nontoxic

medium
care rating

Also known as: common ginger;
Chinese ginger
Family: Zingiberaceae
Grows up to: 40 x 20 inches (100 x 50cm)
Grow a steady supply of spicy ginger

Growing your own ginger inside or out (in tropical zones) can be a revelation that provides not just a steady culinary supply of the spicy, fleshy rhizome, but also beautiful bladed foliage and purple-edged flowers arising from pseudostems (the rolled bases of leaves). Originating in Southeast Asia, its warming, circulation-boosting properties have been known about for hundreds of years.

Planting | Plant two or three rhizomes 1 inch (2.5cm) deep, buds facing up, in a large, deep pot of fertile, well-draining soil or compost.

Position | In temperate climates, grow in a warm, shaded or partially shaded place indoors in winter and move outside when there is no risk of frost.

Watering | Water when the top layer of soil starts to dry out. Your plant will appreciate regular watering but does not like soggy soil, so check that it is always well drained.

Feeding | Fertilizer is seldom required for plants grown in tropical or semi-tropical climates. For pot-grown plants, keep adding fresh fertile soil as more stems emerge.

Also try:
Japanese ginger
(*Zingiber mioga*)

Watch out for:
If your ginger is thriving, the rhizome should multiply and you can dig some up to eat. If not, cut some off at least 2.5 inches (5cm) from the stem.

TURMERIC - *Curcuma longa*

nontoxic

medium
care rating

Also known as: pink-blooming ginger
Family: Zingiberaceae
Grows up to: 60 x 24 inches (100 x 60cm)
Keep planting for a constant supply of
golden roots

Although most people know turmeric as a bright yellow fleshy root or golden powdered spice, it can also be grown as an indoor or outdoor (in tropical zones) plant, as an ornamental or to produce a steady supply of the edible rhizome. Native to India and Southeast Asia, with bladed green leaves and greenish-white, occasionally pink flowers, it can grow quite tall in the wild but can be restrained in a pot.

Planting | For indoor plants, place rhizomes in large, deep pots in late winter or early spring, in well-draining fertile soil or potting compost. Can be grown outside in tropical climates.

Position | Keep plants very warm as they are sprouting; a heat mat can help. They can then be moved to a sunny spot, transferring outside in summer if warm enough.

Watering | Water regularly so that the soil stays moist, every two to three days during the growing season. Water slowly to avoid drowning the rhizome.

Feeding | Feed monthly in spring and summer with a half-strength balanced liquid or organic fertilizer. Do not feed in winter.

Also try:
ginger (*Zingiber officinale*)

Watch out for:
Roots are ready for harvesting when the leaves and stem turn brown, about seven to ten months after planting.

BLACK PEPPER - *Piper nigrum*

nontoxic

hard
care rating

Also known as: common pepper; peppercorn plant
Family: Piperaceae
Grows up to: 78 x 18 inches (200 x 45cm)
Grow your own black, white, and green pepper

Originating from southern India, this perennial climbing vine is now cultivated through the tropics and widely used as a spice and seasoning around the world. The almond-shaped, tapering leaves branch out from a central stem among which clustered spikes of white to yellow-green flowers appear. These then develop into berrylike drupe fruits, ripening from green to red and picked in stages to make green, white, and black pepper.

Planting | Propagate from seed or plant in fertile, well-draining soil or potting soil mixed with sand in a large, deep pot. A trellis can help support the vine.

Position | Grow indoors in partial shade or filtered sunlight in a warm, humid environment, or in full sun for cooler spots. It can only be grown outdoors in subtropical/tropical climates.

Watering | Keep the soil moist but don't waterlog. Raise humidity by placing the pot on a tray of damp pebbles and misting regularly with rainwater or distilled water.

Feeding | Apply a half-strength balanced fertilizer at the beginning of the growing season.

Also try:
chili pepper (*Capsicum annuum* spp.)

Watch out for:
Harvest at different stages of maturation. Drying peppercorns in the hot sun makes them wrinkly.

BAY - *Laurus nobilis*

nontoxic   **easy** *care rating*

Also known as: bay tree; sweet bay; bay laurel
Family: Lauraceae
Grows up to: 60 x 60 inches (150 x 150cm)
Pick leaves for use in bouquet garnis

Some know it as a small tree or large shrub, others for the aromatic leaves used as seasoning in cooking. Bay is also a highly symbolic plant, the handsome foliage signifying victory and high status in ancient Greece and Rome. Either way, it's a lovely plant to grow indoors or out, and can be contained or pruned into a more compact shape suitable for a conservatory, terrace, courtyard, or balcony.

Planting | Grow in a large pot in well-drained fertile soil enriched with compost and grit or shrub compost. Ensure trunks of trees are straight before firming in.

Position | Prefers full sun to partial shade, ideally in a sheltered position. Outdoor plants are hardier, but cover with fleece if at risk of frost, or overwinter inside.

Watering | Water well when first planted and then for a few weeks afterward. Keep soil moist through summer but reduce watering in winter. Mist regularly.

Feeding | Apply a half-strength liquid balanced fertilizer every two weeks from mid spring to late summer. Do not feed in winter.

Also try:
yellow-leaved bay
(*Laurus nobilis* 'Aurea')

Watch out for:
Prune bay in summer with secateurs to keep shape and encourage new growth. Mature plants can be cut back in late spring.

MYRTLE - *Myrtus communis*

nontoxic   **easy** *care rating*

Also known as: common myrtle
Family: Myrtaceae
Grows up to: 60 x 60 inches (150 x 150cm)
A lovely aromatic, pretty-flowered shrub

Native to southern Europe, North Africa, western Asia, and the Indian subcontinent, this hardy evergreen shrub or small tree has thick aromatic leaves and five-petaled white, sometimes pink-tinged flowers that mature into edible blue-black berries when ripe. Historically, brides would include some in their bouquet as a symbol of love and constancy. The flowers can be added to salads, while the berries can be used instead of juniper.

Planting | Grow in a large pot in well-drained fertile soil enriched with compost and grit or shrub compost. Ensure trunks of trees are straight before firming in.

Position | Grow inside in a bright but well-ventilated position. Move outside in late spring or summer to full sun, but return indoors before any risk of frost.

Watering | Keep the soil constantly moist but don't waterlog. Use rainwater or distilled water as myrtle does not like high concentrations of lime.

Feeding | Use a balanced fertilizer on outdoor plants once a year in spring before new growth.

Also try:
variegated common myrtle (*Myrtus communis* 'Variegata')

Watch out for: To train the tree to grow small, like a bonsai, remove spent blooms and clean dead or diseased wood.

LAVENDER - *Lavandula* spp.

nontoxic

easy
care rating

Also known as: English, French, and Spanish lavender
Family: Lamiaceae
Grows up to: 36 x 36 inches (90 x 90cm)
No garden should be without this restful plant

Lavender is one of the most beautiful and versatile herbs to grow, with many ancient therapeutic and culinary properties, including aiding relaxation, combating stress, and adding a sweet, perfumed taste to cakes, bakes, and teas. There are several popular species and numerous cultivars to choose from, including culinary English lavender (*Lavandula angustifolia* 'Munstead') and the tuft-flowered *Lavandula dentata* or *Lavandula stoechas*.

Planting | Plant in the ground or in a breathable container of three parts soil or soil-based compost to one part grit. Plant at the same level as it was in the previous pot.

Position | Grow outdoors in full sun or grow indoors by a sunny, well-ventilated window with at least three to four hours of direct sun a day, moving to a cooler spot in winter.

Watering | Water well when first planted, then once or twice a week during the summer if the weather is hot or the compost dries out. Don't allow pots to stand in water.

Feeding | Lavender likes nutrient-poor soil so doesn't need feeding. Cutting off blooms is the best way to encourage more form. Trim annually in late summer.

Also try:
French lavender
(*Lavandula dentata*)

Watch out for:
English lavender is generally hardy outdoors in colder climates. French and Spanish lavender should be moved inside before frosts.

FRUITS AND VEGETABLES

Lots of fruits, salads, and vegetables can be grown indoors or in containers with a few simple tips—from cut-and-come-again lettuce, microgreens, and celery to strawberries, lemons, tomatoes, and grapes. A great way to have fresh, healthy produce at your fingertips.

LEMON TREE - *Citrus × limon*

nontoxic

hard
care rating

Also known as: citrus lemon
Family: Rutaceae
Grows up to: 13 x 8 feet (4 x 2.4m)
Even without fruits, it smells heavenly

Leathery leaved, white-pink blossomed, wonderfully perfumed lemons are thought to have originated in South Asia, possibly as a hybrid of an orange and a citron. They prefer to be grown outside but can thrive indoors given the right conditions, even providing edible fruit. Choose a suitable variety, such as the compact, year-round fruiting and flowering 'Meyer' lemon or the wrinkly fruited dwarf 'Ponderosa'.

Planting | Plant in a large terra-cotta pot of equal parts soil and sand, grit, or citrus compost with at least 2 inches (5cm) of room around the root ball for expansion.

Position | Grow outdoors in subtropical/tropical climates. Grow indoors in a well-ventilated sunny spot with at least ten hours' full sun. Move outdoors from summer to fall.

Watering | Water regularly through the year when the top layer of compost feels dry. Stand the pot on a tray of damp pebbles and mist regularly.

Feeding | Feed with a high-nitrogen citrus fertilizer every two to three weeks during the growing season of spring and summer. Reduce to once every two to three months in winter.

Also try:
Garey's Eureka lemon (*Citrus × limon* 'Garey's Eureka'); Meyer lemon (*Citrus × limon* 'Meyer')

Watch out for:
Lemons are self-pollinating, but without the help of outdoor bees, you will need to transfer pollen from anthers to stamens with a small brush.

MANDARIN ORANGE - *Citrus reticulata*

nontoxic

easy
care rating

Also known as: mandarin; mandarine
Family: Rutaceae
Grows up to: 10 x 16 feet (3 x 5m)
Opt for dwarf varieties if growing indoors

Mandarins are thought to be native to parts of China, Japan, and Vietnam and are one of the original ancestor species of many popular fruits, including sweet and sour oranges, grapefruits, and many lemons and limes. Although naturally quite a small tree, it's best to choose a dwarf variety for container planting indoors, such as 'Owari Satsuma', with the aim of producing seedless orange fruits in early winter among evergreen foliage.

Planting | Plant in a large terra-cotta pot of equal parts soil and sand, grit, or citrus compost with at least 2 inches (5cm) of room around the root ball for expansion.

Position | Grow outdoors in subtropical/tropical climates. Grow indoors in a well-ventilated sunny spot with at least ten hours' full sun. Move outdoors from summer to fall.

Watering | Water regularly through the year when the top layer of compost feels dry. Stand pot on a tray of damp pebbles and mist regularly.

Feeding | Feed with a high-nitrogen citrus fertilizer every two to three weeks during the growing season of spring and summer. Reduce to once every few months in winter.

Also try:
dwarf mandarin (*Citrus reticulata* 'Owari')

Watch out for: Citrus trees can become stressed and more susceptible to pests and disease due to poor drainage or standing in water.

CALAMONDIN - *Citrus × microcarpa*

nontoxic

easy
care rating

Also known as: calamondin orange; Philippine lemon
Family: Rutaceae
Grows up to: 13 x 8 feet (4 x 2.4m)
Try squeezing the juice into drinks

A hybrid of kumquat (*Citrus japonica*) and a mandarin orange (*Citrus reticulata*), and native to China, the calamondin has heavily scented leaves with winged stalks, beautiful white or pink-tinged flowers, and large, juicy, sharp-tasting fruits. Although it's fun to produce at least a few fruits to eat or squeeze into drinks, the fragrant foliage and flowers make this plant a lovely indoor companion. As with other citrus fruits, it can also be grown as a bonsai.

Planting | Plant in a large terra-cotta pot of equal parts soil and sand, grit, or citrus compost with at least 2 inches (5cm) of room around the root ball for expansion.

Position | Grow outdoors in subtropical/tropical climates. Grow indoors in a well-ventilated sunny spot with at least ten hours' full sun. Move outdoors from summer to fall.

Watering | Water regularly through the year when the top layer of compost feels dry. Stand the pot on a tray of damp pebbles and mist regularly.

Feeding | Feed with a high-nitrogen citrus fertilizer every few weeks during growing season.

Also try:
mandarin (*Citrus reticulata*)

Watch out for:
Can be grown outdoors in slightly less tropical regions in half shade or direct sun.

GRAPEVINE - *Vitis vinifera*

nontoxic

medium
care rating

Also known as: common grapevine
Family: Vitaceae
Grows up to: 40 x 13 feet (12 x 4m)
Take the time to train on wires or trellis

Native to the Mediterranean, Central Europe, and Asia, *Vitis vinifera* is the grapevine most commonly used to produce edible grapes and wine. In the wild, it grows as a liana (long-stemmed woody vine) in humid forests and by the side of streams. As a cultivated crop, it is often trained along wires, creating a small hedge or canopy of palmately lobed leaves with clusters of tiny greenish flowers that mature into bunches of sweet, juicy fruits.

Planting | Grows best in rich, moderately fertile light soil, planted between late fall and spring. In pots, ensure there is enough room for roots to spread out.

Position | Can be grown indoors in a conservatory or greenhouse in the ground or a breathable pot. If possible, plant outside and train the vine indoors through an opening.

Watering | Water thoroughly every week during growing season. Vines with roots indoors will need more frequent watering. Increase outdoor watering in hot spells.

Feeding | Feed with a liquid seaweed fertilizer every four weeks during the growing season. Mulch the rooting area with manure just before growth begins in spring.

Also try:
white early-season grape (*Vitis vinifera* 'Chasselas')

Watch out for:
Needs a few years to establish; cut back to two nodes in winter and then train to shape in the first year.

STRAWBERRY - *Fragaria* spp.

nontoxic

hard
care rating

Also known as: garden strawberry;
Alpine strawberry
Family: Rosaceae
Grows up to: 20 x 20 inchee (50 x 50cm)
Choose alpine strawberries for a compact plant

Strawberries are a widely grown hybrid species of the genus *Fragaria*, cultivated around the world for their fruit and available in a variety of cultivars. Depending on the species or variety, fruits can be harvested in early summer (early); from spring to fall (ever-bearing); and grow with runners or in a more rounded shape. If growing indoors, alpine strawberries (*Fragaria vesca*) are particularly successful as they keep a clumping shape.

Planting | Plant in fall or spring in fertile, well-drained soil or organic potting soil in raised beds, grow bags, a breathable pot, a hanging basket, or a strawberry planter.

Position | Strawberries prefer a sunny but sheltered position, although there are some shade-tolerant varieties. Indoor plants may need help pollinating.

Watering | Water frequently while new plants are establishing and during warm or dry periods. Avoid wetting the crowns and the fruit, as this can promote disease.

Feeding | Feed outdoor plants a high-potassium tomato feed at the start of the growing season.

Also try:
alpine strawberry (*Fragaria vesca* 'Mara des Bois')

Watch out for:
As fruits develop, tuck straw or fiber mats underneath to keep fruits clean.

OLIVE TREE - *Olea europaea*

nontoxic

easy
care rating

Also known as: European olive
Family: Oleaceae
Grows up to: 13 x 8 feet (4 x 2.5m)
A handsome plant that may fruit in time

Native to the Mediterranean Basin area, this popular cultivated crop and ornamental evergreen tree or shrub has a gnarled and twisted trunk, oblong silvery-green leaves, and small, feathery white flowers that mature into small green to purple drupes in mild regions. These fruits are naturally bitter and must be cured and fermented to make them palatable. Or grow one simply for the elegant foliage, silhouette, and symbolism of peace and love.

Planting | Plant in the garden or in a large terra-cotta or wooden container in three parts soil or soil-based compost to one part sand or grit. Cactus soil works well indoors.

Position | Plant outdoors in a warm, sheltered position. Or grow indoors in a conservatory, well-lit porch, or a bright room, moving outdoors in summer.

Watering | Water regularly, allowing the top layer of soil to dry out between. Reduce watering in winter but don't let the soil dry out completely. Can tolerate periods of drought.

Feeding | Feed every month through the growing season from spring to fall with a balanced liquid fertilizer. Olives need regular watering and feeding in order to fruit.

Also try:
dwarf olive (*Olea europaea* 'Arbequina'); Spanish Manzanilla (*Olea europaea* 'Manzanilla')

Watch out for:
Sooty deposits, white waxy eggs, and scales on leaves.

LETTUCE - *Lactuca sativa*

nontoxic

easy
care rating

Also known as: salad; greens
Family: Asteraceae
Grows up to: 8 x 8 inches (20 x 20cm)
Opt for cut-and-come-again types indoors

Salad crops such as lettuce, spinach, chard, chicory, and radicchio can be grown as cut-and-come-again, producing a steady crop of fresh, tender leaves, indoors or out, from spring through to fall. Originally farmed by the ancient Egyptians before becoming popular with the Greeks and Romans, this hardy annual is easy to grow at home, a natural source of iron and vitamins K and A, and a great, packaging-free way to get your fill of greens.

Planting | Sow or plant outdoors in spring in beds of well-drained soil with organic matter, or indoors/outdoors in pots of peat-free multipurpose compost.

Position | Grow in a sunny spot outdoors or in a sunny conservatory, greenhouse, or windowsill, ensuring it doesn't get too hot, which can cause it to bolt.

Watering | Water the soil before sowing to ensure seeds stay in close contact with moist soil. Water regularly so that the soil stays moist, but do not waterlog.

Feeding | Feed with a half-strength balanced liquid organic fertilizer after the first true leaves appear, then once a week for three weeks. Do not get fertilizer on the leaves.

Also try: butterhead lettuce (*Lactuca sativa* 'All Year Round')

Watch out for: When leaves are of an edible size, snip off a few about 1 inch (2.5cm) from the base of the stem. New leaves should grow in their place.

AVOCADO - *Persea americana*

nontoxic

medium
care rating

Also known as: avocado pear; alligator pear
Family: Laureaceae
Grows up to: 42 x 42 inches (105 x 105cm)
Grow from the seed of a previous fruit

Growing avocados from the leftover seeds of a previous fruit is a fun project for all ages, resulting in a tropical houseplant that might even yield its own delicious fruits around ten years down the line. Native to Mexico, these tender evergreen trees can grow up to 70 feet (20m) tall, although constrained in pots they rarely grow taller than a small shrub. Even without the creamy-fleshed fruits, they make handsome houseplants all the same.

Planting | Use toothpicks to suspend a stone, fat-side down, in a glass of water. Let it sprout. Pinch out when 6 inches (15cm) tall, and when bushy, plant in a pot of cactus soil.

Position | Place seed and then plant on a warm, sunny windowsill or in a conservatory with plenty of bright light. Move mature plants outside in summer.

Watering | Water when the top layer of compost is dry during the growth season of spring and summer. Reduce in winter. Yellowing leaves is a sign of too much water.

Feeding | Feed potted plants a half-strength balanced fertilizer every two weeks in summer.

Also try:
Hass avocado (*Persea americana* 'Hass')

Watch out for:
Avocados grown from seed won't bear fruit until they are at least a decade old.

MICROGREENS - Various spp.

nontoxic

easy
care rating

Including: radishes, beet, basil, and arugula
Family: Various
Grows up to: 2 inches (5cm)
Easy to become obsessed once you start

Microgreens are an increasingly popular ingredient used to garnish or supplement soups, salads, sauces, and other dishes. Essentially, they are the stalk, cotyledon leaves, and baby true leaves of edible greens, vegetables, or herbs such as amaranth, radish, beet, basil, cilantro, and arugula, allowed to grow to a maximum height of 2 inches (5cm). Packed with vitamins, they're easy to grow as long as you give them at least four hours of daily sunlight.

Planting | Finely sow, then press chosen seeds into a shallow tray of three parts coconut coir or organic potting soil to one part perlite. Cover lightly with organic potting soil.

Position | Place the tray of seeds on a bright, sunny windowsill or spot that gets at least four hours of direct sun a day. Sprouts should appear within three to seven days.

Watering | Moisten the soil after sowing with a mister. Then mist once or twice daily to keep the soil moist but not wet. Do not waterlog.

Feeding | Microgreens don't need extra fertilization if the soil they are growing in is nutrient-rich. Use fresh soil for each new batch to ensure this is the case.

Also try:
radish (*Raphanus sativus*)

Watch out for:
Take care when choosing which microgreens to grow; the leaves of plants in the Solanaceae family, for example, are toxic.

TOMATO - *Solanum lycopersicum*

nontoxic

medium
care rating

Also known as: Tomato plant; Love apple
Family: Solanaceae
Grows up to: 4 x 2 feet (1.5 x 0.6m)
Some varieties work well in hanging baskets

Native to western South America and Central America, the word "tomato" derives from the Aztec word *tomatl*, meaning "fat thing." Indeed, the fruits that mature from the star-shaped yellow flowers of this fragrant-leaved, naturally vining plant are curvaceous and juicy, ranging from beefsteak to cherry tomatoes. Choose from vining determinate varieties (ripen all at once) and bushy indeterminate varieties (ripen through the season).

Planting | Start seeds indoors in spring in trays of seed compost. Grow on indoors or outdoors in containers or grow bags of fertile organic loose potting soil.

Position | Grow outdoors in full sun. Grow indoors by a bright, sunny window or in a conservatory/greenhouse. Grow lights can help produce indoor crops year-round.

Watering | Aim to keep the soil lightly moist at all times by watering when the top layer is dry. This helps plants to grow and stops fruits from splitting.

Feeding | Use a balanced fertilizer every two weeks until it fruits, then switch to liquid comfrey.

Also try:
golden orange cherry (*Solanum lycopersicum* 'Sungold')

Watch out for:
Shake plants every few days to disperse pollen.

CHILI PEPPER - *Capsicum annuum* spp.

nontoxic

medium
care rating

Also known as: chili; capsicum
Family: Solanaceae
Grows up to: 18 x 12 inches (45 x 30cm)
Keep a supply of mild and hot chilis on the go

The species *Capsicum annuum* encompasses a wide range of peppers, from mild, sweet bell peppers to the hot Longum group, including hot chili, jalapeño, cayenne, and habanero peppers (use caution around children and pets). The alkaloid that generates the spiciness is called capsaicin, measured in Scoville units to determine heat. As well as growing for culinary purposes, white-flowered, bright-fruiting pepper plants can also be grown as ornamental—albeit edible—houseplants.

Planting | Sow in seed compost from late winter to mid-spring. Pot up twice in multipurpose compost and stake with a stick. Store-bought plants can also be repotted.

Position | Grow seedlings indoors in a warm, sunny spot. When plants are around 9 inches (23cm) tall and all risk of frost is gone, they can be moved outside to a sunny spot.

Watering | Allow the top layer of compost or soil to dry out between waterings. Soak thoroughly and then drain. Do not waterlog.

Feeding | Feed every two weeks with half-strength balanced liquid organic fertilizer, from when flowers first appear until the last fruit has been harvested.

Also try:
dwarf chili (*Capsicum annuum* 'Apache')

Watch out for:
Aphids can gather on the soft shoot tips of plants or on leaves. Squash colonies wearing gloves. Do not touch your eyes after touching chilis.

CELERY - *Apium graveolens*

nontoxic

medium
care rating

Also known as: stalk celery; leaf celery
Family: Apiaceae
Grows up to: 20 x 16 inches (50 x 40cm)
Cultivate for the leaves or stalks

This marshland plant has been cultivated since antiquity as an anise-tasting winter vegetable of fibrous stalks, feathery leaves, and spicy seeds. This is another culinary ingredient that can be easily grown on from the "waste" of a previous bunch, simply by propagating the base of the stalks in water before potting up. This method doesn't produce a crop of extensive stalks, but the leaves provide a lovely mild flavor for soups and salads.

Planting | Sow from seed in early spring in seed compost. Cover with perlite. Transplant seedlings into fertile organic soil or soil-based compost in the ground or in pots.

Position | Grow or place in a warm, bright spot, making sure you don't shock plants by moving to a colder place or exposing to chilly drafts. This can cause plants to bolt.

Watering | Water this thirsty plant regularly, keeping the soil evenly moist. It cannot tolerate any kind of drought, which could affect the taste.

Feeding | Dig lots of compost into the soil before planting outdoors. Boost nutrients by feeding with a balanced liquid organic fertilizer a month after planting.

Also try:
stalk celery (*Apium graveolens* var. *dulce* 'Pascal')

Watch out for:
Very sensitive to heat and cold; keep acclimatizing it.

SCALLIONS - *Allium* spp.

nontoxic

easy
care rating

Also known as: salad onions; spring onions
Family: Amaeryllidaceae
Grows up to: 20 x 8 inches (50 x 20cm)
Simply regrow roots in water

Scallions are generally a cultivated form of onion (*Allium cepa* var. *cepa*), the edible parts of which are the long tubular green stems and small bulbous ends, with a mild scent and taste. Many varieties, such as *Allium cepa* 'Matrix', are winter-hardy and grow well outside, but for those without dedicated outdoor space, scallions are also an ideal windowsill or balcony crop to keep close at hand for soups, salads, and stir-fries.

Planting | A fun way to keep a constant scallion crop is to place rooted scallions in water just up to the green part. Even as you chop them, they will grow.

Position | Whether grown from seed in well-draining organic soil-based compost in raised beds or pots, or using the method above, scallions prefer a sunny spot.

Watering | For soil-based plants, water when the top layer of soil is dry. Increase in hot weather. Do not waterlog. Mulch around crops to help maintain moisture.

Feeding | Use a balanced fertilizer when sprouted, and through the growing season.

Also try:
Welsh onion (*Allium fistulosum*)

Watch out for:
Scallions rot in waterlogged soil, so plant them in well-drained soil. Keep weeds away.

INDEX

FURTHER READING

Container gardening

Container Gardener's Handbook: Pots, Techniques and Projects to Transform Any Space by Frances Tophill (Companionhouse Books, 2019)

Container Gardening Complete: Creative Projects for Growing Vegetables and Flowers in Small Spaces by Jessica Walliser (Cool Springs Press, 2017)

Grow: Containers: Essential Know-how and Expert Advice for Gardening Success by Geoff Stebbings (DK, 2021)

Modern Container Gardening: How to Create a Stylish Small-Space Garden Anywhere by Isabelle Palmer (Hardie Grant Books, 2020)

Pots for All Seasons by Tom Harris (Pimpernel Press, 2020)

Houseplants – general

Houseplant Handbook: Basic Growing Techniques and a Directory of 300 Everyday Houseplants by David Squire (CompanionHouse Books, 2017)

Houseplants 101: How to Choose, Style, Grow and Nurture Your Indoor Plants by Peter Shepperd and Martin Oldfield (Wryting, 2021)

How to Grow Stuff: Easy, No-Stress Gardening for Beginners by Alice Vincent (Ebury Press, 2017)

The Joy of Living with Plants: Ideas and Inspirations for Indoor Gardens by Isabelle Palmer (CICO Books, 2021)

The Kew Gardener's Companion to Growing House Plants: The Art and Science to Grow Your Own House Plants by Kew Royal Botanic Gardens and Kay Maquire (White Lion Publishing, 2019)

RHS Practical House Plant Book: Choose the Best, Display Creatively, Nurture and Care by Zia Allaway and Fran Bailey (DK, 2018)

Tiny Plants: Discover the Joys of Growing and Collecting Itty-bitty Houseplants by Leslie F. Halleck (Cool Springs Press, 2021)

The Unexpected Houseplant: 220 Extraordinary Choices for Every Spot in Your Home by Tovah Martin (Timber Press, 2012)

Urban Botanics: An Indoor Plant Guide for Modern Gardeners by Emma Sibley and Maaike Koster (Aurum Press, 2017)

Houseplants – plant care

Dr. Houseplant: An Indispensable Guide to Keeping Your Indoor Plants Healthy and Happy by William Davidson and Jane Bland (Hardie Grant Books, 2020)

Grow Houseplants: Essential Know-how and Expert Advice for Gardening Success by Tamsin Westthorpe (DK, 2021)

Hi Cacti: Growing Houseplants and Happiness by Sabina Palermo (Leaping Hare Press, 2021)

Houseplants for All: How to Fill Any Home with Happy Plants by Danae Horst (HMH Books, 2020)

Houseplants for Beginners: A Practical Guide to Growing and Helping Your Plants Thrive by Rebecca de la Paz (Rockridge Press, 2021)

Houseplants: The Complete Guide to Choosing, Growing and Caring for Indoor Plants by Lisa Eldred Steinkopf (Cool Springs Press, 2017)

How Not to Kill Your Houseplant: Survival Tips For the Horticulturally Challenged by Veronica Peerless (DK, 2017)

How Not to Kill Your Plants by Nik Southern (Hodder & Stoughton, 2017)

How to Houseplant: A Beginner's Guide to Making and Keeping Plant Friends by Heather Rodino (Sterling, 2019)

How to Make a Plant Love You: Cultivate Green Space in Your Home and Heart by Summer Rayne Oakes (Portfolio, 2019)

Leaf Supply: A Guide to Keeping Happy House Plants by Lauren Camilleri and Sophia Kaplan (Smith Street Books, 2018)

The New Plant Parent: Develop Your Green Thumb and Care for Your House-Plant Family by Darryl Cheng (Abrams, 2019)

Plant: House Plants: Choosing, Styling, Caring by Gynelle Leon (Mitchell Beazley, 2021)

Houseplants – propagation

Plant Parenting: Easy Ways to Make More Houseplants, Vegetables, and Flowers by Leslie Halleck (Timber Press, 2019)

The Plant Propagator's Bible: A Step-by-Step Guide to Propagating Every Plant in Your Garden (Cool Springs Press, 2021)

Plantopedia: The Definitive Guide to House Plants by Lauren Camilleri and Sophia Kaplan (Smith Street Books, 2020)

RHS Handbook: Propagation Techniques: Simple Techniques for 1000 Garden Plants by RHD (Mitchell Beazley, 2013)

Root, Nurture, Grow: The Essential Guide to Propagating and Sharing Houseplants by Caro Langton and Rose Ray (Quadrille Publishing, 2018)

Houseplants – history

The Hidden Histories of Houseplants: Fascinating Stories of Our Most-Loved Houseplants by Maddie Bailey and Alice Bailey (Hardie Grant, 2021)

Potted History: How Houseplants Took Over Our Homes by Catherine Horwood (Pimpernell Press, 2020)

Cacti, succulents, and air plants

Air Plants: The Curious World of Tillandsias by Zenaida Sengo and Caitlin Atkinson (Timber Press, 2014)

Cacti by Dan Torre (Reaktion Books, 2017)

Container Succulents: Creative Ideas for Beginners by Kentauo Kuroda and Ayako Eifuku (Tuttle Publishing, 2019)

The Gardener's Guide to Succulents: A Handbook of Over 125 Exquisite Varieties of Succulents and Cacti by Misa Matsuyama (Tuttle Publishing, 2020)

Happy Cactus: Cacti, Succulents and More by DK (DK, 2018)

House of Plants: Living with Succulents, Air Plants and Cacti by Rose Ray and Caro Langton (Frances Lincoln, 2016)

Living with Air Plants: A Beginner's Guide to Growing and Displaying Tillandsia by Yoshiharu Kashima and U (Tuttle Publishing, 2019)

Prick: Cacti and Succulents: Choosing, Styling, Caring by Gynelle Leon (Mitchell Beazley, 2017)

RHS Practical Cactus and Succulent Book: How to Choose, Nurture and Display More than 200 Cacti and Succulents by Zia Allaway and Fran Bailey (DK, 2019)

Succulents Simplified: Growing, Designing and Crafting with 100 Easy-Care Varieties by Debra Lee Baldwin (Timber Press, 2013)

The Timber Press Guide to Succulent Plants of the World: A Comprehensive Reference to More than 2000 Species by Fred Dortort (Timber Press, 2011)

Terrariums and kokedama

Hanging Kokedama: Creating Potless Plants for the Home by Coraleigh Parker (Jacqui Small, 2018)

The Inspired Houseplant: Transform Your Home with Indoor Plants from Kokedama to Terrariums and Water Gardens to Edibles by Jen Steams (Sasquatch Books, 2019)

Terrarium: 33 Glass Gardens to Make Your Own by Anna Bauer and Noan Levy (Chronicle Books, 2018)

Terrariums: Gardens Under Glass: Designing, Creating and Planting Modern Indoor Gardens by Maria Colletti (Cool Springs Press, 2015)

Terrariums and Kokedama: Stylish Ideas for Low-Maintenance Indoor Planting by Alison Mowat (Kyle Books, 2017)

Bonsai, bulbs, and cut flowers

Bonsai: The Art of Growing and Keeping Miniature Trees by Peter Chan (Skyhorse, 2014)

The Flower Garden: A Guide to Growing Cut Flowers on Your Windowsill by Jennita Jansen (Quadrille Publishing, 2021)

The Flower Yard: Growing Flamboyant Flowers in Containers by Arthur Parkinson (Kyle Books, 2021)

The Kew Gardener's Guide to Growing Bulbs: The Art and Science to Grow Your Own Bulbs by Richard Wilford and Kew Royal Botanic Gardens (White Lion Publishing, 2019)

The Little Book of Bonsai by Jonas Dupuich (Ten Speed Press, 2020)

Urban Flowers: Creating Abundance in a Small City Garden by Carolyn Dunster (Frances Lincoln, 2017)

Herbs and edibles

Complete Container Herb Gardening: Design and Grow Beautiful, Bountiful Herb-Filled Pots by Sue Goetz (Cool Springs Press, 2020)

Container Vegetable Gardening: Growing Crops in Pots in Every Space by Liz Dobbs (CompanionHouse Books, 2019)

Grow Easy: Organic Crops for Pots and Small Plots by Anna Greenland (Mitchell Beazley, 2021)

Herbal Houseplants: Grow Beautiful Herbs – Indoors! For Flavour, Fragrance and Fun by Susan Betz (Cool Springs Press, 2021)

How to Grow Your Dinner without Leaving the House by Claire Ratinon (Laurence King Publishing, 2020)

Introduction to Container Gardening: Beginner's Guide to Growing Your Own Fruit, Vegetables and Herbs Using Containers and Grow Bags by Madison Pierce (Nielsen UK, 2021)

The Kew Gardener's Companion to Growing Herbs: The Art and Science to Grow Your Own Herbs by Holly Farrell and Kew Royal Botanic Gardens (White Lion Publishing, 2019)

Botanical style

Botanical Style: Inspirational Decorating with Nature, Plants and Florals by Selina Lake (Ryland, Peters & Small, 2016)

The Green Indoors: Finding the Right Plants for Your Home Environment by Maddie Bailey and Alice Bailey (Hardie Grant, 2021)

Indoor Jungle by Lauren Camilleri and Sophia Kaplan (Smith Street Books, 2019)

Plant Style: How to Greenify Your Space by Alana Langan and Jacqui Vidal (Thames & Hudson, 2017)

Urban Jungle Living and Styling with Plants by Igor Josifovic and Judith de Graaf (Callwey, 2016)

Wild Creations: Inspiring Projects to Create Plus Plant Care Tips and Styling Ideas for Our Own Wild Interior by Hilton Carter (CICO Books, 2021)

Wild at Home: How to Style and Care for Beautiful Plants by Hilton Carter (CICO Books, 2019)

Wild Interiors: Beautiful Plants in Beautiful Spaces by Hilton Carter (CICO Books, 2020)

Gardening for well-being

Houseplants for a Healthy Home: 50 Indoor Plants to Help You Breathe Better, Sleep Better and Feel Better All Year Round by Jon Vanzile (Adamas Media, 2018)

My Houseplant Changed My Life: Green Wellbeing for the Great Outdoors by David Domoney (DK, 2021)

Plant Therapy: How an Indoor Green Oasis Can Improve Your Mental and Emotional Wellbeing by Dr. Katie Cooper (Hardie Grant, 2020)

RHS Gardening for Mindfulness by Holly Farrell and the RHS (Mitchell Beazley, 2020)

RHS Your Wellbeing Garden: How to Make Your Garden Good for You – Science, Design, Practice by RHS, Professor Alistair Griffiths, Matthew Keightley, Annie Gatti and Zia Allaway (DK, 2020)

The Well Gardened Mind: Rediscovering Nature in the Modern World by Sue Stuart-Smith (William Collins, 2020)